The Bright Continent

The
Bright Continent

BREAKING RULES *and* MAKING CHANGE
in MODERN AFRICA

Dayo Olopade

HOUGHTON MIFFLIN HARCOURT
BOSTON • NEW YORK
2014

For information about permission to reproduce selections from this book, write to Permissions, Houghton Mifflin Harcourt Publishing Company, 215 Park Avenue South, New York, New York 10003.

www.hmhco.com

Library of Congress Cataloging-in-Publication Data is available.
ISBN 978-0-547-67831-3

Book design by Chrissy Kurpeski
Typeset in Warnock Pro

Printed in the United States of America
DOC 10 9 8 7 6 5 4 3 2 1

All photographs courtesy of the author, with the following exceptions: Herodotus's map of the world, p. 2, courtesy of David Rumsey Map Collection, www.davidrumsey.com; United Nations poster, p. 5, courtesy of Stefan Einarsson; Kenyan street murals, p. 39, courtesy of Andre Epstein; Boulton's map of Africa, p. 42, courtesy of Geographicus Fine Antique Maps; tribal map of Africa, p. 43, © George Peter Murdock, *Africa: Its Peoples and Their Culture History*; 2009 African undersea cable map, p. 94, courtesy of Steven Song, licensed as BY; 2014 African undersea cable map, p. 94, courtesy of Steven Song, licensed as BY; satellite map of the lights of the world, p. 158, NASA Earth Observatory/NOAA NGDC; and Map Kibera, p. 236, © openstreetmap.org contributors, available under an Open Database License, with cartography licensed as CC-BY-SA.

This book is for Olufunmilayo Falusi Olopade and Christopher Olusola Olopade, also known as Mom and Dad.

CONTENTS

1. Orientation: *A New Map of Africa*   1
   "Just Ask Someone" • The Secret Garden • The World Is Fat • Africa Is a Country

2. Kanju: *The Fine Line Between Genius and Crime*   16
   The Truth Behind Nigerian E-mail Scams • Recycling and Resilience
   The Gray Economy • Naming and Shaming

3. Fail States: *Why African Government Hasn't Worked*   34
   The Runaway State • Vulture Culture • Bad Borders Make Bad Neighbors

4. Stuff We Don't Want: *Doing Bad in Africa*   52
   Keep Your T-Shirts! • Parachute Planning • Villages in Action

5. The Family Map: *The Original Social Network*   67
   Bowling Together • The Information Neighborhood • Health and Help • Brain Gain

6. The Technology Map: *Lessons in Leapfrogging*   91
   The Hockey Stick • Mobile Money • Cluster Economies • "Launch the Damn App"
   One Man's Meat

7. The Commercial Map: *Development for Sale*   121
   Let's Make a Deal • Private School • If You Sell It, They Will Come
   Kanju Capitalism

8. The Nature Map: *To Feed, Fuel, and Build the Future*   157
   The Power Problem • Our Turn to Eat • Charter Cities • Growing Power

9. The Youth Map: *Africa's Demographic Dividend*   191
   "Waithood" • Deliberate Practice • The Right Track • After School Reform

10. Two Publics: *Who's in Charge?*   217
    Exit, Voice, Loyalty • The Strongest State • A Market Test • The Second Coming

   Acknowledgments   237

   Notes   239

   Index   257

A man who uses an imaginary map thinking that it is a true one, is likely to be worse off than someone with no map at all.

—E. F. Schumacher

The Bright Continent

Orientation

A New Map of Africa

THE SEARCH FOR the Nile River took two thousand years too long. The idea of searching is itself crazy: as far as human primates are concerned, the flat pan of water stretching from eastern Uganda to the vast Delta of Egypt has always been there. And yet the first foreign correspondents in Africa — white men from Europe — were caught in an amazing race to "map" the river from tip to tail. Their tales of travel on Africa's waterways and into its dense forests sailed back to newspapers in 1850s London, Brussels, and New York. Sending word of new tribes in Ethiopia, or safe passage to the interior lakes of central Africa, these men laid the foundation for a tradition of sensationalist writing about Africa. It was Henry Morton Stanley, in his 1878 account of his travels in the Congo, who coined the term *dark continent.*

The misunderstanding began before Christ. Herodotus's fifth-century map of Africa left the cradle of civilization looking like an afterthought. (Later, the Mercator Projection sold Africa literally short.) He wrote, "I am astonished that men should ever have divided [Africa], Asia and Europe as they have, for they are exceedingly unequal.

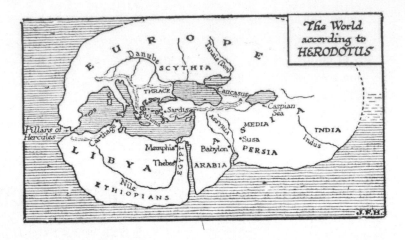

In the fifth century BCE, Herodotus created a map of the world as he knew it.

Europe extends the entire length of the other two, and for breadth will not even (as I think) hear to be compared to them."

For the next millennium, the northward-flowing river puzzled European cartographers. A Greek merchant named Diogenes began a rumor that the source of the Nile lay among the so-called Mountains of the Moon, somewhere in the wilds of "Nubia." As trade suffused the continent's west coast, existing tribes and landmarks were inked with the exquisite penmanship of eighteenth-century European trade schools. But it was not until 1858 that John Hanning Speke "discovered" that the longest river in the world begins not on the moon, but at Lake Victoria.

As news of the White Nile's source rippled through Europe, Major R. E. Cheesman, the British consul to Ethiopia, remarked, "It seemed almost unbelievable that such a famous river . . . could have been so long neglected." Like Herodotus, Cheesman exposed his Western bias. After all, the Nile bridges languages and climates, north and south of the Sahara. It has fed and ferried millions of people since the days of Moses. At the time of Speke's trip, the population living and trading near the source of the Nile numbered almost three million. It might have been easier for the frantic searchers to ask locals where the big river began. A few could have advised them: *here.*

The search for an omnipresent river was not merely inefficient; it charts the dynamic that has defined modern African history. Despite centuries of contact (based largely on slave trading), ignorance and hubris long governed Western impressions of what was seen as an impenetrable unknown — Joseph Conrad's "heart of darkness."

So it was not without precedent that European powers, led by the Portuguese, French, British, and Germans, decided to carve up the African continent using maps and borders of their own creation. At the Berlin Conference in 1884, they drew boundaries that had never existed on the continent, scrumming for natural resources from tobacco to peanuts to gold (oil would soon follow). Their borderlines preserved the gap between foreign perception and African reality that has been difficult to close ever since.

More than a century later, Google showed up. Since 2007, the American Internet giant has opened offices in Ghana, Kenya, Nigeria, Senegal, South Africa, and Uganda and begun translating its most popular American applications to Africa. Maps were a top priority. Google's team of digital cartographers fanned out across the continent, knitting African streets and cities into the fabric of the World Wide Web. The Americans spared no extravagance: a fleet of red Toyota Priuses mounted with cameras circled cities in South Africa to localize Google's "Street View" project — just in time for the 2010 World Cup.

Like the ancient geographers in search of the Nile, the modern Google mappers imported a Western notion of orientation. As anyone who has taken directions in Africa can tell you, we're running a different kind of software. In a developed country, a charming female robot might read out clear directions to a numbered street address. In Africa, however, here's what you get:

If you are approaching from the Tuskys roundabout, stay on Langata Road till you have passed the entrance on Langata Road that would get you to Carnivore. Take the first right turn off Langata Road after this point. Drive down Langata Road for approximately half a second, and take the left turn right before the petrol station

next to Rafikiz. Drive down this road for half a minute. When you
see Psys Langata on your right, take that left.

Confused? These are real — and typical — directions for Nairobi,
the Kenyan capital where I lived while reporting this book. Of course,
Nairobi and many other cities in Africa have roads and districts with
formal names, and some buildings with assigned numbers. But even in
the most cosmopolitan cities, the address is beside the point.

Locals use businesses, billboards, bus stops, and hair salons as a dynamic, alternative framework for navigation. We rely on time, relative
distance, egocentric directions (right or left), and shared knowledge.
In Khartoum, the North Sudanese capital, one prominent local landmark is a building where a Chinese restaurant *used to be.* In the six
months until it was repaired, I gave directions to my home based on a
particularly cavernous pothole. Frequently, the final direction is "just
ask someone."

Anthropologists would call Nairobi streets a "high-context" environment. Such navigation is a holdover from a time when centralized
systems were absent (which, as we'll see, is often still the case). More
importantly, a high-context route from point A is no proof that point
B doesn't exist — it just means you need a different map to find it.

The same goes for modern Africa. Whether you're working for an
American tech giant struggling to standardize navigation, an entrepreneur from Brazil looking for new business opportunities, a French
tourist in search of adventure, a nonprofit trying to improve lives, or a
curious global bystander, you probably don't have a very good map of
life south of the Sahara.

In fact, it amazes me how little the world thinks of Africa. I mean
this in terms of time and of reputation. As a first-generation Nigerian
American, I have personal reasons for paying attention; but what we
all think of Africa when we do is very revealing. In 2010, the United
Nations celebrated the tenth anniversary of the Millennium Development Goals (MDGs) — eight ambitious targets, from fighting HIV
transmission to improving education around the world. To mark the

occasion, the UN sponsored a poster design competition. The winning entry juxtaposed power (leaders of the Group of 8) and poverty (young Africans in line at a refugee camp). The work may be clever graphic design, but the tagline is heartbreaking. "Dear world leaders: We are still waiting." A panel of UN judges validated the biggest lie in modern history: that poor and passive Africans exist only in the shadow of Western action.

If you've read other "development" books, it's easy enough to get that impression. Even as popular discourse begins to question the logic of foreign assistance to the region, the conversation remains focused on how "the West" can improve its performance. Familiar voices on the development beat write prescriptions for everyone from the leaders of the G8 to the infantry of the World Bank to the heads of landlocked countries like the Central African Republic. Though many have spent decades examining the various ruts and bottlenecks in economic growth, it is rare to hear about what ordinary Africans are already doing to help themselves.

This book changes that. As a reporter, I follow the advice of philosopher Ludwig Wittgenstein: "Don't think, but look!" The continent

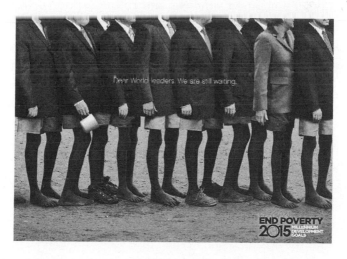

The United Nations held a poster competition to celebrate ten years of its Millennium Development Goals. The winning image juxtaposed power and poverty.

needs to be seen and heard, not imagined and then ritually dismissed. Because when you talk to real people in Africa — shopkeepers, day laborers, executives, or educators — and commit to telling their stories, once-hidden strengths come to light.

The story is as simple as walking to work. Once, my mother and I took an early-morning flight from Kenya to Uganda. We woke before the sun. Riding in a car to the airport, we saw dim shapes come into focus on either side of us. "Where is everyone going?" my mother mused. The figures streaming toward the city center were neither child soldiers on the march, nor mothers queuing for bed nets; they were thousands of ordinary people walking to work. Hundreds of millions of Africans do this every day, waking before dawn to provide for their families.

Nearly every day that I wrote this book, I saw Gladys Mwende working the soil in an open field next to my apartment complex. Technically, she had no right to do so. After moving to Nairobi from the smaller Kenyan city of Machakos, Gladys, her husband, Benson Muthame, and their six children found themselves occupying the abandoned colonial home outside my window. It's a pretty stone and tile structure with two floors of rooms for all the kids — aged ten months to thirteen years. Only its punctured windows and rotting wood cornice reveal that its best days are decades past.

It was bizarre to see this facsimile of rural African life — cooking with firewood, toting water, raising chickens — at a busy intersection in Kenya's largest metropolis. But the land is what matters. As unpaid caretakers of the plot, the family treats its urban farm as though it were a ranch in the Great Rift Valley that keeps the world in coffee, tea, and flowers.

In the spring, they planted rows of maize, careful to leave out the patches of land overshadowed by palm and mimosa trees. While Benson worked as a security guard, the kids who could walk helped Gladys seed and weed the maize, beans, and a shocking stand of sugar cane. Throughout the rainy season, I typed interview notes, read up on national development policies, and watched the green shoots grow. By midsummer, the stalks were taller than all of us. At first harvest, the

Gladys Mwende, Benson Muthame, and their son cultivate one acre in Nairobi. The family of eight lacks a title to the land but produces maize, beans, and sugar cane.

family roasted a few maize husks to sell to commuters at dusk. Cooking my own dinner, I could make out wood smoke amid the exhaust fumes from the bus stop that doubled as a sales floor. But mostly, Gladys told me, they plant to eat, and eat to live.

Michelle Obama would be proud. I marveled at their nerve: the family has no official rights, supports, or farming expertise but like millions of subsistence farmers in Africa, found a way to make one (borrowed) acre count for something. Their quiet commitment is a direct rebuke to the UN poster, and a great example of the bold opportunism that makes Africa's development trajectory so different and exciting.

It's also a reminder of how easy it is to misjudge Africa. Stumbling off a crowded bus or flagging a motorbike taxi, thousands of daily commuters miss this secret garden. To adjacent homeowners, the land is an abandoned eyesore. To government planners, it's an instance of criminal trespass. It took a sustained look — from my bird's-eye perch — to see the land as an essential family asset.

Sharing these hidden triumphs is the best way I know to respond to the depressing top-level narratives that have held the region back. It's why, like many Nigerians before me, I've become a writer. Stories can help to challenge the bad news occupying a thin column in a Western newspaper, or scrolling across the lower edge of a cable news broadcast. The stories in this book fight what I call "formality bias" — the assumption that a rundown house is just that, or that a formal address is the only way to get from point A to point B.

Too often, global institutions, led in part by the UN, as well as macroeconomists, philanthropists, and journalists like me, look away from the figures walking to work, the green shoots in an urban clearing, or the potholes and kiosks that can provide useful orientation. Instead, we focus on Africa's formal organizations and its formal solutions. *How many schools have you built? How many mothers died last year? Was the election free and fair?*

It turns out we have been throwing a party in an empty ballroom. One of the biggest problems with the world's longtime orientation toward Africa is a preference for interactions between governments, or between formal institutions, when the most vibrant, authentic, and economically significant interactions are between individuals and decentralized groups. I've found that informal arrangements like Gladys and Benson's tend to organize daily life — and when it comes to "development," these arrangements sometimes achieve more, better, or faster results.

Take the example of Ushahidi, the Kenyan nonprofit that sprang up in the aftermath of the nation's contested 2007 presidential election. Torn along ethnic lines, supporters of incumbent Mwai Kibaki and challenger Raila Odinga tangled in rural towns and in main cities for weeks. Some 1,200 people were killed and more than 350,000 displaced by the violence. Throughout, the television and radio stations failed their mandate — streaming numbing Muzak while blood ran in the streets. For a terrifying moment, one of Africa's most stable democracies seemed poised to fall off a cliff into chaos.

First by blog, then by e-mail, then in person, a team of Kenyan techies began working on a mapping application that allowed citizens to report violence using their cell phones. Thousands of data points shared using Ushahidi — which means "witness" in Swahili — produced a map with real-time, geo-specific information that sped the effort to restore order and provide relief services.

Since then, Ushahidi has traveled the globe in a multitude of other contexts: monitoring unrest in Gaza and elections in Sudan, Liberia, and South America, following the 2009 swine flu epidemic, tracking oil from the *Deepwater Horizon* spill in the United States, and helping survivors of the 7.0 magnitude earthquake that leveled Haiti in 2010. Both Bill and Hillary Clinton have honored the Ushahidi effort. When Kenya voted on a new president in 2013, a spinoff product, Uchaguzi (meaning "election"), served as a check on governmental action and citizen behavior.

When Nigeria voted in April 2011, Ushahidi was there, too. I spent the month in Lagos — worried. Like Kenya's 2007 vote, Nigeria's prior election was marred by widespread fraud, cheating, miscounting, and delays of game. As the new vote drew near, the civil society organization known as Reclaim Naija reached across the continent for help. Ushahidi was a natural partner, but as its creators consistently stress, the model only works when citizens actually report trouble. And to do so, they need the right phone number.

Ngozi Iwere, the spitfire activist who ran the joint effort, had spent years working on HIV prevention and other health communications strategies in Nigeria. When it came to publicity, she knew exactly where to start. Rather than embarking on a large-scale TV or newspaper campaign, Reclaim Naija enlisted the tailors, the butchers, the car battery chargers, the furniture makers, the masons, the mechanics, the hair stylists, the street vendors, and the men who drive motorbike taxis. As it turns out, many trade organizations meet regularly, collect and pay dues, and chatter constantly about politics. To these communities, Iwere and her team passed on a populist rallying cry (in pidgin English): "If you see any *mago mago* or *wuru wuru* as you dey register or vote, report to Reclaim Naija!"

"It's the most brilliant marketing strategy I've ever seen," said Linda Kamau, a Ushahidi developer who traveled from Kenya to help the Nigerian group with their deployment. The motorbike taxi, or *okada* as it's known in southern Nigeria, carries dozens of passengers daily — a fine perch from which to share reporting protocols in case a ballot box is snatched. (Hair stylists have an even more captive audience.)

The *okada* driver is an odd poster child but represents the new face of development practice — working from the inside out. Previous waves of foreign interventions have been deductive — working from the outside in. They have invested time and money to engineer "networks" of "stakeholders" in "the field" who will promote a prescribed message or enact a binary plan. Like Eurocentric cartographers, many have missed the preexisting platforms that are not only more adaptive, but free of charge.

This book will explore five such platforms — or maps — in sub-Saharan Africa. I focus on the forty-five land-linked countries excluding north Africa because of their shared colonial past and comparatively underdeveloped present. Slavery and imperialism, combined with poor governance, have left the region bubbling with shared frustrations and similar opportunities. As compared with east and south Asia, Latin America, and eastern Europe, the region is also gravely underestimated. My five maps — Family, Technology, Commerce, Nature, and Youth — showcase the unique institutions that bind black Africa together and are building its bright future.

The Family Map is an essential building block. Everywhere I traveled, social relationships defined and improved life. This extended "family" phenomenon is particularly useful in the absence of a government safety net. As we'll see, horizontal networks in and across Africa can save lives, build businesses, and light the darkness. The African family also includes its vast diaspora — an important asset for finance, innovation, and influence.

The Technology Map is the best-kept secret in sub-Saharan Africa — the exciting terrain where need and genius meet. Explosive rates of Internet use and cell phone penetration are creating an entirely new foundation for service delivery, information dissemination, and economic growth. Countless regional ventures are riding this wave of globalization to sensible as well as spectacular ends.

The Commercial Map refers to the markets, large and small, where millions of African consumers find common ground — and novel development solutions. Ventures that match market forces with human needs are inventing a new form of development practice, if not a new form of capitalism itself.

The Nature Map refers to Africa's massive geographic advantages — soil, sun, water, and historic linkages to its east, west, and north. It's increasingly clear that the region's resource wealth goes beyond oil and minerals. Indeed, the future of food production, energy consumption, and urbanization will be developed in Africa. The region is uniquely equipped to accelerate local prosperity and global environmental balance.

Likewise, sub-Saharan Africa boasts an exceptional demographic dividend. It's the youngest world region — 70 percent of the population is under thirty years old. The existence of hundreds of millions of young people on the march from innocence to empowerment has upside and downside potential. The Youth Map is grounded in creative education methods that will make or break the future for all of us.

As we'll see, the region is rich in assets and institutions — if viewed with unbiased eyes. Working together or apart, these informal maps of Africa can be more generative and influential than governments, philanthropies, conventional NGOs, or other formal arrangements. Using them as a compass can supercharge traditional development work in ingenious, effective ways. This follows the basic logic of mapping: only when you know where you are and what you have can you say what you need and where you're going.

A word on terminology: It's hard to write a book about development when you rather hate the expression. But I do. It implies that any given country is "developing" toward something, and that there is only one way to get there. Though I will be using the terms *developing* and *developed,* I think it also helps to describe the world as "fat" and "lean."*

The fat and lean framework is a move away from the antique rheto-

---

* Nate Laurell of the Acumen Fund, an investment firm that emphasizes the social returns of capital, first made the distinction.

ric of First, Second, and Third Worlds, and the more recent "global south" and "global north." Cardinal directions have also been favored (many books about development counterpose poor countries with "the West"), but this orientation no longer makes sense. As even a Eurocentric map will tell you, a great deal of the economic energy of this century is happening due east, on the Asian subcontinent, or with populous trade partners in Latin America. Like "development," this north/south terminology doesn't promote a fair understanding of the world around us.

What is a "fat" economy? I was born in one — the United States. In the wealthy nations of the Organisation for Economic Co-operation and Development (OECD), plenty is normal. Abundance is the average: gross national income (GNI) is about $41,100 per person per year. Problem solving is well beyond the basics of sanitation, vaccination, and electrification. Though it's little consolation to them, even the poorest individuals in fat economies are more comfortable than humans at almost any other point in history.

There are downsides. The United States has the highest obesity rates in the world and grapples with other, more figurative "fat" problems: a subprime mortgage crisis, pay-to-play politics, and an unfortunate taste for oil. Europe, Australia, South Korea, and other fat economies are also struggling to manage the wages of wealth. This decade's rippling, consumption-fueled financial crisis exposed bloat across the OECD. Subsequent "austerity" measures put some fat economies in jeopardy for decades to come.

By contrast, Africa is lean. Among the emerging economies of east and central Asia, and nearly all of the countries in sub-Saharan Africa (the UN groups them as Least Developed Nations), GNI averages just $1,200 per capita. In these lean economies — particularly in Africa — the disease burden is very different. Malaria, HIV/AIDS, and childbirth are among the top causes of death on the continent. Nigeria — where my parents were born — has an alarming infant mortality rate, skyrocketing levels of unemployment, and power outages twenty-six days out of every month.

These difficulties obscure more than a few silver linings. Individual Africans waste less food, owe less money, and maintain a regional carbon footprint that is the lowest in the world. And because the region had been largely excluded from reckless global markets, Africa actually avoided the worst of the financial crisis. As we'll see, many African businesses follow a "lean" model for both operations and finance that can be more efficient. It seems that if the world is progressively tightening its belt, it should aim for the notch marked "Africa."

To clarify the distinction, I often tell the story of Toto, a Japanese company that created the Otohime, or "Sound Princess." The hardware, today installed in thousands of restroom stalls in Japan, realistically mimics the sound of flushing water. The Sound Princess solved a problem of comparative affluence: embarrassed Japanese women were flushing public toilets continuously to hide the sound of their use. Toto's innovation saves them the trouble. The portable, purse-friendly version is a best-selling consumer product.

In a lean economy, toilet-related innovation looks a lot different. In the densest areas of African cities, one time-honored form of waste disposal is the "flying toilet" — which involves bundling refuse into a plastic bag and chucking it as far as possible. It's understandable: far from the automated, sterile public toilets of Japan, more than half the population in Africa's informal settlements lacks the basic dignity of modern sanitation. Waste-contaminated water supplies breed disease epidemics. What's more, fear of urban crime keeps many from using public toilets at night. The "flying toilet" is a stopgap innovation — with obvious drawbacks.

The Umande Trust, a community organization in Kenya, came up with a better plan. With other local groups in Gatwekera, an informal settlement, they built a massive cylindrical biodigester that composts the output of a fleet of built-in toilets. Umande charges a few pennies per use, making about $400 per month. Better yet, the system doesn't drain the water supply like traditional flush toilets, and it creates biogas that powers a community center and heats water for the four hundred residents who also shower there every day.

These disparate innovations for personal dignity define the difference between fat and lean. The Sound Princess joins a parade of novelties for the top of the pyramid: software that will allow you to find a parking spot, to "farm" fake digital crops, to shake your iPhone to simulate the sound of a whip. It solves a problem that arises when the basics (like toilets) are taken care of.

But when the status quo is a flying toilet, anything goes. Lean economies — however challenged they might appear — are an invitation to innovate. If necessity is the mother of invention, Africa's adversities are the mother of necessity.

All this is a fancy way of saying that a general history of colonialism, dictatorship, and poverty has left Africans with a pretty good recipe for lemonade. The next few chapters explain the recipe, and then we get to the lemonade. We're going to see what happens when we examine what the region does best — instead of what its leaders do worst — and give the informal economies and non-state networks that have existed for centuries a legitimate hearing.

This book does not suggest that Africa doesn't have any problems. It doesn't mean all government, all aid, or all modernity is bad for Africa. It's certainly not investment advice, or fine-grained economic analysis. But it will expose the formality bias that is holding back progress — and the bright ideas that can drive *everyone's* future.

It is this convergence of interest that is most important for engagement with Africa. While fat economies have assumed that lean economies should learn from them, it's also true that fat economies must learn from lean ones. The post-crash ethos of doing more with less — less time, less energy, and less money — is a necessary pastime in sub-Saharan Africa, as well as an emerging global imperative.

One last word on methodology: In all of these cases, unless an external source is identified, my knowledge comes from personal interviews. And throughout, I'll be talking about "Africa" — that is to say, a population of nearly one billion people, most of whom I've never met. "How to Write About Africa," an essay by Kenyan writer Binyavanga

Wainaina, has become a widely circulated list of "don'ts" for people such as myself. His satirical counsel:

> Don't get bogged down with precise descriptions. Africa is big: fifty-four countries, 900 million people who are too busy starving and dying and warring and emigrating to read your book. The continent is full of deserts, jungles, highlands, savannahs and many other things, but your reader doesn't care about all that, so keep your descriptions romantic and evocative and unparticular.

I won't treat Africa as one country — reporting across three years and seventeen countries, I witnessed too much diversity to do so. Nevertheless, this book is proudly pan-African. I believe we can learn well from our similar challenges, and perhaps better from our distinct triumphs. Comparing and contrasting the facts of life across the continent is a necessary ambition — of which I've only scratched the surface.

We start with the nineteenth-century saga of mapping Africa because it mirrors the twentieth century of demeaning development efforts. As the MDGs phase out and the twenty-first century of human progress unfolds, we must do better. The ancient searchers along the Nile have the excuse of historical blindness; after all, it took centuries for humans to embrace the very idea of mapping rivers and roads from an aerial perspective. When you're tramping through the jungle, or up a mountain, or across a field, you have no idea how your progress might look from a bird's-eye view, or why it would be useful to see things differently.

When you're thinking of Africa in the context of the wars you've seen, the poverty you assume, or the government you've given up on, you're likewise missing the point. In the age of breakthrough technologies and instant access to information, blindness is no excuse. The stories in this book provide a new compass — not just for the continent, but for every sector of the global economy.

2

Kanju
The Fine Line Between Genius and Crime

ALWAYS WONDERED WHY I never receive Nigerian e-mail scams. Perhaps my spam blockers are too good. Perhaps my obviously Yoruba name deters potential predators, who see me as one of them — wise to and thus exempt from the swindle. Imagine my delight when I received this pitch from an in-box acquaintance:

> How're you doing and I trust that I find you in good health. I'm really sorry to reach out to you this manner and I'm sorry for not informing you about my urgent trip to Scotland. I am here for a Seminar and to complete a project. Presently, I will be glad if I could confide in you and I want this issue to be confidential between You and I because I don't want people to get worried about my situation.
>
> Everything was fine until I got robbed on my way back to the hotel and I lost my Wallet, mobile phone and some valuables during this incident. I'm sending you this message to inform you that am stranded at the moment and need your help with a loan of $3350 to pay up the bills and make arrangements to get back home.

As a bit of an experiment, I copied this message and sent it to a random sampling of contacts. Of the forty people I e-mailed, a few warned me that my account may have been hacked. Most ignored the note. Predictably, no one offered to front the money.

Despite what looks like growing indifference, e-mails like this have made my country famous. While Web-based swindles are common in many countries around the world, Nigerians seem to have perfected the dogged pursuit of international money transfer scams, sometimes known — after the section of the Nigerian criminal code referring to such activity — as 419. Those three digits don't quite do justice to the hundreds upon thousands of elaborate, sometimes hilarious Internet capers that have sullied Nigeria's digital reputation.

As is well known by now, 419 predators blast pleading e-mails asking for emergency loans, or assistance in freeing vast, "trapped" sums of money in exchange for hefty payouts. The classic scam involves a Nigerian prince attempting to reclaim his birthright. Marks are asked to provide Social Security and bank account numbers that allow the criminals to drain vast sums. Some victims are urged to send cashier's checks, or to wire money. Others cite known public figures (the wife of deposed Liberian dictator Charles Taylor, for example), or hint at the opportunity to take advantage of lax accounting and corruption in a distant bureaucracy.

The FBI has reported losses of millions of dollars a year to these scams, which have grown more sophisticated over time. Complex websites and forged ID cards and bank statements are now stock-in-trade for the gangs of scammers who have cornered the market. Tell tale grammatical errors are fewer and farther between. The modern scammer exploits the authenticity of familiarity; e-mails are sent from the real accounts of our acquaintances. From 1995 to 1998, a 419 scam was responsible for defrauding Banco Noroeste in Brazil of $181 million — the third-largest bank heist in history. In 2009, a Nigerian living in Singapore was arrested for trying to defraud the National Bank of Ethiopia of $27 million.

I'd argue the crowning achievement of these "Yahoo Boys" (so called because of the e-mail service that many use to spin their traps) came in 2008, when former US secretary of state Colin Powell found himself onstage at a benefit concert in London, boogying to "Yahoozee," a popular song by Nigerian artist Olu Maintain, glorifying the life of savvy, silent crime that had exploded in Nigeria's backdoor economy. The lyrics tell a flashy story:

> *If I hammer*
> *First thing na Hummer*
> *One million dollars*
> *Elo lo ma je ti n ba se si Naira?**

Thousands of fans appreciated the verse — a form of swagger certification native to hip-hop. But most people see the nuisance e-mails as evidence of moral turpitude — the devil in the digital. I believe the e-mails are proof of a trend that promises to transform Africa at large.

The scams are really about connection. It is no accident that the globalization of 419 has coincided with the spread of Internet connectivity. The late 1990s explosion of Internet cafés in sub-Saharan Africa created shared and slow but cheap connections to the World Wide Web. The most common offenders of the code remain young men who exploit this novel connectivity to make a profit. By subbing in a new location for each manufactured "emergency" — Manila, Mumbai, Madrid — the scammers travel the world, bathed in the light of their computer screens.

The scams are also about disillusion. Of course, cash is a motivation. But the Yahoo Boys' naughtiness also comes from a sense of empty formal alternatives (in fact, the 419 scramble for foreign assets stemmed from the precipitous drop in value of the *naira*, Nigeria's currency). Scamming for a living is one way of exiting an institutional framework that has failed to provide jobs. One youth, having been successfully prosecuted by the beleaguered Nigerian Economic and Financial Crimes Commission, gave an anonymous interview explaining how and why he became a scammer:

---

* How much is that in *naira?*

I come from a poor family in Lagos, Nigeria. We did not have very much money and good jobs are hard to find. I was approached to work for a gang master when I was 15, because I had done well in school with my English, and was getting to be good with computers. The gang master was offering good money and I took the chance to help my family. . . . In the year before I was arrested I earned about $75,000 (£46,000) for my family. I bought my family a better house and drove a BMW. I had mobile phones and laptops and everything that comes with having lots of money.

Then again, 419 is about drive. Nigerians tut-tut about 419 — half joking, half mortified. But its inventors are sometimes the smartest kids in the room: the best with English, critical thinking, and computers. At the very least, they demonstrate a tenacity that is endemic to successful entrepreneurs from Oprah Winfrey to Nigerian Aliko Dangote, the richest man in Africa. In another life, the Yahoo Boys may have enjoyed aboveboard business success. As Apple cofounder Steve Jobs noted in a 1995 interview, a thin line divides genius and crime:

> I know from my own education that if I hadn't encountered two or three individuals that spent extra time with me, I'm sure I would have been in jail. . . . I could see those tendencies in myself to have a certain energy to do something. It could have been directed at doing something interesting that other people thought was a good idea or doing something interesting that maybe other people didn't like so much.

The Yahoo Boys may lack the primary school teachers, the elder mentors, or the Silicon Valley structures to guide them away from criminal activities. Instead, they leverage ambition, resourcefulness, and tools at hand — including their own wits — to pursue a vilified but beneficial livelihood. Equipped with only an e-mail address, these criminals have earned millions of dollars and international notoriety, solving the common African experience of economic stagnation and proving that you can make something from nothing at all.

Academic writer Louis Chude-Sokei, in a wonderful essay on the topic of Nigerian Internet scams, seems to be smiling. "It is hard not to be impressed," he writes. Chude-Sokei believes the scammers are "the public face of West Africa's intimacy with digital media and technology and of Nigeria's refusal to wait passively for either justice from their political system or global charity."* While I don't condone criminality, I, too, refuse to clutch my pearls about 419. From a bird's-eye view, the virtual crime wave begins to look like an amazing new kind of entrepreneurship.

The Yahoo Boys embody a spirit I constantly confront when traveling in Africa. I've begun to call it *kanju* — the specific creativity born from African difficulty. As it turns out, uncertain electricity, clogged roads, and nonexistent social protections can make life tough, but they also produce an extraordinary capacity for making do.

Kanju is why I don't always mind traffic in Africa. For street vendors, the presence of thousands of slowly moving vehicles is an unbeatable marketing opportunity. Thus during "go-slow," as rush hour is known, you can buy water, fruits and vegetables, packaged snacks, mobile phone airtime, mobile phone chargers, and, occasionally, live animals — all through your car window (take that, Amazon). Even if I'm not in the market for children's clothing or fireworks, a road trip offers a glimpse into the dynamism of African commercial life. Just when you think you've seen it all, someone is selling a coat rack balanced on her head.

Traffic marketing is a job for the quick mind with quicker feet. Cars don't always bother stopping to examine wares. Sales can turn on a lingering glance. Once, in Ghana, I silently cheered a vendor I watched sprint 400 meters at what seemed like Olympic record pace. When he reached his target, it turned out that he was not selling but retrieving a bag of peeled oranges he had pushed through the window for exami-

---

* Adaobi Tricia Nwaubani's wry novel *I Do Not Come to You by Chance*, Andrew Apter's "IBB = 419," and Dan Smith's *A Culture of Corruption* all trace this history as well.

nation. Without hesitation, or even a perfunctory show of disappointment, he began to work the adjacent line of irate commuters.

Like the Yahoo Boys', these are not lives to glamorize, but to consider. Mohammed Ibrahim, the Sudanese-born billionaire and founder of the international telecommunications company Celtel, has given it some thought. "I always say Africans are the greatest entrepreneurs," he told me. "Many people wake up in the morning not knowing what they're going to do — but they have to make some money. So they do whatever is needed. If it's raining, you'll go sell an umbrella. If it's hot, you sell ice or some Coke. People try to find ways to make a living, and there's great energy."

He's right, but African entrepreneurship is about more than making a living — it elevates rule bending to fine art. If you want to see the world's most novel business plans, go to the massive, mostly illicit car resale market in Lagos, where a woman drifts through the crowd of potential buyers, selling imitation license plates to those who don't want to brave the car registration authority. Go to the coastal high street of Dakar, where a man is reselling the free headphones and eye masks distributed onboard by international airlines. Go to Nairobi, where Gladys tends her family farm.

Once you start to look for it, this energy is everywhere. Driving on the smoothed dirt roads ringing Lake Victoria in Uganda, I chanced upon the largest speed bump I've ever seen. Rutted roads are no surprise in Africa, but this one seemed calculated — a mountain where there ought to have been a molehill. There was no way around it, and before I knew it, my car had bottomed out. Instantly, a gaggle of young men materialized to "help." They hadn't warned me about the hazard but were happy to perform a rescue — for a fee, of course! I gave them an earful but later laughed at their cunning.

In Yoruba, a language of Nigeria, *kanju* literally means "to rush or make haste"; in English, we might say it is to "hustle," "strive," "know how," or "make do." There are some existing terms that get close to my meaning. *Jua kali* (which means "harsh sun" in Swahili) refers to the resourceful labor in Kenya's informal sector. *"Système D"* and "Article 15" refer to the ecology of workarounds and rule breaking that governs parts of French central Africa. It's *kalabule* in Ghana, *magendo* in Uganda. Political scientist Joel Migdal calls *kanju* logic "strategies of survival — blueprints for action and belief in a world that hovers on the brink of a Hobbesian state of nature."

In other words, Africa's *kanju* culture is more Darwin than Degas, less about subjective beauty than about practical solutions, and doing much more with far less. In fact, the most important thing about *kanju* is that it is born out of everything outsiders pity in Africa. Like the sand in an oyster that creates a pearl, hardship produces an attitude that can be leveraged to attack the same. After years studying informality in Nigeria, Dutch architect and planner Rem Koolhaas reached the same conclusion. In the West, he writes, "there's a sense of infinite choice, but a very conventional set of options from which to choose." By contrast, "in Lagos there is no choice — but there are countless ways to articulate the condition of no choice."

I spent the better part of three years trying to count the ways. Beyond an intense and necessary work ethic, I discovered a rich archive of processes, products, and people that are changing the development trajectory in Africa. They do so by combining the basic ingredients of *kanju* — recycling, resilience, and the pointed irreverence of the Yahoo Boys.

Recycling is the natural corollary to resource scarcity — an integral part of being "lean." I traveled to South Africa a few weeks after the closing ceremonies of the 2010 World Cup. I winced at the sight of football *tchochkes* still cluttering the Johannesburg airport — including thousands of unsold vuvuzela horns. Trying, in my rental car, to navigate the hazards of left-side driving, I heard a story on the radio. A South African woman had created a washing machine from a vuvuzela. It works not unlike a mechanized washer: by poking holes in the cheap plastic casing, she had created a tool to agitate clothing, soap, and water in a bucket.

I parked. With pluck, a bit of creativity, and cast-off materials, this woman had devised a tool to ease the daily chore of the millions who wash in Africa. What's more, she embodied the African attitude I had been pondering for months. *Kanju* solutions, I determined, take inventory: *What do I have? What do I need? What can I do? What can I do without?*

Lynette Denny asks herself as much most days. She is a doctor in the Department of Obstetrics and Gynecology at Cape Town's Groote Schuur Hospital, famous for performing the world's first successful heart transplant. She is ruddy-cheeked, quick-witted, and effervescent in her concern for her country's health and development. On Thursday and Friday afternoons, she drives from the glittering mountain bay to the sprawling Cape Flats, where the population is unanimously black and poor. There, she manages the Khayelitsha Cervical Cancer Screening Project.

In *kanju* style, Denny's clinic is actually two metal shipping containers stacked on top of one another. Nevertheless, her lean staff treats cervixes, tests for HIV, administers medicine and guidance, and, she says, does "everything but operate" in pursuit of women's gynecological health. Low-risk pregnant women give birth here. The clinic also hosts a one-stop rape counseling center. Like many public health services, it is overwhelmed: Denny sees twenty to thirty women per afternoon but has "mastered the art of patients thinking they've had me for thirty minutes when it's been two minutes."

Miles away and years ago, Kenneth Nnebue seeded Nollywood with the same frugal genius. The *N* stands for Nigeria. The rest is self-explanatory. If 419 is the country's most hated export, Nollywood is its most loved. The local film industry makes some of the most profitable original films in the world. Behind Bollywood (sprung from India's Bombay-based studios), Nollywood is second-ranked in the number of movies it produces — up to two thousand per year — and among the world's top revenue generators — $250 million annually by some estimates.

Before he sparked an artistic revolution, Nnebue was an electronics dealer living in Lagos. He found himself with thousands of empty VHS tapes to offload. With several friends and a cheap camera, he shot a short film to fill the space, and perhaps attract customers. The result, *Living in Bondage,* told the story of a man who kills his wife in exchange for a lifetime of vast wealth. Her unhappy ghost keeps him "in bondage" thereafter.

Released in 1992, the campy, Igbo-language film was a fluke—but as disruptive as the Hollywood shift from silent film to sound, or black and white to color. The preexisting national theater and performance culture found a larger outlet for its work. Nigerians saw themselves on film and loved it. Needless to say, Nnebue sold all of his cassette tapes. More importantly, he opened a market of 300 million eyeballs.

It's hard to believe that many millions of people haven't heard of Nollywood; to me, it's as familiar as the smell of shea butter at the beauty parlors where I twist and braid my hair. (Some American salons catering to African women blast all Nollywood, all the time.) I always enjoy the guilty pleasure of watching the latest titles, sucking my teeth with the other clients at dramedic inflection points.

Nollywood movies and soap serials, produced on the cheap and sold locally as home videos (only a handful ever meet a silver screen), are known for melodrama: rolled eyes, waggling necks, and pointed fingers. Beyond the Faustian bargain of *Bondage*, other classic tropes —boy meets girl—are subverted when the girl is barren, or possessed by the devil, or confronts her husband's second wife. Other timeless fables, as when the country mouse hits the city, take on a special significance in a place where recent rural-to-urban migrations have utterly shaken the African social and economic fabric.

The vast majority of Nollywood films are riven with tradition, moralism, superstition, and corresponding godliness—whether Islamic or Christian. More recently, romantic and buddy comedies, heist flicks and gangster dramas, have taken hold of the local imagination. Popular, of-the-moment films like *BlackBerry Babes* (about a maven of women and their smartphone-driven adventures) spawn quick-and-dirty sequels (among my favorite comedies: *Jenifa, Jenifa 2, The Return of Jenifa, The Return of Jenifa 2*).

Until recently, the films have been universally low budget, taking between $40,000 and $200,000 to finance. Unable to fight the tide of copyright violations and piracy—an ecosystem as robust as 419 —movie producers skimp on the front end, scraping together just enough to make and distribute a film. It's no wonder that many are shot in a week, or that a romantic dinner in one offering is staged in the same apartment as a death scene in another.

But the key innovation of Nollywood was never making movies. After all, incumbent studios in the United States had it covered. Selling pirated copies of Disney or Bruce Willis flicks was and remains a brisk business. Rather, Nollywood's innovation was customizing film offerings for a local audience. By offering a more relevant product, shot in local languages as well as English, Nollywood cannibalized an existing market and ran away with it.

For two decades, the industry grew exponentially. Once the barriers to entry had been breached, creatives churned out hits and employed a vast network of hawkers to sell them. Dozens of market clusters sprang up as centers of scripting, editing, printing, and sales. Hundreds of actors and actresses became household names. Thousands of lighting and sound experts, cinematographers, screenwriters, and film editors honed their skills. Digital production democratized the game further. Twenty years after *Bondage*, the highest-grossing Nigerian movie of all time, *Ije*, sold 200,000 copies on the first day it was released and made about $400,000 at the box office. Like 419 scams, the lo-fi, bare-bones, backdoor film economy turned out to be a moneymaker.

The experience of watching a film, however, never changed. Gradually, individuals, some of whom owned VHS machines, could afford DVD players at home. But for the most part, films had to be caught in public, communally, at TV kiosks, "video parlors," or in pubs. From the 1980s until 2004, Lagos didn't have a single movie theater. Elsewhere in Africa, especially outside of big cities, pop-up community cinemas brought a traveling carnival approach to screening films, both African and Western. Informal distribution methods dominated.

Jason Njoku decided to leapfrog the status quo. A serial entrepreneur with a string of failed business ideas behind him, he had slunk from London to his mother's home in Nigeria in 2010. He noticed her penchant for Nigerian content rather than quintessentially British soaps like *EastEnders.* That same year, he launched iROKOtv. The model was simple: acquire rights to African films and put them online.

The venture started with a YouTube channel and quickly developed its own streaming service. "Netflix for Nollywood" now has a library of six-thousand-plus African movies accessible to global subscribers.*

Local viewing is hobbled by what a friend calls "African bandwidth anorexia," but as Web connections proliferate, there's no telling how wide an audience iROKO will find. Certainly, the market is no longer limited to Nigeria and its diaspora; Ghana, Kenya, and other English-speaking African countries have developed their own insurgent film industries.

Other African film distributors like Buni, Wabona, and AfricaFilms .tv are growing, too. The future of Nollywood looks to be a *kanju* fusion of old and new: digital ventures hack an established film infrastructure — itself a mash-up of the Nigerian theater tradition and Hollywood flash. As with the 419 explosion, Nollywood pioneers made something very big from something very small. And, of course, the whole industry would evaporate but for the cadre of self-employed directors, writers, and producers, hustling constantly to make audiences laugh, cry, and pay up.

This anything-goes agility is better called "resilience," now a term of art in sociological circles. It's a shorthand for bouncing back from crisis — whether genocide, drought, or reckless investing. And it has deep, neurobiological roots. The amygdala portion of the brain is constantly scanning for dangers, perceived or real. It's a smoke detector of sorts, helping humans determine whether we are at risk.

Unlike a conventional smoke detector, the amygdala acclimates to your life experiences. As with the body's immune system, there's an ideal balance between nonchalance and defensive responses. And with greater exposure to stresses, our window of tolerance grows, and resilience develops. Some academic literature calls this attribute "hardiness," or "grit" — a character trait in high demand at places from West Point military academy to today's global job market.

---

* In 2011, iROKO spun out a similar service for African musicians — also blindingly popular in local and diaspora markets, but largely unknown in the West.

It's also something kids grow up with in Africa. In my time criss-crossing the continent, rural and urban, I often saw schoolchildren as young as three or four years old walking in neat lines to and from school. Daily, the kids span epic distances — 1, 5, 10 kilometers — along roads alternately dusty and lonely, full of traffic or softened by rains. When my mother was growing up in Nigeria, she had no official cur-few; she was told to come home only when it was too dark to see the lines on her palm.

Helicopter parents in fat economies might be horrified to let their children so far off the leash. But African children walk together, with-out setting off the smoke detector, because they can handle the chal-lenge. Author Paul Tough looked closely at young Americans who were not the smartest in their classes but had, through will and persis-tence, made it from poor neighborhoods all the way through college. He saw what I see in these young Africans: "For young people without the benefit of a lot of family resources, without the kind of safety net that their wealthier peers enjoyed, [grit] seemed an indispensable part of making it to graduation day."

While important, this uncomplaining dynamism and perseverance don't tell the whole story. Resilience is inherently conservative — fo-cused on bouncing back to a prior status quo. Kanju, by contrast, is generative — it's about catapulting ahead. And in my experience, to get ahead in Africa, you sometimes need to play naughty.

The continent's entire commuter culture, for example, runs on col-lective insolence. As day breaks and as dusk falls, those who can afford a lift cluster at junctions across Africa, waiting for *matatu* buses — fourteen-person vans that run hundreds of kilometers per day, along vaguely determined routes, without formal schedules and for fares subject to negotiation. The often-flamboyant décor varies according to the taste of the owner. Many *matatus* boast loud paint and prayer beads, louder reggae music — even back-seat television screens. "Al-lahu Akbar," read one taxi bumper in Douala. "Follow us on Twitter," read another in Nairobi.

The word *matatu* (roughly "30 cents" in Swahili) comes from the affordable 1950s price of a lift along Kenyan roads. *Matatus*, Nigerian *danfos,* Tanzanian *dala-dalas,* Cameroonian *7-places* (the generous inventory of seats in a standard sedan), Mozambican *shapas* — whatever the local term, these vehicles are the primary means of conveyance for millions of Africans with places to go and minimal disposable income. In some cities, the official state-run buses roll by like staid battleships; in most towns, there is no centralized system for moving people, in bulk and at speed. (When living in Uganda, I hailed motorbike taxis so often I took to carrying around my own helmet.)

Matatus likewise fill the gap in nimble, madcap fashion. Other drivers loathe them — understandably. They honk through traffic jams; they hug the curb when so moved; on the open road, they routinely test the mettle of drivers in the opposite lane. Usually the conductor is hanging out of the open sliding door, banging the hull of the van like a jockey, exhorting potential passengers to join the fun.

Transportation in Africa is an unprecedented running experiment in informal economic activity. The cacophony of engines, the constant pinballing of coins and bills, and the reckless merges into traffic have evolved entirely outside the action of the state. Transit is at once a private-sector activity and a massive public good. With minimalist regulations (save shakedowns from the police), the industry in Kenya has swelled to an estimated fleet of thirty thousand vehicles that move millions annually.

Matatus anchor the informal sector that is by definition unregistered, undocumented, and partially excluded from official GDP statistics. It's tempting to think of informality as a symptom of backwardness and disorganization, but the reverse is true. In 2009, a South African Web company called Mocality dispatched an army of agents to walk the streets of Nairobi, collecting basic information from local vendors in order to start an online business directory. Some forty thousand shopkeepers were asked to name their services, their telephone number — and a landmark that would help customers find them.

A startling trend emerged. In a city of four million residents, almost everyone *agreed* about which physical landmarks matter. Everyone in a given district relied on the Globe Cinema, the Caltex petrol station, the South C mosque, the iconic I&M skyscraper, and the like. Likewise, everyone can tell you the rush hour surcharge for a *matatu* ride, or the going rate for roadside sugar cane, cut into neat chunks and sold to commuters with a sweet tooth.

As with high-context navigation, the strength and prevalence of these informal norms distinguish African economies — and are bedrock components of *kanju.* While industrial history and "modernization" theory tend to glorify organization, institutionalism, taxation, legibility, and the rejection of informality, many millions of Africans live every day as a rebuke to this logic.

But why? For the people of all ages self-employed as farmers, filmmakers, day laborers, vendors, drivers, contractors, and the like, the informal economy experience builds vital skills, in arbitrage, innovation, and risk assessment. As compared with richer regions, African informality is acyclical; the gray economy not only provides work in lean times but actually expands during times of economic growth. Often, informal-sector industries are interlinked: one vendor sells used electronics; his neighbor repairs them when they break. It's a remarkably consistent source of employment that, like water in a jar of pebbles, fills every conceivable gap in labor.

There are plenty of tough neighborhoods in which the formal sector does not fully support the labor force. Globally, the gray economy is estimated to be worth $10 trillion; if it were a country, it would be in the top five by wealth. And even in more developed countries, part-time jobs, dog-walking services, jitney cabs, and carpooling schemes are signs of the deformalization of twenty-first-century goods and services.

But in many places in sub-Saharan Africa, the informal economy is the *only* economy — generating, on average, more than half of all economic activity. Movies and transit are the tip of the iceberg. In Lagos, a study by the Institute for Liberty and Democracy determined that nearly 94 percent of the city's businesses operated outside of the law. This labor is worth $50 billion — bigger than both annual foreign assistance to Nigeria ($11.4 billion) and foreign investment ($5.4 billion).

More importantly, development practice tends to overlook this parallel economy. A significant body of experts would prefer that Africans simply color between the lines. Enforceable contracts, property rights, even traffic lights have positive effects on development. But the integrity of Africa's formal institutions is everywhere in doubt—often, as we'll see in the next chapter, with good reason. Consequently, there's a well-defined relationship between rules and the avoidance thereof. All of the vibrant, unusual innovations we'll see in this book are a response to flawed formal avenues for action and expression.

The regional gift for clever hacking exists in part because national leaders have *also* been breaking the rules, even as they are supposed to make and enforce them. Despite the fanfare and spotlight on leadership, Mohammed Ibrahim's $5 million prize for good governance hasn't been awarded for four out of the seven years it has existed. Everywhere, writes Steve Daniels in his book *Making Do,* "the formal institutions we take for granted—law, finance and education—have failed the self-employed manufacturers and traders of the informal sector, who have in turn used great ingenuity and drive to invent mechanisms of production and trade appropriate for a huge popula-

In Dar es Salaam, Tanzania, a roadside fence presents a sales opportunity.

tion of workers." In this climate, *kanju* is not just a means to get by; it is a secondary effect of ineffective central government.

The flip side of informality is corruption, one of the biggest challenges for Africa. The wide reach of graft and rent seeking in regional government will be detailed in the next chapter. But *kanju* is different from simply breaking the rules; it's about coming up with a totally different game. In this conception, informality is more of an escape valve than a corrosive force. In Ghana, *kanju* naughtiness has been a tool to attack the worst types of corruption at their source.

Like most of the entrepreneurs we'll meet, Anas Aremeyaw Anas prefers to ask for forgiveness rather than permission. On a busy side street in Accra, a floppy bucket hat is the only indication that this young Ghanaian has embroiled himself in some of the biggest anticorruption investigations in the country. He wears the hat to keep his face from sight. For a vigilante, overexposure is dangerous.

Anas, known to the public mainly by one name, practices a brand of journalism committed to radical transparency. I report stories armed with a tape recorder, paper, and pen; the soft-spoken Anas uses hidden cameras, microphones, wigs, costumes, and any other means necessary to throw sunlight on corruption in Ghana. A story on bad flour shut down a local biscuit factory. A story on widespread identity fraud sped Ghana's change to biometric passports. A six-month investigation and exposé of the Chinese role in Ghana's sex trade earned him the Norbert Zongo Prize for investigative journalism in 2009.

Unlike most journalists, Anas often casts himself as both reporter and source — as his own Deep Throat. "In my kind of journalism, the key ingredient is to name, shame, and jail," he explains. And so one of his favorite words is *incontrovertible* — a way of describing the meticulous multimedia proofs he marshals over the course of his investigations.

Over seven months, he went undercover at the Osu Children's Home, a state-run orphanage in Accra. Posing as Rev. Abednego Akpabli, local preacher, and Hajia Barkisu, a female trader from Mali, Anas filmed abuses and mismanagement, from locking kids in pens for minor misbehavior to stealing food from their table. When the story broke, the public first gobbled up the sensational drama and then demanded action. Shamefaced, the government cobbled together a committee chaired by the minister of employment and social welfare to test the allegations in the report—the main points of which were corroborated. When President Obama gave a speech to the Ghanaian parliament in 2009, he mentioned Anas as a "courageous journalist" who "risked his life to report the truth."

Anas, whose laconic real-life persona makes his pantomimes and daring seem implausible, also runs a private investigations service called Tiger Eye. He considers himself an equal-opportunity exposer. Neither business cartels nor government ministries are immune. After the first string of successful investigations, the Ghanaian government enlisted him to collect evidence about cocoa smuggling between Ghana and neighboring Côte d'Ivoire. The regulator had deployed police and other ministries responsible for border control, to no avail.

An assistant edits videos for Tiger Eye, the investigations firm and film studio run by Anas Aremeyaw Anas in Accra, Ghana.

"It was clear that the state was in trouble. The state security agencies couldn't solve it," says Anas. After a few weeks of investigation, he found that rent-seeking police forces were the problem. "The security men we were provided to do the work were instead taking money from our own farmers and allowing them to smuggle cocoa out of Ghana."

Anas publishes his findings in local newspapers and has begun producing feature-length DVDs, sold alongside Nollywood dramedies. They aren't the slickest productions, but they pack heat; when we met, he was working on a documentary about revenue leakages in the import and export business. With four months of secret footage gathered at ports across Ghana's coast, he was building a comparative analysis of what Ghana's government borrows from donors, how much is actually given to residents, and how bribes grease countless palms at the borders. The working title of the film: *Enemies of the State*.

With the naughtiness inherent to *kanju*, Anas is twisting the rules of reporting in order to enforce the rule of law. At times, he is also breaking the law — he's been accused of violating privacy rights and other unethical reporting practices. "I admit that I break the law, but eventually it's always in the public interest," he told me, adding that few others are committing time and resources to the transparency beat. Acting out is his way of making change.

Throughout this book, we will return to this theme. We will see, over and over again, mischievous, counterintuitive, and in many cases unprecedented solutions to complex problems born of bad alternatives. Not every person in Africa — or anywhere — has the capacity for the risk taking, creativity, and hustle that characterize *kanju*. But in the cases we'll examine, *kanju* naughtiness is not a liability. It's an asset that often means the difference between suffering and survival.

So rather than deleting 419 e-mails — well, we should probably delete the e-mails — we need to think harder about how and why opportunity looks so different in a lean economy, why so many Africans, held hostage to less functional institutions, play fast and loose with rules. This creative destruction, in the face of frustration, corruption, and in many cases real need, presents a learning opportunity.

3

Fail States

Why African Government Hasn't Worked

S OMALIA HAS LONG represented the quintessential "failed
state." But it's not the only country in the neighborhood. Since
1991, when the end of Siad Barre's dictatorship plunged the nation into anarchy, the northern region known as Somaliland has held
four peaceful rounds of elections, established a central bank, printed
its own currency, and built an elaborate security apparatus that keeps
terror groups like Al-Shabaab at bay. Though Somaliland also borders
the tempestuous Gulf of Aden, virtually no pirates haunt its coast.
During the 2011 drought that thrust the Horn of Africa back into the
news, Somaliland dodged famine, spending around $10 million of its
own resources to cope with the food crisis.

My first encounter with Somaliland's shadow bureaucracy was in
Addis Ababa, the Ethiopian city that doubles as a regional diplomatic
capital. The African Union has frowned upon secessionist movements
since its predecessor, the Organization of African Unity, agreed to pre-
serve colonial borders in 1964. But in Addis, there was no sign of dis-
approval; on a leafy side street, Somaliland's consular real estate stood
near South Africa's. Three female civil servants were delighted to hear
that I was visiting their "country," hand-writing my visa with elegant,

antique script and passing my head-and-shoulders photograph back and forth with great interest.

That was the easy part. The flight into the capital, Hargeisa, remains one of the more harrowing experiences of my life. After Kenya and Ethiopia invaded Somalia in 2011 — in retaliation for the wave of cross-border attacks and kidnappings prosecuted by Al-Shabaab militants — both Kenya Airways and Ethiopian Airlines stopped service to the whole Horn. Undeterred, I scoured my network for tips on how to get to the breakaway state. My best option was an upstart carrier called Jubba Airways, which promised to get me there from the airstrip at Djibouti, the formerly French-colonized Somali nation at the fulcrum of the Indian Ocean and the Red Sea. Holding my breath, I gathered a mound of cash and dispatched a courier to pay for my booking.

After a night of wandering the surprisingly sterile Djibouti *souk,* I arrived at the airport as day broke. There wasn't a soul to be found. After some prodding ("Jubba? Jubba?"), a man in a plastic chair at the airport entrance told me that more intelligent passengers anticipated delays. I felt foolish for not assuming that with informal statehood came informal flight times. Out of local currency, I took a seat on the curb.

Soon enough, I was stamped out of Djibouti and onto a tarmac where a tanklike propeller plane had just landed. Women bearing children and bunches of *khat,* the psychotropic plant chewed across east Africa, clambered into the hold. It was open seating. My seat belt was broken. Down the aisle, a boy snagged a *khat* leaf and put it in his mouth. The airline didn't bother with safety demonstrations or a pilot's welcome. The pilot crackled a firm "Allahu Akbar" as we sped down the runway. And that was it. I pulled on a headscarf and thought happy thoughts.

In the capital, Hargeisa, it was clear that the central Somali government in Mogadishu is as irrelevant as Jubba's flight schedule. Green, white, and red Somaliland flags flew over the parliament building and the twenty-three ministries dedicated to everything from developing mines to taxing the lucrative Red Sea port at Berbera. I paid my way with a mix of American dollars and the Somaliland shillings I was required to buy upon arrival. To hear many locals tell it, all that's missing is formal international recognition.

Dr. Saad Shire, Somaliland's minister for planning, was bullish about independence. He pointed to three main sources of capital for developing states: foreign assistance, foreign loans, and foreign investment. Somaliland's gray status squashes all three. "Very few people will venture to invest in a country that is not recognized," said Shire, equal parts patriot and bean counter. "Independence removes all of these barriers." The imagined flow of investments is not a given; Somaliland remains a place lacking many basic capacities and infrastructures — human, physical, and financial. The state power utility reaches only a fraction of the 1.2 million living in Hargeisa. Everyone else sources electricity privately, at great expense. Sixty percent of the government's budget goes to security and policing.

But more unusual than underdevelopment is the near-unanimous nationalism I encountered. On a continent of invented borders, it was a rare surprise to find a subset of Africans who have affirmatively chosen to share a political community. Edna Adan Ismail, Somaliland's hard-charging former first lady, foreign minister, and current director of a teaching hospital in Hargeisa, explained the unique shape of Somaliland nationalism. "When Somalilanders separated from Somalia, they had this long tradition of taking care of themselves," she said. "They looked after themselves and their country because they wanted to do it."

This communitarianism was born out of hardship. Throughout the thirty-year union between once-Italian Somalia and once-British Somaliland, the Mogadishu government had been openly hostile to the clans in Somaliland, and few national resources ever made it to the region. During the drafting of their constitution, said Shukri Ismail, stirring her drink and shaking her head, "we were slaughtering our own goats, our own sheep, spending our own money collected penny by penny from the community." The only female on the first National Electoral Commission, she believes the fight to survive has been crucial for civic cohesion. "We've tried to build this country from scratch, from the grass-roots level, without any support from the international community."

In fact, foreign interference appears to be a national pet peeve. More than one Somalilander pointed out that the Transitional Federal Government (TFG) in Somalia was born from foreign diplomatic whirlpools such as the Djibouti Agreement and the Kampala Accord. Starting in the fall of 2011, invading armies from Ethiopia and Kenya blanketed the south. February 2012 saw a high-profile Somalia conference with fifty-five delegates in London, and another global meeting convened in Istanbul that June.

At least a few Somalis fault this arrangement for Somalia's present poverty and disarray. K'Naan Warsame, the Somali pop artist best known for the 2010 Coca-Cola World Cup tune "Wavin' Flag," is equal parts furious and fatalistic about this dynamic. "We've had twelve transitional governments since the 1990s, all formed in Kenya, outside the country," he said. "It's like food poisoning — when this government comes into the belly of Somalia, Somalia will vomit." Shire, who helped bootstrap a university in his hometown of Burao, says, "They do not have the legitimacy we have, and they don't feel the duty of accountability as we do."

Somalia's conferenced constitutionalism produced a central government that's the weakest in Africa. By contrast, living without foreign aid and intervention has been good for Somaliland; Nicholas Eubank of Stanford has demonstrated that its constrained resources have led to more inclusive government. As part of a need to share revenues from the port at Berbera, Somaliland kept the traditional clan structure that existed before the colonial encounter. Its constitution empowers a parliament, an executive branch, and also a cluster of trusted elders known as the Guurti.

For all of its rough edges, Somaliland is an example of *kanju* achievement in the shadow of state dysfunction. And it's another reminder of the formality bias that pervades development and foreign affairs. In neighboring Somalia, "we're trapped in this state-to-state diplomatic model," says John Prendergast, cofounder of the Enough Project, a human rights advocacy organization. Against all logic, Somaliland is a comparatively functional government of, by, and for its people. Supporting its mission, says Prendergast, "would be a lot more helpful in the long run than reinventing this broken wheel of central government that for today in Somalia is completely not workable."

It's a tough pill to swallow for observers used to credible, conscientious institutions. But the state framework in Africa is a constant impediment to development progress, because in practice, few Africans trust or validate the work of central government. Reporting this book, I spoke with countless individuals about their lives, challenges, and aspirations. In nearly all cases, the state was more of an irritation than an inspiration.

"Government in Africa — it doesn't deliver the goods," says Aleke Dondo, a tall, no-nonsense economist who works to finance farmers in east Africa. He lamented both administration and execution. "It's bad, and we see it. We see incomplete projects, all sorts of things. That makes you hate the government. Secondly, a lot of promises are made and nothing happens . . . and nobody tells you where the money is gone."

Obiageli Ezekwesili, who left top posts at the Nigerian Ministry of Education and the World Bank, tactfully notes that, in her experience, "much of governance can happen without an emphasis on understanding whether results were accomplished." Ghanaian George Ayittey, who wrote *Africa Unchained,* says that "leaving aside the democratic requirement that a government must be by the people and for the people, one expects at a minimum a 'government' to be responsive to the needs of the people, or at least, to perform some services for its people. But even this most basic requirement for 'government' is lacking." He has called the African state "a mafia-like bazaar, where anyone with an official designation can pillage at will. In effect, it is a 'state' that has been hijacked by gangsters, crooks, and scoundrels."

Ayittey's is an intense but shared frustration. In the run-up to Kenya's 2013 presidential election, Nairobi murals painted in the dead of night offered an insult to venal Kenyan politicians. Sitting leaders were depicted as vultures in business suits, atop thrones of cash, bearing briefcases of ill-gotten gains. Beside one mural on central Koinange Street ran a list of adjectives to "describe your MP": *greedy, selfish, pa-*

In advance of a hotly contested national election in 2013, Kenyan artists and activists began painting murals depicting the political class as vultures.

thetic, missing in action, leech. Another scripted a list of the higher-profile scandals to ensnare government since multiparty democracy resurfaced in 1992. In another, the people of Kenya appear as an indignant chorus, hurling a brick at one guilty-looking vulture.

The mockery makes sense. Even after a decade of modest improvements, many governments in the region are still cringingly ineffective. In Tanzania, as recently as 2011, the state-run air carrier had hundreds of employees — and no airplanes. Perhaps it was a good thing: in 2012, the airport authority admitted that its sole radar system had been broken for more than two weeks.

African bureaucracies become crutches and cover stories for self-dealing. In Swaziland — the last absolute monarchy on the continent — parliamentarians make forty times the average income of the population, and the prime minister gets a cash payment of almost $200,000 when he leaves office. For years in Nigeria, 75 percent of the federal budget went to the cost of operating government, leaving only 25 percent for infrastructure and citizen services. Similarly, Angola allocated just 1 percent of its oil-soaked 1998 budget to public education and welfare. In 2012, its first year of statehood, South Sudan uncovered $4 billion in disappeared oil revenues.

Corruption runs the spectrum from low- to highbrow. I groan when I approach the scruffy roadblocks that line African highways. The police officers on duty aren't necessarily looking for drugs or thieves; they're often looking for "tea" or "lunch" — euphemisms for the payoffs they cadge to get by. In too many countries, even the judicial institutions that are expected to uphold the rule of law have been captured by corruption. Judicial review of executive actions is largely imaginary. Relying on judges to referee contentious power grabs or international trade deals is, per Ugandan law professor Joseph Isanga, "futile and illusory." Saran Kaba Jones, who develops water projects in Liberia, told me about the disenchantment in her country. "For the person who sees an official driving around in a fifty-, sixty-, seventy-thousand-dollar car and building mansions and palaces — they all know where that money is coming from and are still very, very cynical when it comes to government."

Private cynicism is often outstripped only by public incompetence. In Malawi, for example, the seasonal ritual of hoeing, tilling, plowing, and planting is all that keeps its large subsistence farming population from hunger. Every year, Malawians prepare their modest landholdings for the arrival of government-subsidized seeds and fertilizer. The arrangement requires countless hours of labor on the part of the people, and minimal effort on the part of the government. But in 2005, the government botched its end of the deal, failing to procure enough agricultural inputs in time for planting. What's worse, the procurer eventually chosen was on a list of companies affiliated with Al-Qaeda, and Citibank refused to honor the transaction. In a cable published by WikiLeaks, an American diplomat was incredulous: "There are no services in place. . . . It is now extremely likely that Malawians will be in the same food insecure situation for the next year and possibly beyond, for lack of seed and fertilizer."

I've been using the term *fail states* to describe this shabby public service provision. It's a loan from geek culture, in which crying "Fail!"

is a common response to a dashed expectation. "Fail" moments bring your palm to your face — good shorthand for the galling dysfunctions that I found to be common during my travel in Africa.

In Kenya, it's learning that the immigration ministry has "lost" its copy of your work permit application — but can retrieve it for an unspecified fee. In Ethiopia, it's arriving at the airport to find that the power is out (you try landing planes in that event). In Ghana, it's the discovery that your university is on strike (again), and you'll have to wait nine months to finish your degree. In Zimbabwe, it's the smirk that comes from seeing a billboard wallpapered with your now-worthless local currency. In South Africa, it's having an application to start a business returned after six months — because you used blue, not black, ink. In Liberia, it's seeing girls walk miles into the bush to fetch water that should be coming out of the pipes underground. In Nigeria, it's the realization that a promised road has been paid for but not paved. Everywhere, it's the basic understanding that you are on your own.

Of course, "fail states" are substantively different from "failed states," a term that academics apply to the least functional nations on Earth. It's important to distinguish these everyday aggravations from the wars and total political collapse that have characterized Somalia proper.

Likewise, there are many places — south Asia, eastern Europe, Latin America, and fat economies included — where public service suffers, and where the poorest eke out a living in daring, undocumented ways. In his cheekily titled *Lawlessness and Economics*, Avinash Dixit contends that "in all countries through much of their history, the apparatus of state law was very costly, slow, unreliable, biased, corrupt, weak, or simply absent."

But what's darkly comic about the failures of modern African states is the longevity of African civilization. The continent is the oldest continuously inhabited landmass in the world. Yet the head start has not translated into a leg up.

Part of the problem is the states themselves. The modern map of Africa hardly reflects the boundaries of tribes and languages that pepper the continent. The famous 1884 Berlin Conference enshrined

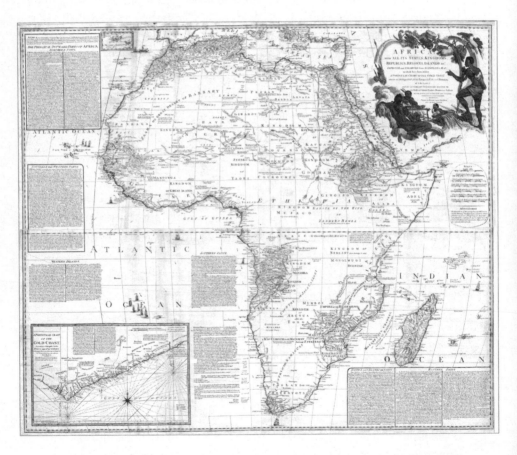

In 1872 — a decade before the Berlin Conference — Samuel Boulton created a map describing the different precolonial kingdoms of sub-Saharan Africa.

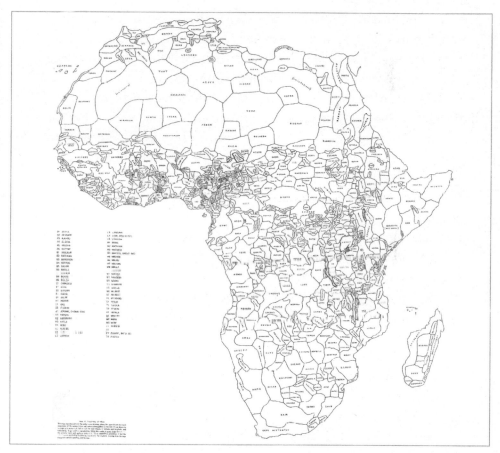

*In 1959, George Peter Murdock attempted to define borders
in Africa based on ethnicity and language.*

regional borders that split major tribes and kingdoms and combined others in a mostly arbitrary fashion. Eighty years later, the Organization of African Unity declared that the colonial borders would live forever. The OAU justified the partition by noting "that the borders of African States, on the day of their independence, constitute a tangible reality." But that doesn't mean the decision was rational, desirable — or even acknowledged. It was another instance of formality bias failing to map facts on the ground.

The truth is that African state divisions are less important than you'd think — and, as with Somaliland, frequently ignored. Seventy-three percent of households in Africa do not speak the official language of their countries (in other developing countries, it's 28 percent). The rural border between Côte d'Ivoire and Ghana is nonexistent — it runs through a village whose residents have lived and traded together for decades. Fulani pastoralists are present in all seventeen west African states. My Nigerian ethnic group has historic ties to French-speaking Benin, the seat of the expansive precolonial kingdom once known as Dahomey. A long decade of armed conflict sent a generation of Africans scuttling between Ghana, Guinea, Côte d'Ivoire, Liberia, and Sierra Leone.

Likewise, in east Africa, "part-time" refugees commute between Congo and Uganda. Despite waves of conflict in the North Kivu region of the Democratic Republic of Congo (DRC), a few sensible souls see no reason to give up their crops and homesteads. Until the episodic fighting passes — and eventually, it does — they head over the border. Western Uganda offers more linguistic, climatic, and ethnic continuity than the southeastern cities, or the Bantu-populated capital of Kinshasa, yoked to the Atlantic by a tiny sliver of coastline. While technically in the same country, it is a culture apart.

Economic interconnections also matter more than passports. The sagging economy in southern Africa — including the DRC and Zimbabwe — has produced a wave of migration into theoretically more stable South Africa. A great consolidation of coastal, trade-linked cities is taking place in west Africa. Already, Nigerian parents send their kids to college in Ghana, where some cross the border with Togo to buy cheaper cigarettes. The introduction of multilane, Chinese-built highways will accelerate the commercial integration. East Africa's biggest cities and economic clusters lie along the Mombasa-Kampala railway, begun by the British in 1896. The tracks are not quite a border, but a seam — one that is far more helpful in comprehending the region.

African borders, like the price of informal sector goods, are highly negotiable because the majority of African nations have a legitimacy crisis. States exist within jigsaw boundaries, lack an organic spirit of nationalism, are prone to division, and are difficult to rule. Their political anatomy was defined by outsiders, and then mismanaged by the ragtag institutions they left behind. They don't represent life as lived.

"When I hear about sovereignty in Africa, I smile. But it's an unhappy smile," says Cheikh Tidiane Gadio, the former Senegalese foreign minister who ran for president in 2012. He notes that European colonizers, with an assist from the OAU, left "fifty-something nonviable countries and states that explain why we are having all of these troubles." He would know: as a diplomat, he's been tasked with conflict resolution involving separatist movements in Mauritania, the DRC, and Mali — not to mention his own country: "The British and French found a way to leave us with Senegal, the Gambia inside Senegal, and Guinea-Bissau in the corner. We used to be the same people and now we have three states — one speaking Portuguese, one speaking French, and one speaking English. . . . We have spent thirty years trying to get out of it."

According to African Studies scholar Pierre Englebert, the continent hosts the highest proportion of illegitimate states in the world.* This history differs from other geographies, including other former colonies like the Philippines, or G20 *arrivistes* such as Argentina and India. Across Africa, Englebert notes, "rarely . . . had the colonial state

---

* The list contains forty-four out of fifty-four countries on the continent — and many of the "legitimate" states (island nations like Mauritius, the Seychelles, and Cape Verde) have boundaries that are obviously defined. The exceptional states — and Botswana is a good example — have had consistent leadership reasonably tied to precolonial political and social structures.

borne any relation to the economic systems, political organizations, and networks of social identification of the indigenous peoples." Arbitrary geographic divisions bankrupted the connection between authority and statehood.

It would be one thing if Africa's new and clumsy states somehow managed to promote progress. But almost everywhere, the project of governing low-legitimacy nations compelled decisions that had nothing to do with economic and social development.* Within its impractical borders, the continent evolved what economists Daron Acemoğlu and James Robinson call "extractive" institutions.

Joseph Mobutu's Zaire is a well-known example. To maintain federal loyalty in a country almost too big to rule, he funneled cash directly from the nation's mines into the pockets of his supporters, sowing the seeds of corruption that persist in the DRC today. To maintain stability, he killed or jailed opposition figures, often in violation of international human rights law. To establish a national identity, he ginned up a cult of the presidency, with white elephant monuments to nationalism, in the form of dams, statues, and palaces. He rebranded the Congo as Zaire and forced the adoption of national dress and a new currency (that he would in short order destroy). In the process, he gutted civic infrastructure and left his people destitute.

In far smaller Sierra Leone, President Siaka Stevens nationalized the diamond industry — but in words only. He systematically issued favorable mining contracts to allies who could mobilize voter support. Despite its resource riches, Sierra Leone's public budget suffered, and smuggling exploded. Reported diamond production (and associated tax revenues) dropped from 595,000 carats to 48,000 carats in eight short years.

At one point, Stevens destroyed the main railroad leading from Mendeland to Freetown. Never mind that it helped move coffee, cocoa, and other cash crops to the coast. He was cutting off his leg to spite his foot: because inland political opposition depended on the

---

* In most countries I visited, for example, all shopkeepers are required by law to purchase and display a photograph of the head of state.

vital pipeline, it had to go. (Perhaps he was right to be paranoid; just hours after his first stint in office, as prime minister, he fell victim to a coup.) Without revenues, civil servants could not be paid and stopped working. The tax commissioner of the capital, Freetown, abdicated his public office and began wheeling and dealing in the private economy. When Stevens stepped down in 1985, after eighteen years, frustrated rebel groups tore the country apart.

The world has watched this story repeat itself throughout the twentieth century. Even if colonial leftovers — say, the British-style schools that educated my parents — persisted in the 1960s and 1970s, they didn't flourish. National leaders rejected the idea of civic responsibility. Self-interested decisions at the center punished ordinary people at the periphery. These decisions wounded the private sector, too: in every year that a single African political party remained in power, firm productivity, growth rates, and sales growth for manufacturing plummeted.

The African National Congress in South Africa is a sterling example of the potential for political rot. Twenty years after the party, led by Nelson Mandela, jubilantly succeeded the loathsome apartheid regime, its membership is beginning to realize that the 1994 revolution was without content. While infrastructure is among the best on the continent, other public service provisions — from schools to health care — remain inadequate. The constitution guarantees access to housing and education, but the majority often enjoys neither. The new black boss looks nothing like the old white one — but profits as ruthlessly. When, in 2012, state police opened fire on protesting laborers at the Marikana platinum mine, killing thirty-four, they seemed to inaugurate an open clash between poor blacks and the country's newest oligarchy.

Even as African citizens have begun to despise African government, outsiders have doubled down on its supposed promise. Since the 1990s, aid interventions have fixated on improving performance at the top of the civic food chain. Donor nations concentrate on civil liberties and the "rule of law" as conditions for giving grants and loans in Africa. Large financial institutions like the World Bank generously fund "good governance" programs in recipient countries. Western-style democracy has become proof of progress.

But holding a vote is not the same as improving government performance or outcomes for citizens. Covering African elections from the ground, I found "free and fair" is only the tip of the iceberg. Frequently, the canniest African leaders organize elections just free and fair enough to get the international monkey off their backs. In 2011, Cameroon held its first "free and fair" election in fifty years of independence. But the vote was a fig leaf for a foregone conclusion — it returned to power the manipulative, autocratic Paul Biya. In advance of election day, Biya's supporters in the massive bureaucracy chanted, "*Cent pourcent!*" referring to projected vote totals for the man who has been head of state since 1982. (The final tally was 77 percent.) Democracy-venerating diplomats urged power sharing as a solution to Robert Mugabe's violent theft of Zimbabwe's 2008 election. In the end, the arrangement so weakened the opposition leader, Morgan Tsvangirai, that he lost the 2013 election to Mugabe outright.

Other celebrated Western habits and assumptions don't map well to sub-Saharan Africa. Take GDP: it's a core accounting standard and the basis of countless economic and aid policy decisions, as well as today's claims that Africa is "fast-growing." But it can lead to errors in calculating consumption and other real growth indicators. Esther Duflo and Abhijit Banerjee have critiqued the GDP approach for ignoring inefficiency and unequal access to resources.*

What's more, GDP is fundamentally tied to the state. Per capita figures are calculated at a national level, flattening variations among rural, urban, and peri-urban residents. Yoked into their respective state frameworks, Mali's populous southern capital appears much worse off than rural Namibia — though arguably the reverse is true. Shanta Devarajan, the chief World Bank economist for Africa, says he has "encountered cases where the minister is not even aware that the

---

* South African political scientist Lorenzo Fioramonti has written a book about why the imported obsession with GDP is hurting African economies.

statistical office is under his ministry." In fact, after decades of mis-
calculations, Ghanaian bean counters "discovered" $13 billion worth
of economic activity left out of the GDP. Nigeria is also scrambling to
recalibrate its figures for, among other reasons, more realistic lending
terms at the World Bank.

Like the bias for Somalia over Somaliland, Western preference for
political and economic formalism has allowed fail states to pantomime
liberal democracy without necessarily achieving progress. Politics have
paralyzed too many nominal democracies. During polling season, says
Ghanaian Kwame Ahiabenu II, who has worked to coordinate election
monitoring throughout west Africa, otherwise absent politicians appear in ethnic strongholds and rural villages, promising new roads and
cement for schools and clinics. Incumbents in Kenya bleed a special
"Constituency Development Fund" to finance their sudden largess.
The day of the vote arrives and, in the majority of cases, ends peace-
fully. The international observers go home. The banners melt from
public walls. Progress on political promises is often deferred until the
next election.

This may sound rather like democracy in modern America — or any
other country with a sagging political tent. But the African instance
is unique. Other lean economies (particularly those with a socialist
history) have built troubled but more mature governments. Even the
American "Tea Party" expects municipal trash collection and working
electricity. Conversely, few states in Africa can boast of a true compact
between citizen and government.

Fail states have slowed the region's development progress — the
eventual justification for the aid interventions we'll discuss in the next
chapter. Perhaps more importantly, fifty years of disappointments
crushed popular expectations of the state.* Blessings Chikakula, a

---

* Illegitimacy likewise explains the worrisome prevalence of militarized opposition
to the African state, responsible for decades of conflict on the continent. "The alien
nature of the state leads each group to attempt to appropriate it or to fear appropriation by others and break away from it," writes Englebert.

schoolteacher in Malawi, told me of the fuel shortages and famines that colored daily life under autocratic President Hastings Banda. "That thirty-year period affected us a lot, and that is the trend in most of the sub-Saharan countries," he said. While there have been recent, semi-organized political protests in Nigeria, Uganda, Sudan, and Senegal, many people lack both the inclination and the time to occupy anything. Comparing Malawi's politics to the Arab Spring, then boiling hot, Blessings said state failures are met with a shrug. "No one has decided to go in the street and march about it — he would look crazy."

All is not lost: for all their defects, fail states play an overlooked role in modern Africa. The crisis of faith in African government has forced dynamic *kanju* responses from ordinary people. There's a reason Anas takes such liberties in his reporting, why Gladys and her family are in no hurry to pay property tax, why one wealthy Nigerian friend spends thousands of dollars a month on his own electricity generation. It's why I wound up carrying my own motorbike helmet around Uganda. "Everywhere," writes Achille Mbembe, the great Cameroonian academic, "the delinquency of the state produced a culture of *débrouillardise* and of do-what-you-must, and a decline in the national identity."

When institutions are broken, playing by their rules becomes a laughable proposition. Where political freedom, social protections, and economic opportunities have failed to materialize, ordinary people have taken ownership of their fate — tearing down the assumption that states matter more than their alternative arrangements. In an odd way, the fail state has created millions of libertarians.

It's a sensible posture: the coming century will be dominated by forms of organization both smaller (think family) and larger (think Facebook) than the state, forging new allegiances on issues ranging from security to epidemics to trade. Dr. Shire agreed that "countries become less strategic as more and more economic communities form, and as more regional integration develops. . . . The boundaries of states become less relevant and important."

Somaliland is the tip of the iceberg. In Mombasa, Kenya's coastal metropolis, city residents and entrepreneurs established a hyperlocal "complementary" currency to deal with the scarcity of official Kenyan shillings. In "Bangladesh,"* an informal Mombasa settlement with a large merchant population, the invented "Bangla-Pesa" functioned like a promissory note for the barter economy. Traders could use the notes to facilitate everyday commerce — buying eggs or oil or lumber — and redeem them for cash later. In roughly one month of operations, the currency allegedly boosted trade by 20 percent.

Of course, there's a fail state wrinkle: virtually since independence, Kenya has labored to enforce its colonially bequeathed nationalism among an incredibly diverse population. In the past decade, the government has clashed with an outlaw political group known as the Mombasa Republican Council. Like Somaliland, the group points to historic marginalization and calls for an independent nation of ethnic, religious, and linguistic homologues. Sporadic attacks and protests followed by violent state reprisals have sharpened the conflict in recent years.

Which is why, when government officials caught wind of Bangla-Pesa, they mistook it for a secessionist plot. Never mind that the people of "Bangladesh" were more interested in economics than in politics. State police jailed the printers for forgery, too blind to see the ingenuity behind the dreaded insurrection.

The prisoners were released after paying stiff fines. But the episode neatly captures the best practices of *kanju* and the petty instincts of the fail state. Too many politicians, economists, and diplomats overlook the alternative institutions that matter to ordinary people. They discourage the region's successes while clinging to support for its bad borders, bad leaders, and bad habits. And when it comes to official development planning, the habits are even worse.

---

* Some informal norms borrow from the language of the state: in the DRC, "Article 15" is an invented constitutional provision that endorses hustling and hacking to get by. Co-opting the distant nation of Bangladesh is an equally good joke.

4

Stuff We Don't Want
Doing Bad in Africa

J ASON SADLER WEARS T-shirts for a living. In 2010, as an
extension of his Florida-based marketing enterprise, the American entrepreneur launched an initiative called "1 Million Shirts."
He encouraged individuals to send him $1 and at least one old T-shirt
—which he would then bundle and ship to "Africa." In an interview
with *Time* magazine, Sadler laid out his agenda: "All I'm trying to do is
trying to make something good happen and motivate people to get off
their butts, get off the couch and do something to help."

He wasn't the first sartorial altruist. Anyone who has traveled in
the developing world has seen the fruits of the practice firsthand. At
a hospital in Malawi, I met a woman wearing a "Harvard Volleyball"
T-shirt. (I don't think she was on the varsity squad in Cambridge.) Investor and philanthropist Jacqueline Novogratz's best-selling memoir
The Blue Sweater is named in honor of an old and beloved sweater
she had given to Goodwill as a teenager. The sweater finds its way to
a poor child in Rwanda and reminds her that "our actions—and inaction—touch people we may never know and never meet across the
globe."

In one narrative of globalization, this kind of connectivity is a feature, not a bug. But in sub-Saharan Africa, secondhand clothes are bad
for business. In west Africa, the textile industry is the biggest industry
aside from agriculture. When bales of free clothing flood local markets, they put tailors and clothiers and textile laborers out of work. In
1997, Nigeria's textile industry employed 137,000 workers. Six years
later, the number had plummeted to 57,000, largely as a result of free
clothing from fat economies. In the past decade, Malawi's largest textile manufacturer has closed, and similar companies in Mozambique
and in Uganda, where 81 percent of clothing sold is secondhand imports, are teetering toward bankruptcy. In Zambia, garment industry
workers have staged strikes in protest of this importation. Ethiopia
and Eritrea have outright bans on worn and used clothes. Mali, one
of the largest cotton producers in sub-Saharan Africa, has not itself
produced a single T-shirt.

This absurdity isn't lost on locals, who deploy colorful names for
the secondhand swag. In Ghana, they are known as *broni wa wo*, or "a
white man has died." In Togo, it's dead *yovo* ("white person") clothes.
The sinister cast seems warranted: Kenyan economist James Shikwati
calls such "gifts in kind" the destructive junction "where overwhelming helpfulness and fragile African markets collide."

In short, the T-shirts are SWEDOW — "stuff we don't want." In
2010, an anonymous aid blogger coined the term and its handy acronym to describe the poorly reasoned development planning that has
little use — or does actual harm.

One step ahead of Sadler, TOMS Shoes turns SWEDOW into
profit. The company offers conscientious consumers the satisfaction
of helping people while shopping. Their model donates one pair of
shoes to poor communities around the world for every pair of shoes
sold. Unfortunately, the model ignores the fact that plenty of poor
people have shoes, both on their feet and (like T-shirts) available for
local purchase. In the end, it exploits shoeless victims as a brand dif-
ferentiator. My first encounter with the for-profit corporation was at
a tony "awareness"-raising event in Manhattan's meatpacking district,

at which guests were urged to leave their shoes at the door. The bare-foot party was intended to approximate the harm shoeless kids face every day.

Unknown to most revelers: the true tragedy of bare feet is not shoe-lessness, but poverty — the inability to afford shoes, or much else. For many families getting free TOMS shoes, a steady job — making say, shoes — presents a more permanent solution. While TOMS claims to be evolving toward local sourcing, its disclosures have been opaque. As of publication, the company has manufactured the vast majority of its products in China — where, writes Richard Stupart, "it's presum-ably cheaper to make two pairs of shoes and give one away than it is to get people in a needier community to make one pair of shoes."

If you have seen the 1995 film *Clueless* (one of my favorites growing up), you'll recall that at one point the protagonist, played by Alicia Sil-verstone, is pestering her Beverly Hills peers for donations to victims of a natural disaster. When questioned about the wisdom of sending downhill skis to a tropical climate, she pouts: "Some people lost all their belongings — don't you think that includes athletic equipment?"

Of course, skis are beside the point. Like many micro-aid projects targeting Africa, buying shoes or sending gifts in kind privileges West-ern convenience as much as the intended recipients. It doesn't get at the larger structural reasons for the supposed problem, or offer flex-ibility in determining the ultimate solution. Worse, it reinforces the notion that the less fortunate are unable to provide the most basic ne-cessities for themselves. It's a presumption repeated in the 2010 UN poster, and a corollary to the formality bias that fixates on engineered states. Like bad geographers, amateur philanthropists "aid" an Africa of their own invention.*

In reality, footwear manufacturing is a booming industry in the region (where leather and rubber are abundant). Bethlehem Tilahun Alemu, owner of soleRebels, exports shoes from Ethiopia — whose shoemakers are among the biggest producers on the continent. She

---

* What's more, in parts of the continent accustomed to a constant stream of aid workers, NGOs are soon as members of a formal institution not unlike the state.

sees her work as a direct counternarrative. "It's not only a shoe we're selling. We're saying African people can work and offer something out of Africa. It's not like we're taking things from outside people," she told me in her airy flagship store in Addis Ababa. "We can create, build, and sell a product."

In the weeks after Sadler — who had no prior contact with development policy — announced "1 Million Shirts," scores of practitioners joined an outraged Internet pile-on, pointing out the economic and cultural folly of the endeavor, that there is little evidence that the less fortunate want what the more fortunate do not. In an open letter to Sadler, Senegalese entrepreneur Mariéme Jamme fumed: "How would Americans feel if we reverse the project and ask Africans to collect their old T-shirts and send them to the USA? Would Jason wear one? I think not."

Within days, Sadler took the heat to heart. He wrote an extended apology for his idea, noting: "That money will now be going to help people build wells, schools, homes, etc. The specific places and regions where this will be happening will be defined shortly and we want to make sure we get it right this time and don't generalize anything." Months later, the whole thing was scrapped. Poor Sadler learned the hard way that aid is not about aid, but about design.

Channeling charity from fat economies to lean ones in Africa is a fifty-year habit, with a dubious payoff. Where nations like South Korea and Indonesia began the 1960s in economic circumstances comparable to those of nations like Nigeria and Côte d'Ivoire, their African counterparts have had nowhere near the same success in blunting poverty and competing on a global footing.

Zambian economist Dambisa Moyo has written a popular book, *Dead Aid,* claiming that foreign aid is responsible for the divergence, and that all assistance to Africa should be eliminated. Along with wasted time and wasted funds ($1 trillion, by her estimate), she blames outside-in decision making for the continent's woes. Her logic — and accounting — has been roundly debated. Defenders of aid point to the great impact of humanitarian assistance in addressing public health

crises like HIV, tuberculosis, and malaria. It's true that without donations from abroad, many millions in Africa would suffer.

But she's right about the design flaws. Most forms of aid to Africa come attached to foreign agents. Most international NGOs still
depend on a model of external funding that can pervert incentives.*
Wealthy nations that deliver foreign assistance to Africa sometimes
add an exploding caveat: the appropriation must be spent to purchase
goods and services from the donor. In many situations, earmarked aid
leaves the recipient country soon afterward, in the form of salaries,
per diem allowances, and "hardship pay" for employees of the World
Bank, JICA (Japan), DFID (Great Britain), SIDA (Sweden), SNV (the
Netherlands), Norad (Norway), or the rest of the alphabet soup.

"Tying" aid in this way is estimated to increase the cost of intervention by between 15 and 30 percent. Yet the practice persists: the share
of UK aid contracts going to British firms is on the rise, and the United
States allocates $3.19 billion a year — nearly a third of its budget — not
to the needy abroad, but to ten large domestic corporates. During a
flood in Mozambique in 2000, "tied" American aid compelled flood
workers to procure, then ride Harley-Davidson motorcycles from outpost to outpost, "like some breed of medical Hell's Angel," according to
Stupart. "Fascinating to behold, but utterly wasteful."

The evolution of charity from pure good into deadweight didn't
happen overnight. It is the result of centuries of mismapping Africa.
In the seventeenth century and continuing through the turn of the
twentieth, colonial arrangements conscripted African economies into
service of the great powers of Europe. After the Second World War,

---

* To encourage giving, the industry is fixated on decreasing the "overhead ratio"
— what proportion of donations is spent on administration versus action. This has
led many nonprofits to hyperinflate the value of donations (like T-shirts). World Vision, the Christian charity operating in sixteen countries in Africa, accepted 100,000
articles of merchandise wrongly congratulating the Pittsburgh Steelers on winning
Super Bowl XLV (they lost). Though the shirts were virtually worthless, they were
logged as donations worth $11.65 each on average — a piece of legal but manipula-
tive accounting designed to reassure donors that World Vision is efficient.

the same great powers — having discovered the success of the Marshall Plan to rebuild Europe — applied the idea of aid to anything else.

As the twentieth century progressed, foreign powers divided the continent again, often according to Cold War allegiances. The United States backed despots like Joseph Mobutu in the Democratic Republic of the Congo for his anticommunism — but didn't bother to follow the money once disbursed. The Soviet Union did the same in nations like Ethiopia, Angola, and Mozambique. As we've seen, these politically motivated subsidies provoked some of the worst corruption the world has ever seen. In the 1980s, the rot in aid-soaked African economies began to show. Productivity in badly managed national industries sank. In response, the International Monetary Fund (IMF) and the World Bank began a series of painful "structural adjustment" programs to liberalize lean economies.

Once the Berlin Wall fell, strategic aid was largely moot, and governance began to take a front seat. Donors introduced conditionality into the same aid flows: Stop starving and jailing and warring and stealing and you can have this bag of money. Hold an election, and win what is behind door number three! For rich governments, dangling assistance in front of a corrupt regime seemed better than the sticks they were weary of wielding.

But it didn't change much. Even as a wave of liberalization and democratization swept over sub-Saharan Africa in the 1990s, per capita income decreased. Sundry international development policies turned out to be poorly matched to dynamic circumstances on the ground, and in some cases counterproductive. As Johns Hopkins professor Deborah Bräutigam and others have demonstrated, aid flows are inversely related to government function: for every dollar of foreign assistance donated to developing states, government spending drops by 43 cents. In exchange for World Bank aid, Kenya's government promised — and failed to implement — the same labor, agricultural, and educational reforms five times in fifteen years.

For years now, the donor economy has been both inefficient and out of touch. UN or World Health Organization funds are disbursed to country managers or large philanthropies, which partition support to large international NGOs, which may then contract with smaller ones closer to the ground. The Bill and Melinda Gates Foundation, for a powerhouse example, solicits and funds grant proposals that circle the globe but keeps most employees in its Seattle headquarters. Whether it's direct charity from individuals or bilateral earmarks sent from fat economies, the big pile of goods and money tumbles through a meta-bureaucracy of agencies and aid workers.

This century, a new wave of intervention has begun, branded by journalist Nick Kristof as the "D.I.Y. Foreign-Aid Revolution." With this phrase, Kristof refers to the daring do-gooders who leave fat economic life behind to make a difference in their own patch of the developing world. He is onto something: as social solidarity has turned global, grass-roots charity has broadened from the domain of nineteenth-century missionaries and twentieth-century Peace Corps volunteers to include millennial church group service trips, goodwill semesters abroad, and bright-eyed "social entrepreneurs" a bit like Jason Sadler. Kiva, Vittana, MicroPlace, and other micro-funding platforms allow armchair philanthropists to make a difference.

The more personalized aid movement coincided with the end of dogmatic Cold War subsidies and shifted the focus from politics to people. (RED) products and credit cards, celebrity adoptions in Africa, and the persistence of Bono were only the most visible signs of the new paradigm. Internationally recognized advocates amplified existing battles, for AIDS patients in need of cheap retroviral access, debt forgiveness to flailing African governments, or peace processes in Darfur. Jason Sadler was just the latest iteration.

As in Sadler's case, none of these good intentions can replace good intelligence. The data are clear: besides promoting dependency among donees and groupthink among donors, the whole spectrum of foreign assistance to Africa risks misreading the story on the ground. And when external interventions — like borders — don't map onto reality, they are counterproductive.

Edna Adan Ismail, the midwife whose hospital in Somaliland receives both cash donations and foreign gifts in kind, told me about a donated MRI machine that broke soon after it arrived. Exasperated, she pointed out that the cost of the equipment would have trained forty to fifty midwives, who could have a more durable impact on public health. Holly Ladd, who works with the UN Foundation, described a project to combat measles in partnership with the Red Cross. Her team wanted to know how far a community of mothers would be willing to travel to obtain immunizations for their children. They asked study participants how many kilometers they had walked that day. "The mothers had no answer for their question," says Ladd. "They weren't measuring their lives in kilometers — they weren't using watches."

Rebecca Enonchong, a warm and energetic businesswoman based in Cameroon, told a story of UN Women, the agency for women's issues, attempting to teach older women in rural Uganda how to use Microsoft Excel. After weeks of training, a handful of women could run the program, but the price tag for the intervention reached $600,000. "Had they used one hundred dollars — or one thousand dollars — and bought cell phones for each of those women . . . it would have had a much more profound impact on the society." She shook her head. "But they never ask what the community needs. They sit in an office in New York . . . and they have no idea of how we live."

In early 2012, an American NGO called Invisible Children produced a video about its longtime lobbying for the capture of Joseph Kony, the Ugandan leader of a cultish and brutal militia known as the Lord's Resistance Army. The video featured a white American father teaching his white American child the basics of terrorist activity thousands of kilometers away. The short film doubled as a call to action — or rather, buying the NGO's "action kits."

The simplistic narrative was designed to increase awareness among non-Ugandans — which it did. Over the course of nearly 100 million views on YouTube, *Kony 2012*, as the film is known, sold the chance to "fix" a complex geopolitical problem simply by watching a movie. It also downplayed important facts: Kony had left Uganda years prior, and the United States had already committed military resources to hunt him down. Worse, it amplified and reproduced a narrative of Africa in crisis, when Ugandans themselves had been trying to move on.

Kristof defended Invisible Children against "armchair cynics." To critics of this style of advocacy, Kristof likes to tell a parable about starfish washed up on the beach. A small girl is patiently picking up the starfish and flinging them back into the ocean. When asked why she is bothering — knowing she can't possibly throw them all to safety — the girl picks up another starfish and tosses it into the surf, saying, "But I have helped that one."

Kristof does yeoman's work covering poverty and rights in some of the most valuable real estate in journalism. He's met Edna Adan Ismail, too. He must be aware that surviving and thriving in a less developed region of the world is complex — nothing like lying passively on the beach. And yet glamorizing foreign mediators fundamentally disrespects the poor. Nigerian author Teju Cole calls this "The White Savior Industrial Complex," in which "a nobody from America or Europe can go to Africa and become a godlike savior or, at the very least, have his or her emotional needs satisfied." (The idea, enshrined in the UN poster, has also been called "The White Man's Burden," after a Rudyard Kipling poem.) Absent local input, or better, agency, the best-laid plans for development become "stuff we don't want."

Perhaps the high-water mark for SWEDOW arrived in 2000, when the United Nations ratified its ambitious Millennium Development Declaration. Representatives from the 189 member countries gathered in New York to chart a new course to speed human development. Their map is as follows:

1. Eradicate extreme poverty and hunger.
2. Achieve universal primary education.
3. Promote gender equality and empower women.
4. Reduce child mortality.
5. Improve maternal health.
6. Combat HIV/AIDS, malaria, and other diseases.
7. Ensure environmental sustainability.
8. Develop a global partnership for development.

Leave aside for a moment whether the goals are good (who doesn't want to improve maternal health?) or whether they are being achieved (in Africa, most are not). The Millennium Development Goals (MDGs) are designed from the outside in — part of the same monologue that brought us 1 Million Shirts.

This has led to some big problems, such as relying on formal indicators to tell a story. Goal 1, for example, measures poverty based on people living on $1.25 a day. But when you work as a traffic vendor, a seamstress, or a farmer, your income is likely so variable as to make the benchmark meaningless. Some days are flush, and others impossibly lean. The formal framework can't capture that.

Goal 2, for another example, focuses on increasing enrollment in primary school. African countries have been sprinting toward this goal; enrollment in central, west, east, and southern Africa jumped from 58 percent to 76 percent between 1999 and 2008. But the new norm has also left millions behind. Poorly paid teachers are frequently absent or unready to teach a curriculum that is both dreary and dated. Many just skip the subjects they don't know well. Classrooms are bulging, and some students show up too hungry to learn. The focus on primary schooling devalues high school, college, and vocational training. The millions of Africans who have left school "half baked" are out of the loop entirely.

The outside-in design has failed to link different goals with one another. The simple connection *within* goal 1 between reducing hunger and reducing poverty is agriculture, which happens to be the single most common source of income in Africa. Helping the poor grow more and better food is a stellar defense against poverty *and* against disruptive food shortages on the continent and beyond. Amazingly, however, the MDGs leave out agricultural investment.*

The British journal *The Lancet* published a ten-year, more-in-sorrow-than-in-anger analysis of the MDGs, claiming that the specificity

_____

* More shockingly, the MDGs, drafted in 2000, make no mention of climate change — which will disproportionately affect sub-Saharan Africa.

of goals 4, 5, and 6 distorts planning in the broader health system. As a result, malaria money is for malaria only, and HIV treatment is just that. In Kigali, I had a long talk with Betty Mutesi, a cheerful, apple-cheeked young woman who works with the Rwandan Ministry of Finance on MDG compliance. She lamented the lack of integration. "If I have retrovirus access, at the end of the day even if I give you the medication and you don't have food to eat, it's a problem. It's not about medication alone."

That last bit gets at the heart of the problem with outside-in aid. Deductive planning misses the interconnected nature of progress everywhere. Family planning, youth employment, digital inclusion, a free press — to name a few goals that were left out of the MDGs — are key ingredients of progress. While they will release new goals for 2015, the 193 countries and fifteen agencies of the UN are anatomically ill equipped to generate a more nuanced vision.

The design flaws might be frustrating on their own. But the MDGs have become a cut-and-paste template for governments seeking to make policy and also qualify for additional foreign assistance. Here, formality bias and donor hubris work hand in hand to limit creativity. Ministries convene stakeholder meetings and official government events and commission "poverty reduction strategy papers" that ceaselessly invoke the MDGs. About a dozen countries — including Ghana, Rwanda, Kenya, Tanzania, and South Africa — have adopted "Vision" plans that photocopy the MDG framework as official national policy. In Rwanda, says Mutesi, "they were telling us: Don't invent the wheel. Go with the MDGs and the Vision 2020 paper, and check if whatever you want to introduce is in line."

As presently structured, the donor economy empowers the wrong people. In a 2009 debate with Dambisa Moyo, Stephen Lewis, who served five years as the UN envoy on AIDS in Africa, pointed out that her critique of aid says "nothing about the intrinsic nature of aid itself. It says everything about donor governments, multinational corporations, and the World Bank and International Monetary Fund, who were perfectly content to use aid in the most manipulative and destructive ways imaginable." Add to the mix clueless do-gooders and predatory recipient states, and you see the scope of the problem.

In 2010, Teddy Ruge, a Ugandan writer and consultant, watched the United Nations General Assembly celebrate ten years of the MDGs. Over the course of "UN Week," celebrities, philanthropists, and heads of state swarmed Turtle Bay in New York City for committees and panels and parties. Some popped in to orate and network at Bill Clinton's Global Initiative, which often meets the same week. Because of the MDG anniversary, much of the 2010 conversation was about the poor — but nobody invited the poor. "They were numbers. They were figures. And they were invisible," says Ruge.

He decided that the bad habits of African development practice don't have to stay that way. "I said OK, fine — if you're not going to invite the poor to participate in the caviar and wine, then I'm going to take the microphone to the village and see what, if anything, they know about the MDGs." And so in November 2010, in the village of Kikuube in northwestern Uganda, Ruge set up a stage, aimed some cameras, and plugged in a speaker.

The conversation that followed was unprecedented — and not just because it was streamed live on the Web. Local residents arrived at a conclusion that the planners of the Millennium Declaration had not. "They realized that everything that they do is connected," he says. "If you invest in education, that investment in education affects community health, community health affects business in the community, business in the community affects health, well-being, and education — everything is interconnected."

In this sense, the Villages in Action effort seems to complement the Millennium Villages Project. The MVP is the brainchild of Jeffrey Sachs, who midwifed a poverty reduction partnership between Columbia University and the UN that now covers over half a million people in fourteen villages across the continent. To its credit, the project recognizes the interlocking requirements for real development and approaches education, health, and income generation all at once. In all of the target villages studied, malaria and infant mortality are down, water quality and farm yields are up. City migrants have returned to some of the villages.

Sachs has the right idea about decoupling from government: more resources need to reach the bottom, not the top, of African economies. But the program is expensive — up to $12,000 per household by one calculation. One of the villages in question received a cash influx amounting to 100 percent of its local economy. With that kind of investment (and publicity), it's no wonder that things are looking up. But the funding Sachs would need to expand beyond the fourteen current villages is astronomical. Like most conventional aid, the MVP is hobbled by its dependence on outside money and talent.

General questions of sustainability haven't slowed the philanthropy industry, which has been urging wealthy nations and individuals to give more. Smaller donor organizations continue to depend on bequests and sponsorships. Bill and Melinda Gates, with Warren Buffett, have embarked on a personal crusade to swell the pile of money earmarked for development assistance. Consistent with his cash-intensive approach to progress, Sachs never tires of asking fat economies to pledge beyond current levels. In a 2004 speech to African heads of state, he encouraged them to travel the world with hat in hand, "to call boldly and persistently for these funds to be increased." In this decade, African philanthropists like Ibrahim, Patrice Motsepe, and Tony Elumelu have begun to copy the foundation-and-donation model.

But money matters less than design: just as state borders don't always capture historical context, enrollment doesn't mean education, grants don't produce prosperity, and more women surviving childbirth doesn't mean social equity. At an event in Kenya during which Melinda Gates and other development experts lectured on ways to achieve the MDGs, Muchiri Karanja, a local journalist, stood up to state the obvious. "I don't think we need millions of dollars to do these things," he said. "We don't need millions of dollars to make sure we treat women with respect. Do we need money to put more women in leadership positions? We don't."

Africans are speaking out, to anyone who cares to listen. At the first Villages in Action gathering, Milly Businge, Ruge's mother and the chairperson of Kikuube, delivered the keynote address. She hadn't heard of the MDGs as they were being drafted but had a message for their architects: "We would like the entire world to know simply that we exist, and that we are empowered, we live, and we are real and not just a story. We would like you to know how we stand, how we survive, how we study, how we grow, our successes and our failures."

Rather than waiting — as the UN poster suggests — or launching a march on fail states, many people I encountered are making their own arrangements. "We provide our own education, we provide our own health care, our own electricity, our own water supply, our own waste disposal," says Ngozi Iwere, the Nigerian organizer who has long occupied the trenches of small-scale development work. "So what do we need local government for? I am a local government."

This book is not an argument for anarchy. Even as Africans bemoan the fail state culture, many hope for better. Strongmen die; piecemeal reforms take root; there were some thirty elections across the continent in 2011. The benefits of intelligent government and liberal democracy are undisputed. And Africa — as with fractious, 1700s Europe — would probably not be better off should its political map follow its ethnic contours. But the exciting alchemy between historic failures and decentralized cultural responses has the power to change the framework for development in Africa.

Likewise, this book is not an argument for drowning aid in a bathtub, as debt-shocked legislators in fat economies would have it. Certainly, global charity has improved African lives, even if at the end of a long chain of intermediaries. Large entities such as the Gates Foundation and the Global Fund to Fight AIDS, Tuberculosis and Malaria have invested millions in health in Africa, with impressive results. In his book *Getting Better,* development economist Charles Kenny points out that infant mortality has decreased, and life expectancy has increased. Literacy rates in sub-Saharan Africa are up, and more African countries are graduating from the bottom rung of the World Bank's Development Indicators, to "middle-income" status.

New research trends look more closely at what works in development and what does not—based on the method of randomized controlled trials now standard in medical research. The multidimensional poverty index, developed in 2010 by Oxford University, tries to capture a more informal picture: of nutrition, access to electricity, years of schooling completed—even what your floor is made of. And after a decade of foot-dragging, the UN released a landmark Human Development Report that zeroes in on agriculture as a way for Africa to be food secure and prosperous in the future.

But there's no shame in calling out a donor economy that is still wasting time and resources, or in critiquing the state-centric model that is both arbitrary and destructive. Even those experts who argue for a "big push" to get Africa on the formal development trajectory can acknowledge that it makes no sense to push in the wrong direction, using the wrong map.

The historical, political, and cultural framework I have outlined suggests that trusted, non-state networks may be the nimbler means to improve outcomes in sub-Saharan Africa. If the fail state drives both underdevelopment and brilliant, collective alternatives, it makes little sense for aid to continue flowing through palaces and parliaments. Neither does it make sense for development "solutions" to be hatched from afar, and implemented by outsiders, or governments with no better authority than force of habit.

The MDGs will expire in 2015, and a new round of goal setting for Africa is already under way. The next wave of well-meaning philanthropists, businesspeople, students, and activists must acknowledge the non-state structures and informal shortcuts that can help accomplish a whispered goal of some aid workers: to put themselves out of business.

5

The Family Map
The Original Social Network

O N THE SHORES of Mozambique, the Indian Ocean flogs the coast at high tide. The rocks are slippery and the waves high, and dozens of women are at work. Swaying with the force of the waves, some stand waist deep, prying clams and mussels from the stingy rocks that face the sea. The children who cannot yet work — or walk — are under the watch of the mother who has most recently given birth. She will earn a reprieve from work until another mother takes her place, while still enjoying a portion of the group's daily take. This informal child care solution enables the larger group to continue wage earning, despite having children who need constant attention in the shifting tide.

The true strength of social relations in the village of Inhaca struck me as I drove away from the worksite. Several women were walking to market, crowned with plastic bags of their daily catch. One bag had broken. The woman offered her day's work to my driver to carry to town ahead of her. We took the valuable parcel, no questions asked.

I didn't get her name, but I later marveled at how simply these arrangements achieve shared goals without passing through the car wash of government or charity. In my travels, I met so many people

Women in Inhaca, Mozambique, share child care responsibilities while they work.

— and not just women in Mozambique — who rely on tips, favors, and cooperative forces.

I was surprised to find that this fellowship extends to sex workers in Nairobi. Prostitution in the city is an open secret. After dark, a roughly organized confederation of street hawkers, sex workers, and night watchmen depend on one another for security and income. One longtime sex worker told me about the reciprocity in her trade. "If you're working the street, the other girls are your best security," she said. "You make professional associations. It's like a bank. They'll give you a loan and you give in exchange some collateral or security. Like, I'll give you three clients of the five I pick up. Or you can wear my hair." She laughed at the idea. "Even the most simple and unlikely interaction is always a way to build security. It's not built on affection, but it's a way to survive."

These strong ties invert the fail state problem: within the state, interactions can be asymmetric, deferential, and occasionally predatory; without the state, relations tend to be symmetric, reciprocal, and more supportive. What's more, one arrangement drives the other: African social networks are strong *precisely because* central systems are weak, and because getting along together is better than bowling alone.

Bowling Alone is a work by Harvard professor Robert Putnam that bemoans the self-segregation of American life. In the wealthier world, neighbors are strangers, business is rarefied, and inequality mounts. We convene in coffee shops — not to socialize, but to cruise the Web on electronic devices. We are less religious, from smaller families, and less social as a result. The *American Sociological Review* showed that in 2006, one in four Americans had no close friends or confidants — a huge leap in isolation from just twenty years prior. In *Join the Club*, Tina Rosenberg observes that fat economies have a "blind spot" about the importance of social circles: "We believe we don't have time for people; we already have enough friends; we want to keep our private lives private."

In much of Africa, however, the accumulation of colonial history and fail state culture has left a different legacy. Without formal financial or political resources, the grass roots has had to design informal workarounds. Social capital has become an important currency. Repeat interactions build mutual goodwill. Social boundaries collapse, and favors become less extraordinary. Objects themselves are subject to a different sense of ownership. Everyone uses the water pump. Everyone uses the cell phone charging station, or the public toilets. Vehicles are a shared asset — the car in Inhaca was mine and my driver's and the woman's, too.

When I think about it, I realize I've shared all manner of conveyances — from speedboats to *matatus*. In Rwanda, a truck collected me for a farm visit. I expected a ride back in the same vehicle. Because we were all going to Kigali, I offered the pickup bed to a gaggle of farm workers. Only after two hours of chatter and traffic did I realize that they were doing *me* the favor of bunching up like sardines. The truck was their normal commute, and I was the interloper.

Even as they've weakened in fat economies, social ties in Africa are robust — often stronger than more formal affiliations. In fact, everywhere I traveled, kinship and proximity mattered more than citizenship. Protocol was as important as politics. Language can trump law. I am more likely to identify myself — and be identified — as a member of my Yoruba tribe than as a Nigerian citizen, because of my name. Likewise, Yoruba has a particular word for thanking someone who is older, and another for thanking someone with less social status. Mothers are often identified by the name of their first child — a sign of the close tabs kept within the community.

This contextual intelligence, and the unusual salience of human relationships, is the essence of Africa's Family Map. It's why schoolchildren travel in packs. It's why the tacit final instruction in African navigation is often "just ask someone," and why, nine times out of ten, it works. Interdependence powers much of daily life in Africa. In my experience, it's rare to find individuals truly fending for themselves. Kin looks out for kin; a willingness to turn a favor one day often pays off the next. Expected mutuality is what transforms *kanju* culture from Hobbesian chaos into a social compact grounded in social networks.

"People don't recognize that what glues African communities together is governance at the community level," said Iwere, the Ushahidi Nigeria activist. "Just go visit any little village or any little town. What is keeping it together? It's the way people have organized themselves to keep public space clean, how they bury the dead, how they share and access the land for farming and economic activities. Which has nothing to do with this government we're talking about."

Though *family* is a term of art — certainly not limited to blood relations — the Family Map of Africa defines and supports life without a state safety net. As we'll see, it anchors diverse development solutions, from health care delivery to off-grid energy sales.

The first feature of Africa's Family Map is not charity, but solidarity. Family is grounded in positive affiliation — recognizing yourself in those around you. Such solidarity transforms identity into action. Remember why our anonymous 419 scammer first got into the game: he wanted to help his family. Tribe alone can trigger the solidarity instinct: in the DRC, kinship ties among the Kasai people are so powerful that they transcend possessions. Certain goods, like food and water, are presumptively shared. Vanessa Mulangala, who grew up in Kinshasa, told me, "If someone came and rang the door and asked for water, I would have no choice but to give it to him."

On some level, this identification is what is meant by a "nation." It is not an administrative or mandated relationship. Mulangala shares belonging based on geography, history, ethnicity, and culture. (This is a sharp counterpoint to the statehood that has failed so many.)

But solidarity can extend to strangers as well. A favorite anecdote of mine comes from a Canadian working on water projects in Malawi. He finds himself standing at a broken ATM, out of cash, trying to get from the city of Blantyre to the capital, Lilongwe. He shakes out his bag for a few coins but is short about 50 cents for the bus. He devises an elaborate plan to trade cell phone talk time for the shortfall:

> The first person I ask just gives me a funny look (probably at least in part because I was speaking in Chichewa), smiles, and then hands me the money I need. I try to get her phone number to pay her back, and she declines with a laugh. That's life here. And that is the answer. The glue that holds things together. People. Each other. When you can't always rely on services, when the world's not always that predictable, you turn a little more to the people around you.

When the Gates Foundation earmarked $5 million to try to convince Ghanaian mothers to give birth in hospitals, the grantee, a physician, convened a village meeting to solicit community buy-in. The doctor was prepared to offer cash in exchange for assistance with transport. He was surprised when local minibus drivers suggested a *kanju* fee structure: the drivers would be happy to help the women in labor — but rather than profiteering, they settled for getting to jump the line for passengers returning to their village. The proposal makes sense only when you realize that the going rate for helping a friend is often free.

Maybe the best example of such solidarity is Davis Karambi, who is from a small village in north-central Kenya called Ikumbo. Raised by his grandmother, he knew she could not afford school fees past the eighth grade. He recalls thinking, "Whether I am going to high school or not, I will put all the effort with the little resources I have to make the best out of it."

In annual nationwide exams, he came in first in his class and in his entire public school district. His jubilant grandmother sold a cow to raise half the money needed for his freshman year of high school. But as the second semester began, Karambi was kicked out when he couldn't pay the rest of his tuition. Unbowed, he went straight to the headmaster. "I told him if he could manage to let me be in school — even if it's on credit for four years — I would work in his house for sixteen, twenty years, whatever it is." The headmaster couldn't cover the cost on his own but pointed Karambi to a major, overlooked asset: his hometown social networks.

Karambi returned to his village, whose residents had celebrated his performance on the national exams. As word of his problem circulated, and with help from the headmaster, "for the first time I saw a lot of people turn up with firewood, with pawpaw [guava], with sugar cane, trying to auction anything they had to keep me in school." In pieces, the village managed to pay for Karambi's high school education — and has since helped similarly talented young people who just need a break.

Collecting 10 shillings (less than 10 cents) at a time from a population quite poor by Kenyan standards, a communal fund has built a new secondary school and now ensures no Ikumbo resident will have his or her wings clipped by financial concerns. "Eventually we became so well organized that most of the systems now run on their own," says Karambi, who is recently married, living in Nairobi, and working in global public health. Over lunch, he identified the importance of social networks: "The biggest resource you have to go through school is not money, it's the drive. If you have the initiative even when everything is falling apart, people will take note of what you are doing."

This kind of community finance has firm roots in lean economies. But it has particular resonance when other financing options are absent — as is the case for millions of Africans (we'll read more about that in Chapter 7). An academic study in Nigeria found that families either owe or are owed money from an average of 2.5 other families — and unlike a traditional bank loan, the terms are flexible enough to accommodate blips in income for both lender and borrower. A short borrower could pay back less than the principal, and a lender in crisis could be reimbursed *more* than the principal loan. While families in the study were not immune from economic shocks, horizontal relations softened the blow.

Of course, the success of these arrangements depends on communal intelligence — basically, knowing other people's business. In a village several kilometers from the nearest paved road, the news that Karambi needed help with school fees spread like wildfire. This is the second part of the Family Map. Aside from selfless help, social networks hold a remarkable ability to transmit information effectively and rapidly.

There's an obvious reason: within Africa's densely knit social networks, privacy is a scarce commodity. In Kenya, it was fairly unusual for me — a woman in her twenties — to be living alone and unmarried. Multigenerational households are standard. The woman in Mozambique wouldn't have trusted her catch to my driver if she hadn't known exactly where to find him later that day. Elizabeth Eze, a friend who spent a year living in rural Tanzania, confirmed that family and community tend to be much more inclusive. Joking about her failed attempts to establish privacy, she faced the facts· "My inner circle now includes an entire village."

The social feedback loop is a valuable, flexible tool. Development practices that rely on proximity, familiarity, and trust can more readily spread necessary information. In Ghana, researchers found the uptake of new crops and techniques had a strong correlation with the habits of respected "master" farmers. What we might call the grapevine, the researchers call an "information neighborhood." Clusters of neighbors all engaged in the same trade watch one another closely — and know who's successful and who is not. When it comes to agriculture, success is measured at harvest time and can sway decisions made at the next planting. In order to convince farmers to use fertilizer, or make the switch from sorghum or cassava to a more lucrative crop like pineapples, converting a widely observed plot was incredibly effective.

Likewise, misinformation is one of the top barriers to the uptake of responsible practices from contraception to hand washing. In Dar es Salaam, Tanzania, I talked up a cluster of men selling charcoal. Every day, they travel up to 17 kilometers out of town to gather wood for making charcoal, which they stack high atop well-greased bicycles to sell at dusk. Four days of charcoal costs about 8,500 Tanzanian shillings, or $5. Kerosene is just as expensive. Dirty energy was a huge part of local household expenditures. When I asked them about solar panels — for sale in an electrician's shop, up a winding staircase about 200 meters away — the vendors badly overestimated the cost. They assumed a basic installation was 800,000 shillings, or $500, when it is actually $30.

As it turns out, even the lowest quintile of earners can afford solar solutions — especially because they are already paying a premium to exit the system in dirty ways. I explained to the men how much cheaper the green solution might be for them. They rightly worried about losing their livelihood as charcoal producers, and about the quality of the solar products for sale in local markets. And they didn't seem to believe the price I'd just verified. I walked away frustrated. I had earned their acquaintance, but not their trust.

In neighboring Uganda, women are emerging as the better ambassadors for solar adoption. It's a subversive adaptation of the cosmetics sales market in fat economies. In thirty-five markets outside of Africa, "Mary Kay ladies" sell blushers and eye shadow to female peers — perhaps earning a pink Cadillac. In Uganda, Rwanda, and South Sudan, Solar Sister has recycled the franchise system. The organization loans interested women, mostly homemakers, a handful of solar lamps and teaches them about their benefits. The entrepreneurs are then dispatched to their communities, where it's up to them to make sales. For each solar lantern sold, the women make 10 percent of the suggested retail price.

The nonprofit's system of sales training and recruitment — and it's not the only one to encourage female entrepreneurs in Africa — is a welcome source of livelihood for the more than four hundred registered "sisters." It's part of an off-grid energy renaissance we'll discuss more in Chapter 8. But the scheme is most interesting as an example of effective horizontal networking.

The sisters are a useful source of knowledge in the market where solar lanterns are alien and underdog. Local brokers can explain the function and value of renewables much more effectively than centralized marketing schemes. With a little education, "many families are going to look at it as affordable, and you don't have to worry about it," says Evelyn Namara, who runs the Uganda program. "You will light up your house for the rest of your life."

More than statistics on climate change or years of sales experience, the sisters' best asset is proximity to information neighborhoods. They have preexisting ties to the markets they enter (most of the Ugandan sisters are recruited through formal and informal women's groups). And they come armed with a social value proposition — success. Like the dolled-up makeup slinger, the women themselves model the product. Paired with the resulting bump in income, some become higher-status role models to others.

Just as women are crucial to getting clean energy products out from the cities and into homes excluded from the national power grid, they are central to the entire function of the social safety net. As caretakers, laborers, decision makers, or entrepreneurs (at least some of the time), Africa's women are overlooked brokers of behavioral revolutions.

It's impossible to talk about women and social networks in Africa without describing Tostan, an advocacy group that has nudged thousands of communities in Senegal and the Gambia to stop the practice of female genital cutting. The tradition of removing all or most of a young girl's clitoris and labia is thousands of years old. The Senegalese parliament officially banned the practice more than a decade ago (the Gambia has no such law). But until very recently, the cultural practice continued to affect millions of women on the continent every year.

The persistence of cutting had to do with the persistence of social norms. For a millennium, well before Islam (which is followed by 94 percent of Senegalese and does not condone the practice) hit the region, cutting was, roughly, like wearing white on a Western wedding day. It was a universal, irrevocable precondition to the marriage all families want for their daughters. In villages outside the smallish major cities like Thiès, girls were cut to help them find partners in nearby intermarrying villages. Scholars found the convention was oddly binary: most villages were either completely practicing or non-practicing. Predicting a girl's likelihood of being cut was a matter of determining whether nearby homes cut, too.

Demba Diawara, an influential imam in Senegal, linked up with Tostan, which has spent more than twenty years working on health and general education for women in Senegal, the Gambia, Djibouti, Guinea, Guinea-Bissau, Mali, and Mauritania. They knew that any strategy for changing minds had to redefine boundaries and norms — rather like introducing neon-green trousers as acceptable wedding day attire. If a critical mass of community members could be convinced that cutting was the greater harm, many more might follow.

The first Tostan-brokered renunciation came in 1997. Fittingly, the first family Diawara lobbied was his own. In Keur Simbawa and ten interrelated villages, he made a case against cutting grounded in fact and proximity. Though a body of evidence both medical and psychological supported their opposition to cutting, Diawara and Tostan discovered that a public declaration worked wonders. A soapboxed statement in Senegalese towns had the same effect as a master farmer in Ghana switching to pineapples. Once village A broadcast its intentions to forgo cutting in the future, villages B through Z weren't far behind.

But the same cultural and spiritual mechanisms for change can just as easily prevent it. Religion is a complex form of social solidarity in Africa; identification as a member of a particular faith can be stronger than as a member of a nation or state. Countless Africans — my family included — have depended upon religious organizations to backstop state failures. My grandfather had his first day of school, beginning at age eighteen, because Anglican missionaries saw it as their duty to teach. The commitment to education they bequeathed is almost certainly why I am writing this book.

But faith has destructive network effects, too. The reckless "prosperity gospel," in which pastors extract tithes in exchange for salvation, is responsible for keeping many devoted African Christians in poverty. I've attended church services where the liturgy is an afterthought — circulating the offering basket is the main activity. Likewise, Islamist movements in Mali, Nigeria, Somalia, and elsewhere have shown a troubling lack of interest in economic and social progress, preferring instead a rights-curtailing brand of Islamic law.

Jibrin Ibrahim of the Centre for Democracy and Development in Abuja believes the *erosion* of family is responsible for the acts of religiously motivated terror groups like Boko Haram and Al-Shabaab. "Both Wahhabi Islam and Pentecostal Christianity have removed the influence of the family," he says. "They say, 'Listen not to your mother and father; they will not guarantee your place in heaven. Listen to your pastor, listen to your preacher, listen to your imam.' With the loss of control of the family, anything becomes possible."

In Senegal, however, the same concentric circles of faithfulness and family that fueled genital cutting helped to stop it. Diawara's social network worked to stop the tradition because the social network began the tradition. Men and women had to pledge to renounce the practice *together* and hold one another to the pledge. As practicing villages intermarry with nonpracticing ones, the cycle is broken permanently. In this instance, community norms proved as powerful as — and reached further than — state action or inaction.

The social education approach also works for more general health issues. Despite all the hand wringing (much justified) about public health in Africa, remember that we know a lot about general medicine and have developed fixes for the big health plagues. We have pills to fight malaria, treatment regimens for tuberculosis, and — at long last — improved access to antiretrovirals (ARVs) for HIV. But that doesn't mean the fixes reach their target. As Rosenberg points out in *The Social Cure*, "People do throw back lifelines, especially when their culture tells them to." In South Africa, for one example, ARV uptake has been inhibited by misinformation, stigma, and a swirl of other factors that are hard for bureaucracies to address. With enough pressure, African governments may get a drug to a pregnant patient, but, writes Rosenberg, "the job is not done until she puts it in her mouth."

Good intelligence in the hands of African health consumers is often the best medicine. And like a common cold, life-saving information best circulates within networks of repeated interaction. Community norms are a powerful tool.

In practice, this favors more decentralized models for health delivery and patient management. Directly observed treatment, short course (DOTS), for example, is now the leading method to stop tuberculosis from spreading, or taking on frightening mutations. While the World Health Organization emphasizes government buy-in, the method is built on horizontal relationships — it requires another person (initially, a nurse or doctor) to watch the TB treatment pills go down.

Over time, DOTS has expanded to pair patients with less official sponsors, such as clergy, school employees, or fellow patients. These untrained volunteers share responsibility for compliance over the lengthy treatment cycle. Like the Solar Sisters, their value is not fancy training or particular expertise in health care. Rather, they are sourced from the patient's information neighborhood, which triggers an additional incentive to keep the patient TB-free. DOTS was born in Tanzania in the 1980s and has been successfully adapted for HIV in Malawi. Researchers hope to use the community-based model for noncommunicable diseases like hypertension, diabetes, and schizophrenia.

Especially with these tricky chronic diseases, social connectedness can have as great an influence on survival as the drugs. Celia Dugger reported on groups of AIDS patients in Mozambique who are bolstering one another's will and ability to live with the disease. The patient clusters support one another with taxi fare to appointments and encourage one another to turn a cheek to the social stigma surrounding their status. "If I'm sick and isolated, kept at home, I'm considered a dead body, though still breathing," said one patient. "But when a person is in a group, he feels, 'I'm sick, but I count.'"

Locally generated feedback loops and monitoring are proving essential to all kinds of development work. It's mapping again: if you know where people are, both literally and figuratively, you can reach them and get them to do something they are not personally or culturally inclined to do. It's similar to the push within the world of microfinance to lend to groups rather than to individuals — it helps to police loans in less hierarchical and institutional ways.

The Family Map helps solve another problem in health access in Africa: the lack of remote clinical services. Thirty-six of the fifty-seven countries with critical health worker shortages are in Africa. Though health budgets across the continent are propped up with foreign assistance, and philanthropies carry much of the load as well, comparatively wealthier urban populations still benefit more from government health spending. In Mauritania, for a glaring example, 72 percent of state hospital subsidies benefit the richest 40 percent of the population. Godwin Godfrey, a Tanzanian doctor, trained as a surgeon in an 850-bed hospital serving fifteen million people in northern Tanzania. When he returned from a stint in Israel, he was the only pediatric heart surgeon in the country — and the waiting list of patients was 500,000 strong.

It's hard to overstate what a crushing inconvenience it is to be sick in rural Africa. Patients in underserved areas must forgo a day's labor to wait outside a distant facility, where they aren't assured of an appointment, much less a solution. Health care professionals hate these postings, located far from basic luxuries and the communities they know best. Facilities lack physical resources like x-ray machines and blood reagent equipment. The lack of consumer traffic in turn justifies neglect, a vicious cycle of worsening care.

The Family Map expands the definition of caregiving, which helps someone like Dr. Godfrey enormously. Task shifting, for example — in which a nurse is trained to do some of the functions reserved for a doctor, and a community health worker is trained to do the work of a nurse — has been incredibly effective in covering the gaps in skilled labor. Community health workers are more likely to understand hyperlocal medical histories and nonmedical fears, superstitions, and concerns. Decentralization puts simplified tasks and familiar faces at the front lines of care.

Without formal regulation or explicit guidelines, nearly half of the countries in Africa have already begun to use non-physician clinical workers to perform minor surgeries. In Tanzania, non-physicians perform 84 percent of C-sections, hysterectomies, and laparotomies for ectopic pregnancy. In Mozambique, the figure is 92 percent. In Angola, the Kalukembe Hospital is a rural facility with 180 beds and *zero* on-site doctors. Since the 1980s, the nurses who plug the gap have been trained in techniques that save lives where the Ministry of Health (which doesn't recognize the program) does not reach.

Public health practitioners in Africa hotly debate how to optimize many populations' reliance on traditional healers. Many Africans — 80 percent on average — turn to cheaper, trusted caregivers in their information neighborhood. But traditional remedies can lead to badly set bones, home birth fatalities, or herbal "cures" that have no proven physiological benefits. Likewise, there is no evidence that HIV and cancer can be prayed away.

In response, the WHO has focused on formal standards — increasing the registration and research of traditional remedies — rather than engaging the people who are trusted to dispense them. This risks dismissing a potential source of health information and treatment provision. Giving informal healers Western diagnostic tools, or drawing them into a referral system for conventional medicine, may allow for a gentler transition to better care.

Training and empowering local actors can make a difference in who sees a doctor, and who takes a pill. But *prevention* — the cheapest health intervention of all — is harder. In fat economies, we know that smoking kills, that eating right is smart, that exercise matters, and that regular checkups can save our lives. But that doesn't mean we act accordingly. In Africa, HIV prevention is a high-wire example of the need for better persuasive methods.

In South Africa, which has experienced the worst epidemic on the continent, the disease is no longer denied. Where once the minister of health advocated garlic and lemon juice as a curative measure, the efforts of the Treatment Action Campaign and other global advocacy organizations have put drugs in the hands of more than one million adults in the country. Infection rates are falling—but not fast enough. About 5.5 million South Africans live with the disease, and, distressingly, young people across the continent are spreading it. By now, it's not because they haven't heard of AIDS. Rather, it's because they miscalculate their risk.

In a study aiming to prevent new HIV infections among teens, young Kenyan girls were shown a video explaining that older men were more likely to carry the virus. Over time, the self-reported relationships with these men shriveled to dust. Compared to other methods, the scare tactic was the cheapest and the most effective. And a bit like the farmers who adopt the practices of a neighboring plot, the teens were more likely to cut off a "sugar daddy" if they knew other girls were changing their habits as well.

But what if the sugar daddy never got the disease? Male sexual health has been an overlooked strategy within the AIDS NGO community. While HIV disproportionately affects women in Africa, in practice, male behavior tends to determine public health outcomes. "A woman can try to negotiate safe sex with her husband from today to tomorrow. She gets beaten, she gets thrown out, and her parents will send her back and say, 'Don't disgrace our family,'" says Iwere. "But if a man made a conscious decision that he should use a condom, automatically the women in his life are safe or safer." The same logic has spurred the movement to circumcise men as a means of containing the epidemic. African patriarchy may be a regrettably persistent norm, but it can also help target interventions against a disease still ravaging families in the region.

If talk of enlisting teenaged peer pressure, male machismo, and quack doctors sounds unwise, remember that the Family Map is as unwieldy as the concept of family itself. Nepotism and tribalism are prominent features, as are corruption and self-dealing. These attitudes pervade government, but also companies large and small. McKinsey asked over 1,300 growing businesses across sub-Saharan Africa why they were not expanding. Along with lack of cash flow and poor infrastructure, many pointed to a lack of trust in employees. In this climate, employers are biased toward known kinship circles or information neighborhoods, leaving outsiders out of luck for work.

This is a minor irritant compared with cronyism in government. Even in nations like Botswana that are more respected for good governance, multiple members of President Ian Khama's family occupy key ministerial positions. Like the backslapping "old-boy" networks around the world that swap meritocracy for familiarity, nepotism in Africa can lead to poor performance or, in the worst cases, bloodshed. Some fail state institutions come to be dominated by a certain ethnic clique — an arrangement that has incubated resentment and violence for successive generations in Liberia, Sierra Leone, Chad, and more recently Côte d'Ivoire.

In many of these situations, contentious identity politics are the only politics. Whether across one-party or multiparty rule, voters in dozens of African countries consistently splinter into religious, clan-based, cultural, linguistic, and geographic factions for purposes of political presentation. (In Kenya, taking a vote is like taking a census.)

Aggressive identity politics dominate where genuine nationalism has failed to take hold. As Daniel Posner points out, identity politics also correspond with resource allocation from a fickle central government.* "Where politicians woo support by promising to channel resources to would-be voters," he writes, "ethnicity provides a cue that helps voters distinguish promises that are credible from promises that are not." Never mind that many promises are not credible; bloc voting is another loophole by which canny leaders keep power while delivering very little.

Contrary to popular perceptions, violent interethnic conflict is often tied to resource battles — clashes not of civilizations, but of economic and environmental interests. Cattle rustling, retaliatory home invasions, and even arson have all been documented in the tense areas of Africa where multiple climates meet and natural resources are

---

* In this way, African voters align both ethnic and economic interests.

scarce. When disappearing pastures and shrinking water tables overlap with cultural and religious borders, competition tends to amplify these divisions.

Nonetheless, the generosity and intelligence of authentic social networks in Africa are among the essential building blocks of regional hopes. They are also a good defense against fail state threats. For years after independence, in rural northwest Tanzania, the cash-strapped socialist government raided cattle. In the 1980s, after the predatory practice intensified, the community responded, each person according to his or her abilities. Rich peasants organized a common fund to pay off state security officials to protect the property of contributing households. Because the poor couldn't afford the bribe, they formed alternative, decentralized police forces in each village, controlled by informal popular assemblies.

Likewise, when American first lady Michelle Obama visited South Africa, she praised the informal "parliament of Soweto" for its exceptional community organizing functions during that country's struggle against apartheid. "When the congregation sang their hymns, activists would make plans, singing the locations and times of secret meetings," she said. "Church services, and even funerals, often became anti-Apartheid rallies."

Along with solidarity and communal intelligence, a third aspect of the Family Map is reach. The microscopic connections that link Africans together in towns and compounds also support extended kinship networks that span the entire globe. Today, African diaspora maps are reverse models of colonialism — Anglophone Africans flock to Canada, the United Kingdom, Australia, even India. Francophones are more likely to be found in Europe, and lusophones have a foothold in Portugal and Brazil. Everyone comes to America — Sudanese in Atlanta, Somalis in Minneapolis, Ethiopians and Eritreans in Washington, DC. The francophones run New York.

The rap on African diaspora — or more pejoratively "exile" — communities has been that they are a net negative for Africa. "Brain drain," as some call the widespread twentieth-century migration of Africans to fat economies, swiped the best professionals away from their home countries at just the moment they were needed most. As a result, for every one physician in Zimbabwe there are 6,300 patients, and in the Gambia, 9,300. In Ethiopia it's 45,400 patients per physician, and in Liberia, it's 71,400 to one. There are only 120 doctors and 100 nurses in South Sudan.

Yet diaspora communities retain a burning stake in the day-to-day at home. At a State Department conference on diaspora engagement, former secretary of state Hillary Clinton correctly noted that diasporas "are, frankly, our Peace Corps, our USAID, our OPIC, our State Department rolled into one."

I count myself an example. My parents left Nigeria as students in 1983 — one year before the coup that plunged the country into a decade of dictatorship. But they built a life that never gave up on home. When I was growing up, our spare bedroom in Chicago was constantly occupied by aunties and uncles (only some of whom were blood relations) staying over while they found their local footing. I spent my childhood bathed in Yoruba language, food, and family. It wasn't until I was a teenager that I understood why my parents never bought gasoline from Shell. They believed that the Royal Dutch company was systematically destroying the Niger Delta and killing kin. Miles from home, we were expected to make what difference we could.

As Nigeria eased out of military rule, our trips home, laden with Tylenol and sturdy shoes, became more frequent, for longer stretches of time. My parents began teaching and researching at their alma mater in Ibadan. I tagged along. I traveled on my own, in concentric circles beyond Nigeria. Over fifteen years, this constant tether to west Africa — its tempo, traditions, and loyalties — set me on the path to this book.

When I took a job as a political correspondent in Washington, I found myself chewing over politics and development issues with friends and family in the African diaspora. Guinean immigrants to the United States have developed a clever way to do the same thing across the entire country. Each week, Mamadou Barry, a Guinean living in central Ohio, puts together a radio show on topics of interest to his peers in America. "Radio show" is a generous moniker: he doesn't have a radio frequency, or rights to broadcast, or fancy recording equipment. He doesn't have any journalism training. But he does have a telephone. And so does everyone he knows.

And so for several hours each week, GuineeView broadcasts a vibrant "talk show" using free conference call software. American users, often from francophone west Africa, dial in and join a conversation linking past and present, home and away — with a collaborative twist. When the host has a question for the audience, he asks it — and in conference call form, listeners can dial the hash key to weigh in.

There are hundreds of other African immigrants who make similar efforts to debate, inform, and engage with diaspora circles. Fréquence Ganndal transmits in French and Fulani, with some religious programming as well. *The Jacques Roger Show*, hosted by an Ivoirien in Washington, DC, covers a news area from Burkina Faso to Senegal. Listening spikes as you'd expect: during the electoral crisis in Côte d'Ivoire, or after the 2008 death of Guinean president Lansana Conté, when reliable news sources were few and far between.

Conference call radio shows are a classic *kanju* hack, democratizing flows of information to and from Africa. It's light-years ahead of incumbent technologies: buying phone cards in African specialty stores (which my family still does), or sending paper letters with friends of friends who are heading home (which my family still does). Even e-mail, Skype, and Web and cable news can't replicate the kind of chatter that might take place at home. The shows create a familiar, new-world analogue to the radio medium (until the cell phone arrived, the most pervasive and important form of communication in Africa).

The most impressive example of modern diaspora engagement must be Dahabshiil, a money transfer service born in Somalia. The company allows users to drop off cash in Minneapolis and pick it up in Mogadishu or Mumbai — and the other way around. Abdirashid Duale, the Dahabshiil CEO, manages billions of dollars in international remittances. He is a trim and focused man who jets between Kenya, Somalia, the United Kingdom, and the Middle East.

In 1970, Duale's father began trading as a remittance broker, manu-

ally trafficking goods between Somalia and the Gulf states and passing
the proceeds back to Somali families. By 1988, he'd made the business
the leading such service in the region. Unfortunately, a civil war that
year dispersed over 500,000 Somalis, including Duale and his surviving family members, as refugees, all over the world. It was an unhappy
time, he says. "We lost family and friends and left our homes and everything we knew. On the other hand, it challenged us to adopt and
innovate in the difficult situations." The Duales were lucky to land in
London, where Somali immigrant presence is strongest. "My father
recognized the opportunities this presented to help displaced communities to send money back home."

Dahabshiil started again from scratch, this time setting up outposts
all over the diaspora that enabled the fractured community to keep
together. "It is in the Somali culture to help one's kith and kin, so the
business has a natural cultural heritage," he says. Because decades of
government failure had left Somalia without any commercial banking
services, Dahabshiil was (and still is) one of the only ways to make
financial transactions for hundreds of kilometers around the Horn.

The business has expanded to 144 countries since then, and the
platform now enables Ethiopians, Sudanese, Rwandans, and Ugandans to send money around the world. Duale introduced the first deb-
it card program in Somalia and employs nearly five thousand people
worldwide. During recent food and conflict situations, it's taken on
a humanitarian bent: the UN, Oxfam, and Save the Children rely on
Dahabshiil to smooth their operations. Diaspora remittances are a
force to rival formal aid; every year, $21.5 billion flood sub-Saharan Af-
rica from abroad. It's all the more incredible to learn that most of that
money is still transferred family to family, and under $200 at a time.

Governments in the United States and elsewhere have tarred Dahabshiil with tenuous links to terror networks, including a one-time
employee in Pakistan who was detained at Guantanamo Bay (no further ties have been established).* But even with its potential to be used

---

* In 2013, Barclays announced that it would no longer honor transactions to "black-
listed" countries — Yemen, Poland, Bangladesh, Pakistan, Sri Lanka, and Somalia.

for money laundering, Dahabshiil is a net positive for development. African diaspora communities use services like Dahabshiil to support those unsheltered by the fail state. Far from an informal scourge, it's a huge asset.

Finance is not the only use for the African diaspora. Semhar Araia, an Eritrean American with a decade of experience in policy circles from the Horn of Africa to the US Capitol, founded an organization called Diaspora African Women's Network (DAWN) that seeks to capitalize on the skills and knowledge of women straddling multiple worlds. If Anglo, European, or Asian tribes have dispersed and assimilated into new contexts, Araia's path from Eritrea to America left an umbilical tie to the Horn. "I don't think there's any other community as connected as Africans," she says. "Our migration around the world is still new."

Dahabshiil is a money transfer service that manages to get cash to and from some of the most neglected markets in the world. This sign advertises a branch in central Hargeisa, Somaliland.

DAWN focuses on what Araia calls "role modeling." Diaspora Africans are micro-politicians and development consultants, micro-financiers, and, increasingly, micro-ambassadors. Experience with comparatively stronger civil societies in fat economies offers a template for organizing abroad. This includes using Africans' casual communitarianism as a tool for home country development. "Think of all the church fundraisers, your community national holiday celebrations — think of when a disaster strikes at home, how easily we can amass resources," says Araia. "We organize in our sleep but we take it for granted."

This is the silver lining of Africa's years of human export. And slowly, government institutions are leveraging the Family Map. The US State Department, with Araia and other stakeholders, has begun to recognize the importance of diaspora engagement. "What the State Department might call diplomacy, you might call a phone call home. What we call foreign affairs, you call family affairs," said Maria Otero, the undersecretary of state.

As the example of Dahabshiil shows, sometimes the most troubled countries have the most committed diaspora. Forced from home rather than choosing to leave, they invest in the success of lands they expect to repatriate one day. For similar reasons, diaspora has been essential to liberation struggles in Africa. The Eritrean civil war was diaspora funded, and (controversially) the country maintains a 2 percent tax on nationals wherever they are. During the effort to rebuild Rwanda after its genocide, it was communities abroad that fed the project of renewal — just as they had funded and fed rebels led by President Paul Kagame in their three-year guerrilla war against the Habyarimana regime. Political and economic exiles were indispensable to South Sudan breaking free of the abusive Khartoum government. When, in 2011, South Sudan earned its independence, more than twenty-five years in the making, many streamed back to start afresh.

The verdict is still out on South Sudan in particular, but Liberia — thousands of miles away — gives a snapshot of how diaspora pays development dividends in post-conflict situations. In Monrovia, which spent the bulk of the 1990s under fire, I met with Saran Jones, a polished, pragmatic thirty-year-old who spent most of her life in exile. Her story is typical: Her family dodged the beginning of the end of civilian rule in Liberia. She bounced from neighboring Côte d'Ivoire to Egypt, France, and then the United States. In 2005, after leaving Harvard College, she joined the millions of Africans sending money to support a relative in school. In 2008, as the dust settled from more than fifteen years of civil war, she finally came home. And what she saw made no sense.

When I visited Liberia myself in 2011, I could understand her consternation. Just outside the capital city, ancient water pipes sprouted from the grass, at times attached to nothing but a crumbling wall of a bombed-out house. The once-grand beaches of Monrovia had been annexed as informal settlements that — by virtue of being built on sand — lack clean water and toilets. When I walked the beach, residents washed and splashed in the ubiquitous Atlantic Ocean. Inland, open creeks did quadruple duty as sites for drinking, cooking, bathing, and disposing of human waste. Everywhere, sanitation infrastructure had been gutted by war.

Soon after her own visit, Jones founded FACE Africa, a traditional NGO focused on water security. She and a close family friend began by going door to door, conducting a needs assessment in Grand Bassa, a county anchored by ArcelorMittal, the global steel giant. "We're going for basic, low-tech water solutions," she told me during our meeting in town. "Our first project, we tried using a fancy sophisticated solar filtration system and it was a complete disaster. You don't have the local knowledge to manage this." They've since determined that building wells and repairing old ones, relying on local contractors and local skills, is the surest way to meet immediate water needs.

Jones returns when she can and runs the nonprofit with clear eyes about the difficulties of filling the government provision gap. "We don't get much support from government," she says. "We go through them for the necessary accreditation . . . but pretty much everything is done independently." While traditional charity works have filled the gap for many Liberians who lack access to safe drinking water, FACE has also found itself cleaning up after earlier, abandoned aid projects.

One of the wells they repaired was installed by Mercy Corps in 2004 but broke within two years and lay dormant for five more before FACE refurbished the hand pump, with local help and funding from Procter & Gamble.

County by county, the grass-roots project is attempting large-scale, long-term solutions to state inaction. Of course, Jones is nowhere near her goal of clean, safe drinking water across Liberia. But there is much to learn from the homegrown effort. Traditional NGOs tend to cluster around main cities, leaving out the far-flung places (think Davis Karambi's village) where needs may be greater. Diasporas, by contrast, are willing to invest time and money in fragile communities. Their fluency in high-context African societies — whether in business, social work, language, or navigation — has been a huge asset.

In Liberia, I also met Shawn Winter, a twenty-three-year-old Canadian returnee who says it was the news of Ellen Johnson Sirleaf's 2005 election that brought him back. "It's meaningless to be in a country where you've already acquired knowledge, you're there, you have bills, you have this and that to attend to — when you could be doing something to improve the economy of your country."

Shawn is not alone. He conveyed the mix of ambition and obligation echoed in the many conversations I've had with Africans in the diaspora. We'll meet many more such bridge characters, working in areas from agriculture to technology to corporate finance. They are evidence that a younger generation of diaspora kids have re-engaged the African economies that spent the 1980s and 1990s exporting people. Rather than laboring in middle management in fat economies, many experienced young Africans have set off for home, setting up "move back clubs" to support their transition. This is the secret solace of the 2008 world financial crisis: Africa's brain drain has become "brain gain."

Family, loosely defined, carries built-in incentives and efficiencies. It is both weapon and shield. And luckily, it's abundant and free. While it's the least objective and thus the most mired in challenges, it is also one of the oldest non-state networks in Africa.

Our next map, however, is brand-new.

6

The Technology Map

Lessons in Leapfrogging

N 1997, WHEN an American plane touched down in Côte d'Ivoire, a water well was waiting for Larry Summers. A few hours from the thrum of Abidjan, the nation's largest city, a village had been living without clean water for years. This was a tolerated inefficiency. Women and young children fetched water over long distances or drank the unsafe output of boreholes and crude wells.

Enter USAID — the agency for global development created by President John F Kennedy in 1961. Eager American engineers dug a well for the village's residents. The official christening, of course, required official Americans. The baptist: President Bill Clinton's brilliant, often-rumpled deputy treasury secretary. First by plane, then by car, and finally by boat, Summers made his way to the US-sponsored spigot. With one turn, fresh water graced the lives of the villagers.

As Summers crossed the lagoon back toward the main road, the noise of dipping paddles gave way to a digital chirp. An aide fumbled for the sound. "Secretary Rubin needs to talk to you," he said. Summers's boss was on the phone — worried about the US budget deficit, perhaps, or the brewing Asian debt crisis. He took the call and they paddled on; as he recalled with a grin, "I was able to be talking to

Washington with a perfect connection and nobody was thinking very much of it."

The source of Summers's delight lay not in pipes beneath the earth but thousands of miles overhead, within the constellation of communications satellites hidden by the afternoon sky. Since the 1980s, satellites have offered Internet and mobile telephone access around the world. Today, this architecture of connectivity powers more than secure calls between Western dignitaries. It touches every element of contemporary life. In Africa, these connections have offered millions the chance to depart their geography, class, religion, or culture and access a world out of their sight — but now within their reach.

Cell phone adoption in Africa is best described by thinking of a hockey stick — the shape of the graph plotting the sharp increase in new users over the past decade. Summers's trip was not the beginning, but it's a useful place to start: since Rubin made his call to Côte d'Ivoire, the continent has become a $56 billion mobile ecosystem, with over half a billion subscribers; there are now ten times as many cell phones as landlines south of the Sahara. In 1999, fewer than 10 percent of Africans lived in areas with mobile phone coverage. Today, that number is more than 60 percent. Those owning phones were clustered mainly in Arab north Africa and South Africa; by 2012, 650 million people in sub-Saharan Africa — from tiny Gabon to sprawling Sudan — had subscriptions.* Multinational telecoms like MTN, Vodafone, Orange, and Bharti Airtel are competing for eager consumers, improving connectivity and dropping prices. Basic "dumb phones" have been runaway bestsellers. When Nokia sold its billionth handset, it was to a Nigerian.

The speedy uptake of mobile technology took even Africans by surprise. In 1999, Kenyan telecom Safaricom projected that the market *might* hit three million users by 2020. Seven years short of that deadline, Safaricom alone has seventeen million subscribers. These users run the gamut — from busy executives who rely on BlackBerry's mes-

---

* Over the course of writing this book, I have had to revise that statistic upward multiple times. I expect the final number in print to be outdated.

saging service to reach contacts abroad, to housekeepers who manage appointments with their phones. My paternal grandmother — born in the 1920s in a British colonial authority — today uses her phone to keep track of church affairs. If you are working or looking for work, your phone is essential. When I visited a woman who mothered three young children in Kibera, a low-income district in Nairobi, the topic turned to cell phones. She brandished the Nokia 1100, which has been termed "the AK-47 of communication" for its utility and ubiquity. Her model was secondhand, but working, with the upstart YU telecom, to link her to networks ten times as powerful as those that connected Summers to Washington.

In northern Mali, chords of the lilting, beautifully pitched folk songs for which the country is known now travel along a digital vector. Countless local music fans use battered "dumb phones" as proto-iPods. The phones can both store and play back the MP3 stylings of legendary musicians like Ali Farka Touré and modern rappers like Iba One. The cultural practice of sharing and circulating songs of sorrow, praise, or rebellion has been upgraded for the electronic age; the same memory card can be removed and circulated among other phones at will (Bluetooth technology makes syncing tunes even easier).

As phone ownership enters the cultural mainstream, sub-Saharan Africa is being plugged in — literally — in some places for the first time. In July 2009, SEACOM, a 10,000-mile-long fiber-optic cable rose up from the Indian Ocean. The giant sea creature, funded by African and American venture capitalists, now connects South Africa, Mozambique, Tanzania, Kenya, and Djibouti — previously, according to Kenya's former president Mwai Kibaki, "the longest coastline in the world without a fiber-optic cable connection to the rest of the world." The gold rush is on: another lightning-fast connection is snaking down Africa's west coast. Between 2007 and 2011, Africa's Internet capacity leaped from 340 Gb to 34,000 Gb per second. By the end of 2012, no fewer than eight new undersea fiber-optic cables wired the continent for broadband access, north to south. By 2014, it is estimated that 69 percent of mobile phones in Africa will have Internet access.

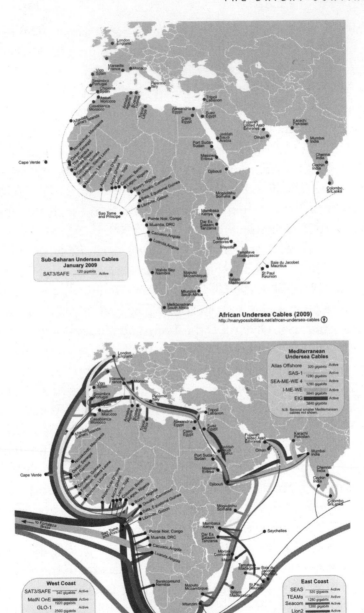

From 2009 to 2014, broadband infrastructure in Africa has become both ubiquitous and transformative.

It takes only a cursory glance at *this* map of Africa to see the enormous potential for connectivity to change the continent. Speaking to me about his 2005 book, *The End of Poverty,* Jeffrey Sachs lamented having published before connective technology exploded in Africa. "It would have been a different book," he said.

Technology has four main features relevant not just to Africa, but to the world. It is democratic, market based, innovative, and increasingly effective for development. Combined with *kanju,* African tech leads us to smart, lean solutions in health, financial services, and retail distribution. And that's just the beginning.

The potential of technology is grounded first in its seismic redistribution of power. Around the time Summers took his boat ride, *Wired* magazine published a feature on undersea cables that explained why digital connections matter:

> Wires warp cyberspace in the same way wormholes warp physical space: the two points at opposite ends of a wire are, for informational purposes, the same point, even if they are on opposite sides of the planet.

Wires transform London into Lusaka, and vice versa. The shift from mobile calling to mobile Web allows ordinary people across the African continent to access the same information as the wealthy world. Electron-to-electron connection has inverted the traditional division of authority in society, eliminating hierarchies across Africa. Ken Banks, an anthropologist with early exposure to the African tech scene, notes that for most African users "centralized means 'remote,'" while "distributed" now signifies "local." In other words, your phone puts you at the center of something. The world is not quite flat, but it's increasingly difficult to segregate the center from the periphery.

Funke Opeke has logged years of experience in the wired world order. A Nigeria-trained engineer who rode the dot-com boom in the United States, Opeke left a job at Verizon in 2005 to return home as a chief technical officer of South African telecom MTN. She soon struck out on her own as CEO of Main One, one of the private companies that are dropping fiber into the sea.

A map in her central Lagos office shows that Main One will cover all of Africa's west coast, from Morocco to South Africa; the last mile of connectivity will be sold to local Internet, television, and phone operators. She believes she is selling more than Internet access. "Information is empowering. It's empowering first to our young people, in terms of education and business opportunities and sources of employment," she says of her venture. "To businesses who are ambitious enough to participate on the global scale, it gives those skills and capabilities better visibility to engage with people around the world and participate with an equal footing."

Web access figures aren't there yet; urban elites are far more likely to be streaming, tweeting, and e-mailing than rural or less wealthy counterparts. But Africa's best challenge to Craigslist started in sleepy Limbe, Cameroon. Its creator, Fritz Ekwoge, has a moon-shaped face and easy smile that belie a ruthless entrepreneurial mind. He learned to write computer code at age sixteen—without a computer. Unable to afford a laptop or desktop, he borrowed a friend's TI-82 calculator. "In exchange for me using it I had to write software for him to pass his math exams," he says now, laughing.

Far from being a disadvantage, this hardship has made Fritz one of the most versatile programmers on the continent. When he was still in high school, he created a protocol for simple cell phones that could turn electronics on and off remotely. It was a prank, but it established his reputation for clever hacking and laid the seeds for the mobile industry entrepreneurship he has cultivated since.

In 2007, Ekwoge founded Kerawa, a website to host classifieds. Like his computer skills, this venture was born of *kanju*. Upon graduation from polytechnical school, he needed to move to the major city of Douala but could not for the life of him find an apartment. To fill the market hole, he coded Kerawa and began selling ads and soliciting postings. Quickly, Web users in Cameroon and nearby Ghana and Nigeria began trading goods and services online. Today, Kerawa transmits listings from forty-three different African countries (plus India). It ranks among the top thirty most-visited websites in Cameroon— beating out Craigslist itself.

Ekwoge long ago quit his job at accounting multinational PricewaterhouseCoopers — a wild leap for most young Cameroonians. But his venture underscores the second important fact about technology in Africa: commercial markets are working. The explosion of charity support in Africa is founded in part upon the idea that the continent is too poor to help itself. Corruption gums up the wheels of commerce, and the impoverished African can't afford anything — least of all markets (we'll talk more about commercial networks in Chapter 7). But the advent of mobile phone technology has offered an unequivocal rebuke to this logic. Without aid or subsidy, Africans are willing to build and buy the tools of this new world order.

Like so many other aspects of the *kanju* creative ecosystem, individual adoption of mobiles has come out of necessity. Landlines are bad, or

Mobile phones have enabled a wealth of innovative business models,
from basic charging and repairs to more advanced financial
products like savings accounts and insurance.

nonexistent (in fact, I've *never* used a landline in Africa). Fail states interfere as well: most businesses in Kenya, where I lived, have had to wait an average of one hundred days for landline connections to be installed — in most cases, following a bribe paid to the parastatal institutions responsible for providing services (the average amount: $117).

What's more, the unreliable infrastructure makes basic information highly asymmetric. What is the price of tomatoes on the coast? Did the teacher show up today? Has the baby come yet? The cost of not knowing the answers to these questions can be high — and without a mobile, the cost of finding out can be just as expensive. For firms and ordinary people, these explicit and implicit costs are a reason to join the mobile public square.

In Niger, for instance, traveling to a market to figure out the price for a cash crop may gobble between two and four productive working hours. A brief phone call between a producer and vendor provides the answer in a fraction of the time, and at half the cost. Phones change market behavior — Nigerian grain traders with mobiles have more connections and a wider sales radius, which increases the price they can get for their goods. The opportunity for clever arbitrage is not limited to the pulsing African metropolis: especially in rural areas, recharging mobile phones is a brisk, profitable, informal-sector business model.

It's thus no surprise that Africans spend on average 10 percent of their daily wage on mobile airtime. The figure varies by country and income, but the proportion is amazing. It's as though an individual making $30,000 a year spent $3,000 on phone calls. The demand for connection in Africa is real and growing, born of both improved purchasing power and greater sophistication about value. The economic rationale for investing in connectivity is nearly bulletproof. This logic will only strengthen as data-enabled phones proliferate. In 2010, Jim Balsillie, then CEO of BlackBerry, described the popularity of his device in emerging markets. He asked, "Is this the most expensive phone, or by far the cheapest TV you've ever heard of?"

On the supply side, African technology is proving to be among the most exciting growth industries in the world. It's appropriate that

Mo Ibrahim, the first African billionaire, made his money from a cell phone company. When it comes to profitability, mobile phone services in east Africa now rival beer. African mobile technology companies like Vodacom, MTN, and Tigo have followed in Ibrahim's footsteps, replicating the scramble for Africa — this time, for its consumers. Opeke is bullish about the potential. "People are willing to pay. They have a need that you can quantify in economic terms, and we as a private venture can organize and raise the capital to satisfy individual aspiration."

The ensuing price wars have been an entertaining and beneficial side effect. When, in 2010, Airtel — then Zain — dropped its calling rates in Kenya from 6 shillings a minute to 3, and SMS rates from 3 shillings to 1, observers gasped at the bold move to undercut market leader Safaricom. With 80 percent of the subscriber base at the time, Safaricom could afford to look the other way. Yet, within a month of Airtel's announcement, Safaricom had also slashed its rates. The undersea cable business — three of the new cables are backed by private investors — is likewise good for consumers: since the cables arrived, the wholesale price of fiber-optic connections has dropped by a factor of ten.

Devices are being marketed just as aggressively, and in ways tailored to African markets. Phones with prepaid minutes offer strength, speed, and flexibility to users, without the Western hassle of contracts and premiums. As cheaper handsets flood the market, prices are dipping to meet Africans at their purchasing point. These are no longer simply "dumb" phones like Nokia's ubiquitous 1100; in 2011, the Chinese company Huawei introduced the IDEOS, a top-flight touchscreen smartphone, for $80. Innovations in function only enhance the enormous strides made in market structure and price.

The advent of mobile and other connective technologies has had its own discrete impact on economic development. In South Africa, according to researchers Stefan Klonner and Patrick Nolen, phone coverage correlates to a 15 percent increase in employment — and women are the chief beneficiaries. Another much-cited 2006 study found that a 1 percent increase in mobile penetration in a given country produced a 0.6 percent increase in national growth rates. For many African nations in which the late twentieth century produced flat or negative growth, the introduction of mobile telephony is like a sudden stimulus package.

The best and brightest example of converting connectivity to cash comes from Kenya's M-Pesa, which transforms a twelve-button mobile phone into an ATM. The idea is simple. Customers deposit cash onto their mobile phones at one of the thirty-seven thousand official M-Pesa kiosks in Kenya. By producing identification, a phone number, and a PIN code, they can withdraw it at another kiosk, perhaps hundreds of kilometers away.

Because mobile technology is the building block of many regional innovations, it helps to know some basic facts: In Africa, cell phones are generally not linked to specific networks. A SIM card holds a user's number. And rather than establishing postpaid plans, with contracts and credit checks, mobile phone companies generate revenue from prepaid airtime scratch cards ranging in price from just a few minutes of talk to weeks of data downloads. The cards, sold universally at corner kiosks, hold special code numbers to load "credit" for the individual user.

This produces some typically *kanju* uses — multiple family members sharing a simple phone, swapping the SIM card depending on who wishes to make or receive a call. Those who can afford it have developed the habit of owning multiple handsets to use on multiple networks. (The extra phone serves as insurance against service outage.) In response, Samsung came up with a phone to store two SIM cards at once — a lean economy innovation that has since been marketed to wealthier users who need to balance work and personal calls.

This adaptability extends to actual minutes used. In 2005, Safaricom rolled out Sambaza, a service that lets customers send prepaid airtime to other subscribers. Callers used to real-life barter and arbitrage began using the system as a type of e-currency, swapping phone credit back and forth to settle debts or trade favors — with no transaction costs. To its credit, the telecom paid close attention to the trend and in 2007, with British Vodafone and backed by DFID, Britain's development agency, launched a new product to allow *actual* money transfers between any two subscribers (for a tiny fee). I used M-Pesa to pay my cable bill, or a taxi driver, or a small businessperson, without any cash changing hands.

This demonstrates the third result of technology adoption in Africa: a flood of unprecedented innovation. M-Pesa enables a range of financial services. In the event of emergency, funds can be wired to relatives or friends simply by using their phone number. Payment and collection of debts do not require face-to-face interactions. Many users "store" funds electronically in their Safaricom accounts—a kind of rudimentary savings scheme. In Africa, credit and banking services barely exist—about 80 percent of the population is unbanked, and the majority of Africans south of the Sahara have no access to credit. As a result, a significant proportion of Africa's *pesa*—which means "money" in Swahili—has been hidden in mattresses or in boreholes.

M-Pesa offers security, convenience, and empowerment—not to mention a long-sought ability for individuals in poor countries to build assets. The immensely popular service is now used by 65 percent of Kenyan households, and transactions amount to some $20 million *daily*—equivalent to 50 percent of Kenya's annual GDP, and growing. In a society that is openly patriarchal, mobile money is gender balanced: women send money as often as men.

As a phone company offering, M-Pesa was technically not supposed to exist. At inception, local banking partners bailed on Safaricom—all found a mobile money venture too risky. The ultimate product was a clever workaround that found a way through loopholes and oversights in regulation—and eventually forced the hand of the state. (Kenya issued a special license to Safaricom, permitting the telecom to operate as a financial institution.) This is an important triumph of *kanju:* in economies where banks are powerful, and complex financial products are common, M-Pesa simply would not have developed. Governments elsewhere in Africa have hobbled the spread of mobile money, using regulation to seek rents from an innovation that has transformed and energized Kenya.

But the genie is out: Africa's mobile commerce has seeded a radically new concept of cashlessness around the globe. Parrot programs like Paga, EcoCash, Splash Mobile Money, Tigo Cash, Airtel Money, and MTN Mobile Money have sprung up in dozens of other countries. The Senegalese company W@ri built software that powers e-payments, payment cards, and virtual accounts in twenty-two countries. Africa's example is already pressing the global community to reexamine the delivery of goods and services. A 2012 survey of global financial habits found twenty countries in which more than 10 percent of adults reported using mobile money. Of them, fifteen were African—with more than 50 percent in Kenya, Sudan, and Gabon, and *one-third* in Somalia—the great "failed state." In a pleasing inversion of development logic, the share of adults using mobile money in fat economies in Europe and the Americas is as low as 1 percent. Africa has leapfrogged way ahead.

Such generativity is a common feature of disruptive technology.* Like personal computers, credit cards, Amazon, or eBay, M-Pesa is a platform that has changed the scope of what's possible. Hundreds of businesses piggyback on M-Pesa in order to provide value-added services. In Nairobi, one of the biggest conveniences for me was paying electric and other utility bills using mobile money. Ticket sales, micro-insurance, and e-commerce are some popular business models that use mobile money. Kopa Chapaa and M-Shwari are two credit services based on mobile money—users can borrow funds and earn interest on deposits using their cell phones. Mobisol and other energy vendors install solar systems in poor households and let users pay for them over time with mobile money. Businesses can more easily and securely pay informal or part-time labor and, rather than missing the bank teller who leaves by 4:00 p.m., can deposit the day's cash earnings with a mobile money agent.

But in Africa, tech isn't everything. *Kanju* is still the killer app. Almost as important as the M-Pesa innovation is the network of kiosk owners who have been conscripted into the access-to-finance scheme. In Somaliland, the ZAAD money transfer system deploys the vast net-

---

* For more on the topic, see Jonathan Zittrain's work on "The Generative Internet."

work of retailers of *khat*. A 2010 study of M-Pesa found that users tend
to strengthen and consolidate extended networks beyond immediate
relatives. The technology turns phone contacts into potential lenders,
borrowers, or collaborators in financial activity. Our maps layer on
top of one another; mobile money works because it leverages social
networks. Technology helps live social networks transition into virtual
ones, and vice versa.

One example of this occurred at TEDGlobal, held in Arusha, Tanzania, in 2007. For the first time in its history, the popular conference
on technology and design brought together one hundred fellows from
across the continent. Kenyan-American technologist Erik Hersman,
engineer Juliana Rotich, and former Google Africa policy director
Ory Okolloh met, stayed in touch, and leveraged their personal connections to build, with David Kobia, both Ushahidi and later BRCK
— a rugged, low-cost wireless modem designed for developing world
Web access. "We wouldn't be here if it were not for the Internet," says
Rotich, the executive director. "We were very disparate, but one thing
we had in common was the Internet and blogging. It's not a recipe, but
a catalyst — a key connector."

The world is littered with "cluster economies" — specialized zones
where proximity accelerates progress. Think Milan for shoemaking,
Detroit for cars and Motown, Las Vegas for gambling, or the Pearl
River Delta in China for the world's plastic, toys, and textiles. Silicon
Valley attracts tech talent and capital because of the existing concen-
tration of both. Today, the same thing is happening in Africa. Steve
Daniels, in his wonderful in-depth study of Kenya's informal economy,
defines local manufacturing clusters as "an intricate web of relationships and transactions, [operating] with its own collective efficiency,
so long as there are minimal losses in the connectors — usually guaranteed by close proximity and established social relations."

The same mechanics of plastic production are being deployed in
Africa's burgeoning digital economy. A nondescript white building in
bucolic Buea, Cameroon, houses ActivSpaces, a tech cluster established with the help of Bill Zimmerman, an ex-Microsoft developer

with a passion for Africa. Coders and dreamers can rent a desk in the open-plan office, sharing coffee and testing pitches on one another. Similar spaces, committed to clever hacks and mutual uplift, have sprung up at Akendewa in Côte d'Ivoire, Jokkolabs in Dakar, EtriLabs in Benin, iLab in Liberia, Hive Colab in Uganda, and the Co-Creation and Wennovation Hubs in Nigeria.

The best-networked and largest of these labs is Nairobi's iHub, an airy workspace with a chartreuse décor that, from 7:00 a.m. until late, plays host to events involving government ministers, Silicon Valley visitors, and local developers. Founded in 2010 by Hersman with support from the Dutch NGO Hivos and the Omidyar Network (run by eBay founder Pierre Omidyar and his wife), the venture has attracted over ten thousand registered members, who pay to enjoy the blistering-fast Internet connection and the community of like-minded developers. On a typical day, three dozen technologists from around east Africa are hacking in huddles, building new applications for the local market — with breaks for foosball and Pete's Coffee.

On one afternoon, a young programmer sports a yellow tee blaring Mark Zuckerberg's motto: "Move Fast and Break Things." Jessica Colaco, the office manager, cups her hands to make an announcement: TEDGlobal will be streamed live all week. In part because of its fast Web connection and in part because of the networked approach of its founders, iHub keeps one foot in the fast-moving world of global technology, and the other firmly grounded in the start-up, collective culture of *kanju*. "The iHub sees itself to be a link with all these corporates, academia, universities," says Colaco. "We open up the boundaries here."

There are plenty of whiz-bang tech hubs the world over. But in African tech communities, the fail state makes clustering particularly effective. For emerging market entrepreneurs, institutional uncertainty heightens all the typical worries of an early mover. Around a table in Lagos, I met a group of Nigerian programmers — aboveboard cousins of the Yahoo Boys. They named state power failures as one of the key hurdles to building start-ups. After all, bootstrapping is hard enough without having to think about electricity.

The majority of the programmers I spoke with were completely self-taught — the victims of a listless educational system. "A lot of people encounter courses in computer science or engineering courses in university, [but] it's wholly inadequate," says Dejo Fabolade, a consultant and Web developer with a decade of experience in Nigeria's tech scene. "This is the Wild West stage of Nigerian Internet entrepreneurship, in which we can't depend on those well-laid infrastructures to be successful."

"As young guys, we face a lot of challenges. You're running a business and you're the president, secretary, and cleaner — there's a limit at which you can grow," adds Dele Odufuye, the executive director of Tsaboin, a Nigerian tech consultancy. "At a point I was attending to more than twenty people, more than fifty, and everybody wants your attention at the same time. . . . And in a situation where the infrastructures are not there, you have to connect a lot of dots together."

Coworking spaces share the burden and create a new information neighborhood that members use to learn from one another. "There's no centralized platform for us to do this," says Valery Colong, a programmer from Buea, Cameroon, who serves on the board of ActivSpaces. "If you come together and meet people who have the same passion like you, it gives you a sense that you're not alone and gives you the courage to act on your business." Colong has been working with his friend Ebot Tabi on and off for ten years. He has also partnered with Al Banda, whose background is in real estate, on an online platform to search for and sell properties in Cameroon. Says Banda: "It's a division of labor. They may need to concentrate on the tech part of what we're doing, and I may need to concentrate on the business part. It's a lot easier than trying to do it all yourself."

Negotiating hardships breeds strong ties among micro-enterprises, whether industrial or digital. In the plastic economy, according to Daniels, ventures "work together to share labor, technology, and materials. When an entrepreneur gets a large order, he might ask a friend to take on some of the load. Or when supplies are tight, he might ask the friend for a loan of materials. Pooling of resources ensures that they are used efficiently by those who need them. . . . Trust is one of

ActivSpaces, a coworking hub in Buea, Cameroon, allows programmers,
marketers, and quants to share space and talent.

the most valuable assets." Despite the globalized tools, Africa's digital
economy still looks like the informal economy on the streets outside.

While the scale of these clusters is nowhere near as large as those in
Shenzhen or in Detroit, Africa's planned tech hubs anchor the Technology Map. Odufuye is proud of what his friends in Nigeria managed
to do with bare-bones support: "We may not have a Silicon Valley location right now, but I can say we have a Silicon Valley experience going on."

The explosion of these hubs has merited east Africa a flattering nick-
name: the "Silicon Savannah." (In South Africa, it's the "Silicon Cape.")
This comparison to California is instructive. Investors and technologists who travel between the two communities describe worlds apart,
yet connected. Mbwana Alliy, who worked as an angel investor at i/o
Ventures in San Francisco, sees African technology as the hot new
space for real innovation. "In Tanzania, where I'm from, I see cool

technology more and more," he says. "Remember, we don't have to have a PC revolution — we skipped that. The catchup is more interesting than anywhere else in the world."

In California, where "me, too" ventures and sky-high valuations for photo-sharing and social messaging applications have bored or spooked the most adventurous investors, African technology is an exciting alternative. "People say, 'Hey, I missed out on China and India — I don't want to miss out on Africa,'" says Alliy. In this spirit, he brought Russel Simmons, the cofounder of Yelp and an early employee of PayPal, on a visit to east Africa in 2010. Despite having worked with online payments for much of his career, Alliy told me, "[Simmons] saw M-Pesa and said, 'Whoa, what the hell is this?'"

Alliy and Hersman are making connections, real and virtual, between established and emerging markets. In 2012, the two, with a third partner, Paul Bragiel, established a $5 million VC fund for tech ventures called the Savannah Fund. But culturally, some links already exist. A key facet of *kanju* is flexibility — on-the-fly improvements that counter overdetermined planning instincts. Speaking at the first ever Tech4Africa conference in Johannesburg in 2010, Hersman described Ushahidi as "a small organization that dislikes hierarchy and being told what we can't do — one that questions everything, embraces innovative thinking." He described a madcap, three-day timeline from conception to launch, driven by only one overriding goal: "Launch the damn app."

This attitude is why I'm convinced the most impactful innovations of the future will come from lean economies. Call it the imagination differential. The problems — or in business-school-speak, "pain points" — facing wealthy, well-educated entrepreneurs in fat economies are galaxies away from those facing African technologists. Hermione Way, a British entrepreneur who interviewed two hundred start-ups in the California cluster, gave this difference as the reason why California produces "Groupon clone after Groupon clone, yawn . . . yet another social media dashboard, a cloud-based enterprise solution or, worse still, another photo sharing app . . . they're building technology to solve trivial issues."

By contrast, Tayo Oviosu, CEO of Pagatech, a Nigerian mobile payment company, left Stanford looking for another spoon. "The guy who invented the spoon," he says, with sincere reverence, "he might not have known what he was doing, but he changed the world." Having spent years working in the United States as a technologist for Cisco Systems, Oviosu found himself sitting in the airport on his way home to Lagos. He began a list of twenty ventures that could pass "the big-idea test" and make a difference. "The primary criterion was impact," he says. "I wanted to say in forty years that I had done something."

His list of ventures ran the gamut—from hair extensions to fast food—but two ideas stood out. Number ten: mobile payments. Number eleven: banking the unbanked. Oviosu soon realized that these goals operated in tandem; a company that leveraged the explosion of mobile phone usage in order to allow Nigerians to build wealth would do good *and* do well. From the boarding gate, he called his cousin, his friends, and his parents. He had found his spoon.

Of course, the technology boom bears the risk of diverting Africa's best brains into trifling apps and first-world problem solving. But *kanju* keeps African innovators from aping Silicon Valley's flaws. Ushahidi's BRCK modem comes with an eight-hour backup generator built for African blackouts—a solution that also works in fat economies, where drained iPhone batteries expose the limits of even the sexiest technology. At the fourth annual Maker Faire Africa—a celebration of hacking and creative recycling that captures Silicon Valley's early cyberpunk spirit—a quartet of Nigerian teenaged girls presented their riposte to the Japanese Sound Princess. Rather than a toy to mask the sound of urine, they had built a generator that runs on the stuff. (One liter gives you six hours of electricity.)

Likewise, Fritz Ekwage's tech heroes are classically California—Jobs, Gates, Larry Ellison—but his tech instincts are all Africa. "I have grown up with calculators, not computers," he says. "So I was trying to push the limit of what that simple device could do." This has translated into a contemporary obsession with high-utility apps for low-budget phones.

Ekwage runs an "app store" for the most unlikely of machines: the

Nokia 1100. It works because his customers are eager to improve their lives with mobile tech; the three most popular paid apps in his store are for job offers, learning English, and inspirational messages. Another application allows individuals without fast Web access or constant electricity to be alerted by mobile when they have received new e-mails. When we tried it with my e-mail account and Nokia feature phone, I was delighted to see the first several characters of my inbox messages arrive directly via SMS. "I'm making Nokias into BlackBerrys," Fritz told me with a grin. "BlackBerry should be afraid of me."

African technology innovation changes the game in fail states. Bitange Ndemo, head of Kenya's information and communications ministry, which has been a rare leader on tech policy, described the proliferating connections and their disruptive impact on his country as a "virus": "It has to kill something. It will kill the current inefficient systems, it will kill the corruption we have, and it will create completely new systems." David Aylward, who works with the UN on these issues, marvels that "this has all happened without government planning except for the regulatory side, and mostly without government investment."

This demonstrates the fourth essential feature of the African tech revolution: appropriate technology can supercharge development. In lean economies, connection means more than ringtones and talk time — it means coordination and planning in space and time. M-Pesa is a marquee example. It is a user-generated solution to a problem that had eluded development economists and aid practitioners for years: how to meaningfully improve the financial lives of the poor.

In recent years, a movement branding itself as Information and Communication Technologies for Development (or ICT4D) has advocated even more integration of technology and social services. Nigel Snoad of ICT4Peace often tells the story of a Sudanese refugee who obtained the mobile number for the head of the UN mission in Darfur, after he had toured a camp hosting tens of thousands of the war displaced. Rather than waiting passively for assistance, the woman took action and composed a text message: "I didn't get the plastic netting you promised."

At scale, direct requests like this would be an administrative night-mare — starfish flinging defined. In 2005, Ken Banks, an ICT4D veter-an, adopted a tech fix for those who *don't* stumble across a well-placed NGO staffer. The system, called FrontlineSMS, allows any mobile phone owner to send a bulk text message far beyond his or her im-mediate circles. Installed on any desktop or laptop computer, the free, open-source software becomes a digital megaphone that can be help-ful in a wide variety of situations — party invitations, reminders about schoolwork, and, in some cases, vital health information.*

Medic Mobile, built on the skeleton of Frontline in 2009, allows clinical workers to reach huge populations with information about drugs when they arrive, appointments when they are needed, and reminders that malaria season is nigh. Previously, rural community health workers had to walk or bike tens of kilometers to submit data and other progress reports on health services. During the initial pilot in Malawi, reporting with cell phones saved hospital staff 1,200 hours of follow-up time and some $3,000 in fuel for motorcycles. Today, ver-sions of the patient management tool operate in Cameroon, Kenya, Mali, Uganda, and South Africa, as well as in Haiti, Honduras, India, and Bangladesh.

Frontline is another *kanju* technology. Distributed data manage-ment leapfrogs the frustrations of the status quo. Instead of requiring patients to commute to health care, health care can reach people where they are — through the simple magic of a text message. Importantly, the platform is two-way. Enlisting users as monitors generates data sets for better service delivery. Just knowing when a child has been born, for example, offers a boost to immunization services, where the timing of childhood vaccinations is essential to their efficacy. The abil-ity to quickly summon or dispatch an ambulance (even if it is a bicycle) or a skilled birth attendant is the number-one factor in determining whether women live or die in childbirth. In the absence of state-run "911" emergency services, Mobile Medic is a life saver.

---

* Northern Ugandans, in partnership with Al Jazeera, used FrontlineSMS to rebut the *Kony 2012* video.

As you might imagine, African health policy and practice are ripe for streamlining. The field consumes reams of paper and cash, for concerns from family planning to malnutrition. It's a sector that economists and development experts fret about daily. But for all the subsidies and conferences and meetings between ministries, some of the most exciting innovations in African public health rely on simple, existing tools and connections.

Mxit, for example, is the biggest virtual social network you've never heard of. Built as instant messaging technology, it boasts fifty million users in sub-Saharan Africa, and in South Africa it has more users than Facebook, MySpace, and Twitter combined. Unlike, say, Facebook, Mxit has proven a tool for socially conscious developers, generating more than mindless advertising, or Words With Friends. Mxit offers a foundation upon which others can build high-context solutions for Africa. Its Hello Doctor application, one recent success story, brings cloud-based medical services — symptom checkers and live chats with practitioners — to a captive audience. It's an information management and dissemination tool. Users who are already spending their days in the Mxit family can now access tips and updates about their health.

One of the most impactful ICT4D tools in Malawi is "upcycled" from eBay. In 2000, right around the time the UN was drafting the MDG framework, an American company was offloading "net appliance devices" — basic low-frills computer monitors. They were designed at the height of the dot-com tech boom but were a dud in the Western market.

I grew up hearing the Yoruba proverb "One man's meat is another man's poison." A Canadian named Gerry Douglas followed the same logic. He purchased two hundred of the castoffs online, for $20 apiece, and brought them to the Malawian city of Lilongwe. A team at a nonprofit called Baobab Health began hacking. "We were basically upgrading them," says Soyapi Mumba, a programmer on the original team who leads software development for Baobab, "adding a touchscreen component on it, changing how it uses power and things like that."

The upcycled computers, first deployed in a pediatric ward, have been transformative. They are now used at six hospitals and clinics across Malawi, electronically registering patients when they walk in the door. Pioneered in partnership with Lighthouse Trust, a Lilongwe-based health provider, the electronic data system (EDS) deploys customized software for different medical needs. The software guides the health worker through a series of basic inputs: a patient's name, mobile phone number, and past visits. At the clinic treating AIDS patients, the EDS asks for the time since diagnosis, or the due date for a cell count analysis. At the maternity ward, the system wants to know how many times an expectant mother has already given birth. At the tuberculosis clinic, follow-up appointments are entered.

Most of the clinical workers have never used a computer before, says Oliver Gadabu, a researcher at Baobab. "The closest they have come to a computer is a basic cell phone." A touchscreen flashing foolproof instructions — rather like the devices that log orders at a restaurant — bridges the distance. Doctors now know when a patient was last seen, for what, and by whom. They know who has had malaria or been tested recently for HIV. With mobile phone numbers, they can call patients who have missed an appointment. X-ray technicians can see a patient's previous scans dating to 2005. EDS enables "point-of-care" use as well, in which the computer is live in the consultation room with a patient — an innovation few fat economies have accomplished.

The project was born of dire straits: at the time the EDS was first created, Malawi's HIV infection rate was 15 percent. The segment of the population between the ages of fifteen and fifty had been brutally culled, and the number of orphans was nearly one million. Today, 900,000 of the country's fifteen million people live with HIV, and patients on ARVs abound. The overcrowded hospitals exacerbated the preexisting lack of doctors and nurses. At "high-burden" clinics like the Lighthouse Trust, nurses and clerks took up to five days to prepare quarterly data reports on patients, sometimes closing the clinic in order to do so.

What the system needed most of all was time. "If you come to see a nurse or a doctor, most of them don't have time to find out your patient history," says Mumba. "It's, 'I have just a few minutes, what's your problem? OK, this is the medication'"

Miraculously, the EDS makes time. I watched a machine spit out labels at the maternity ward at Lilongwe's Martin Preuss Centre. EDS has issued 1.1 million individual patient ID numbers since 2001, and the average patient check-in time has dropped from twenty minutes to about fifty-seven seconds. New patients got new bar codes, and old patients were scanned into the system instantly. Crosschecking shows the data gathered are just as good as the paper. The careful design showed — or rather more impressively, didn't show.

In the same way that Ekwage makes dumb phones smart, Baobab strives to deploy technology fit for Africa. It seeks more effective solutions than the broken, donated MRI in Somaliland or the UN's exorbitantly expensive Microsoft Excel training scheme for Ugandan women. Traditional desktop and laptop computers succumb to power surges, viruses, and airborne dust in places like Malawi, and donors or governments find themselves replacing them every year. By contrast,

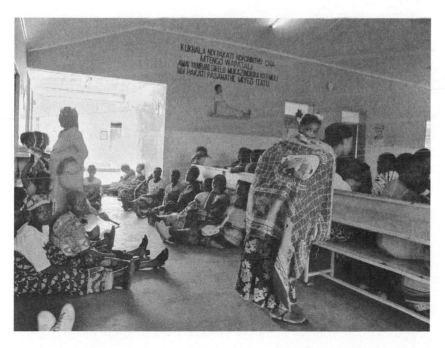

Baobab Health uses simple touchscreens to streamline record keeping in Malawi health clinics, where overcrowding has been a huge problem.

the Baobab models consume tiny amounts of power, are easy to use, test, and replace, and are robust enough to last for years.

The secret is local talent and design. In an open workroom in the center of Lilongwe, Baobab hosts more than a dozen Malawian programmers skilled in hardware and software engineering, and steeped in the design challenges unique to Africa. "We put in computer systems that are well designed for our settings, for the developing world in general," says Mumba. "We try not to just take a computer system that's designed elsewhere but ask, 'What are the components, what are the features that we need?'"

I grilled the engineers about whether hacking old computers makes more sense than importing fancy tablets or "One Laptop" Toughbooks. They made a good case for upcycling. "We don't have to wait for someone to fly to the country to fix any challenge we face with the software we develop here," says Gadabu. "We think of these problems from the moment we begin engineering the solutions we deploy."

Electronic medical records aren't an African invention. But they show extreme promise where the floor for health services is so low. Better data management helps doctors, nurses, community health workers, and laypeople give and receive better care, despite strained resources. The electronic accounting means fewer drugs get stolen or lost in the shuffle. When clinics run out of medicine, we know. And for diseases like tuberculosis, the ability to monitor patient compliance helps prevent monster strains from spreading.

The Centers for Disease Control and Prevention and USAID have since supported Baobab with small grants, as has the Malawian Ministry of Health. The software has attracted notice in Rwanda, Kenya, and Zambia. Mumba created an open-source Firefox extension that has been downloaded almost 100,000 times.

Growing up with clean water, adequate nutrition, and two trained physicians for parents, I have been lucky to avoid some of the worst of African public health concerns. I was vaccinated for measles and polio before I can remember. I've never had to cook food indoors over an open charcoal flame   the cause of common respiratory illness among young women across Africa. I've never had to worry about having a family before I am ready, or contracting HIV from a patriarchal sexual partner. The advantage stretches back to my being born in a hospital — a technology more than half the continent does without.

In 2011, however, I got malaria. It's common enough; every year, 174 million Africans contract it from infected mosquitoes in tropical regions. But it's a nasty disease and a shameful drain on productivity and health in Africa. It's a leading cause of child mortality and 10 percent of the continent's disease burden — serious enough to be among the Global Fund's big three villains and the source of countless awareness campaigns.

I was bitten in Nigeria. And it was definitely my fault. I loved being home, but I hated the preventive pills that for years had protected me from malarial bites but left me with wild dreams and a bitter taste in the back of my throat. And so for a month of covering my country's national elections, I bailed on the meds and recommended bed net, figuring I would join the millions of other Nigerians making do without. Quickly, however, I joined the ranks of those for whom malaria is a debilitating and potentially deadly disease.

The parasite brews in your bloodstream for weeks. I happened to be in Chicago for Mother's Day when I was flattened with fever, chills, muscle pain, and dehydration. My parents, who have slain multiple bouts of malaria between them, felt sorry for me, but also sure they had the problem under control. My dad gave me some medicine he had bought in Nigeria. There, malaria treatment pills are not only more readily available, but they retail for a few dollars — much less expensive than in a US pharmacy.

After a miserable night, I got worse and grudgingly checked into the hospital. There, confusion reigned: a simple blood smear to check for the malaria parasite was showing up negative. I was put through a barrage of tests, for typhoid, meningitis, or worse. I submitted, bleating, to a spinal tap. After two days of intravenous agony, I was on the road to recovery — but not without a bill approaching $16,000.

When my fever cooled, I got hot again. I'd had an unpleasant introduction to the variance between fat and lean health care. Virtually anywhere in Africa, malaria diagnosis and treatment would have been easier and cheaper. Doctors would have had fewer high-tech machines with which to torture me and confuse themselves. I could spend a month in a Kenyan hospital for a tenth of my American bill. But it held different dangers. In fact, the medication that my dad had procured in Nigeria was almost certainly fake.

As it turns out, in many fail states, if you're sick, *and* you've made it to a hospital, pharmacy, clinic, or whatever you can afford to access, *and* a qualified doctor has prescribed a useful drug, the pharmacy still has two options: the designer drug and the generic version. In most cases, the poor will go for the cheaper version. (So do consumers the world over.) But instead of generics approved by federal regulators, African patients are frequently ingesting either toxic chemicals that can harm them, or diluted medications, which, as in my case, do nothing at all. Even designer drugs are suspect: in a 2012 study, Nigeria found that fully 84.6 percent of malaria pills on the market were fakes — despite having good registration numbers from the National Agency for Food and Drug Administration and Control.

Fat economies might have a central solution to the scandal — regulation, sanctions, screening. Not so in fail states. Gaps in policing expose millions of people to this free market uncertainty. Some African governments have made an effort at enforcement, raiding markets and confiscating shipping containers. But there have been few prosecutions or high-level arrests. Drug companies and distributors have tried everything else — but within porous and corrupt institutions, holograms, bar codes, tamper-proof seals, and even registration numbers get hacked. Without effective government oversight, credulous African consumers had no way to forestall health disasters.

West African innovators have created a truly elegant response. Today in Nigeria, pharmacy customers find that some drugs come with a scratch-off label that reveals a numeric code. With a free SMS, the patient can verify whether the drug is real or fake. The simple, red-light-green-light system was repurposed directly from the scratch card economy associated with mobile phones. With the ease of loading airtime, the service gives consumers ownership of their consumption of health products. And for drug makers wary of recalls and public relations disasters — not to mention revenue lost to the black market — the encrypted code on every product is a million-dollar idea.

The innovation is the brainchild of Bright Simons, who may have the perfect name for an African social entrepreneur. Simons grew up in Ghana and came of age at a time when pro-democracy movements and mobile technologies hit his region with twin force. After time as a university student known for rabble-rousing activism, he wanted to stop talking and actually do something that made a difference. "I thought entrepreneurship was really cool, that you could really build something you can use to make your lives better."

Simons had been working with farmers in Ghana on fair trade practices and organic certification. He paired his experience with reputation verification in agricultural trade with his graduate study of China in Africa. Like mobile phone usage, Chinese business dealings with African governments and companies had begun to hockey-stick in the early 2000s, bringing with them a spike in counterfeiting — particularly medicines.

The obscene statistics on antimalarials are the tip of the iceberg. Among twenty-seven other drugs on the World Health Organization's essential drug list, 48 percent of those sold in Lagos and Abuja did not have enough of the active ingredient. Up to 30 percent of medicines sold in developing countries are counterfeit or crappy (to use the scientific term). As demand for drugs in clinics and hospitals has increased, fast-moving, relatively expensive drugs have become a lucrative part of the global black market — worth $200 billion annually. Amoral criminals hijack the goods that actually make a difference in Africa: high-end antibiotics, antidiabetic drugs, and antiretrovirals used for treating HIV/AIDS.

Simons began mPedigree in 2007 as an explicit social response to a public health catastrophe. mPedigree's first pilot program, in 2008, put scratch codes on liquid Tylenol for toddlers in Ghana. The model worked just as planned. After receiving small-dollar grants from business competitions and foundations in the United States, Simons and a growing team began constructing partnerships with telecoms operating in Nigeria, Tanzania, Ghana, and Cameroon. His approach was to get pharmaceutical companies interested in the service, and to use telecoms to make it available to ordinary Africans (the mobile network operator would front the cost of the SMS). To both sides, Simons stressed a kind of corporate social responsibility to protect consumers. By 2010, he had received a glut of international praise for his efforts and funding from bigger partners. He'd gotten all the major telecoms in Nigeria to agree on one number for consumer feedback. Hewlett-Packard came on board to manage the label printing and code generation.

Over the same time period, a company called Sproxil launched a similar service. Founded by another Ghanaian and one-time mPedigree employee named Ashifi Gogo, Sproxil has secured $1.8 million in equity funding from the Acumen Fund and has more than two dozen employees in Nigeria, Kenya, Ghana, India, and the United States. Both companies have earned the approval of relevant government regulators, and both partner with multinational companies: mPedigree works through telecoms Airtel, Orange, Glo, and MTN. Sproxil supplies codes for Johnson & Johnson and GlaxoSmithKline, as well as local drug distributors. Their work has been recognized by big names in development: Gogo by the Clinton Global Initiative and Acumen, Simons by the World Economic Forum and Ashoka. In 2012, Sproxil celebrated its one millionth SMS verification request.

Both ventures are learning a lot about how to expose fake drugs in Africa. Neither operation prosecutes offenders; instead they pass on valuable data to government actors on the hook for stopping crime. When three hundred blisters of Lonart, a popular antimalarial drug, went missing in Nigeria, Sproxil was able to track the range of serial codes to a local pharmacy and, eventually, the distributor who had stolen the product. The data are equally attractive to companies, which can track the geographic clustering of fakes, or the repeat offenders who are stealing their brand.

The system also encourages community policing, says Gogo. "It's a deterrent," he notes. "Any consumer that walks into a pharmacy can say, 'Hey, I texted in a fake,' or, 'I have a hotline for the Nigerian FDA and I'm going to call them now and they're going to close the shop.' For two fake drugs you sell, you're going to lose your shop. So you better cut the crap."

The ICT4D trend is sometimes caricatured as a humanitarian movement — saving babies with cell phones. And yes, many of the tech entrepreneurs I encountered were building ventures that plug a social hole. But as mPedigree begins to show, ICT can also help solve more mundane and commercial inefficiencies.

Retail distribution, for example, is a dominant source of fail state headaches. Goods are expensive because they must be transmitted across high-tariff borders and badly maintained roads; rural communities have little access to commodities produced at a distance. Products from Coca-Cola to early childhood vaccines have to labor through the baroque distribution architecture that seems designed to keep both necessities and luxuries out of the hands of ordinary people.

Virtual City aims to ease the circulation of goods and services in east Africa. Founded by John Waibochi, a thirty-something Kenyan engineer trained in Michigan, Virtual City markets itself as "a mobility solutions company" that concentrates on supply chains in Africa. "How does a commodity leave from a smallholder farmer to first-level processing, second-level processing, all the way out to export? And what are the inefficiencies there?" asks Waibochi. It turns out there are lots of them. Moving a container inland from Senegal to Burkina Faso costs $10,000 (and waiting time at fifty-five different checkpoints).*

His business, which bested entrants from fifty-four countries to win a $1 million mobile innovation prize from Nokia, uses mobile technology to "automate the entire value chain," he says. "We will automate the buying process of a smallholder farm using mobile devices, mobile weigh scales, mobile printing, smart cards for the farmer, whatever — and capture that accurately and honestly."

African corporations, research institutions, and small and medium-size enterprises prefer to concentrate on their core business, whether it's gathering medical information or selling milk. But in the absence

---

* Rail in China, by contrast, could transport goods the same distance for $1,000.

of first-world distribution networks, they need help. Waibochi admits that the lean economy is a key driver of demand for his business, and that Virtual City would have struggled just five years ago. "You may find you have started this initiative or this company to do this great product, and you spend 60 percent of your time running the company, whether it's dealing with power issues or dealing with cost issues, or dealing with the Internet going down," he says. New connective infrastructure and widespread mobile usage enabled him to sand down the business of doing business in Africa. His generative solution improves the consumer choice of millions.

The Technology Map isn't just about clever apps. Rather, it is a platform for self-direction. It helps people to exit systems over which they have no control — and to make better decisions where they do. Talking with me about Ushahidi, Juliana Rotich made the case for locally grown projects. "As participants in the new knowledge economy, [we] have the opportunity to create apps that serve the needs of everybody — and we're not going to wait for Western developers to create apps for us; we're going to do it ourselves."

This is why technology matters in Africa: it is unbiased — supporting both formal and informal economic activity. It reduces information asymmetries and helps to repave well-worn paths of development policy. And it's an ironic foil to government dysfunction — deployed as a solution to problems that central institutions have shown themselves poorly equipped to tackle.

Larry Summers's Ivoirien well is an important point of contrast. It may still exist (though the half-life of such aid projects is often short), but the mobile phone in Summers's hand has surely evolved — to be smaller, stronger, and linked to a faster network with more people. It is this exponential value that gives African technology the power to break the chains of institutional failure: rather than doing good in a single corner of a single village in a single country, modern connective technologies create a world of opportunity accessible literally from thin air.

7

The Commercial Map
Development for Sale

DURING THE WAR for secession between Sudan and South Sudan, virtually all commercial banks were blocked from the southern region. According to local legend, South African Stanbic Bank earned hero status by ferrying suitcases of cash from accounts abroad and hand-delivering them to the rebel front lines — by helicopter at times. In 2012, Stanbic made a triumphant official return to a newly independent South Sudan and turned a profit after only nine months. It's a fitting reward for the bank's wartime customer service, and proof that markets can make it in the toughest neighborhoods in Africa.

Commerce seems to thrive in the cracks and crevices of fail states. Where bureaucracies have overlooked local needs, smart producers like the "Bangla-Pesa" printers have found a way through. Even Melinda Gates enjoys pointing out that Coca-Cola is able to distribute its products cheaply and universally when international drug companies cannot. I'm always amazed that *khat*, the leafy opiate sold throughout east Africa, makes it from farm to table every day, even as government wheedling and tariffs stall formal trade.

Outsiders have consistently neglected markets on the continent.

Aid flows and "poverty porn" reinforce the notion that there's no money in Africa. Economists engage with the continent from the top down, focusing on dispiriting macroeconomic factors such as GDP per capita, fluctuating interest rates, and donor-funded government budgets. Commodities tycoons in bespoke Western suits worsen the image. When Ugandan Andrew Rugasira tried to launch his product, Good African coffee, with investors and distributors in the United Kingdom, he ran into serious prejudice. "People were expecting Idi Amin," he says. "No one makes any distinction between older generations of African businessmen and the new generation." Fear of what is known euphemistically as "political risk" is overstated; the World Bank's Multilateral Investment Guarantee Agency, which compensates investors in case of coups, expropriations, and other externalities in developing countries, has paid out only six times in the past twenty-five years — and only twice in Africa. Like our Nile mappers, international institutions and investors miss the simpler story: commercial activity is a powerful, shovel-ready network in Africa.

Here is some prosperity porn: Africa provides a higher rate of return on investment than any other developing region of the world — including the celebrated "BRIC" nations of Brazil, Russia, India, and China. Seven of the ten fastest-growing economies in the world are African. Behind the dusty feet in the UN poster, the African middle class is booming. Its members are not oil barons or oligarchs. These are the people who have steady jobs, who own property, perhaps even a car (though it may end up parked halfway through the month when gas prices pinch). Health emergencies don't knock them to the mat. They indulge in tiny luxuries in the form of a movie ticket, imported sweets, or a fancier mobile phone and make larger investments in cable television, home computers, or a decent private education for their children.

In 1998, business strategists C. K. Prahalad and Stuart L. Hart first introduced the business world to consumers at the "Bottom of the Pyramid" — the "BOP" for short. The BOP is the most numerous and least wealthy demographic around the world (the well-off inhabit the top of the pyramid). The African Development Bank estimates that

there are now up to 350 million people at the *middle* of the pyramid
—a population the size of the United States making up to ten times
the poverty benchmark of $2 per day. This doesn't mean there aren't
massive inequalities in virtually every African economy. Or that the
African "middle class" looks like its equivalent in a fat economy.

But the conventional stories and statistics about money in Africa
no longer apply—if they ever did. "A low GDP per capita says that
Nigerians can't afford mobile phones. Yet there are over 60 million
mobile subscribers in Nigeria," says Zain Latif, a private equity investor focused on sub-Saharan Africa. "Obviously something doesn't add
up." This century, huge opportunities exist for producers who can peer
past historic blinders. They'll find highly complex local, regional, and
global markets that enjoy near-universal participation. As it happens,
Africans are willing and able to buy or sell just about anything to just
about anyone—if the price and product are right.

When it comes to human development, African commerce has
three built-in advantages. In the first place, commerce is common—
both widespread and shared. Even the least well off can join in the supply and demand for goods and services. Second, commerce is accountable, in every sense of the word. Parties to even the smallest roadside
transaction agree to specific terms for which both are responsible. It's
a banal fact but, in the context of distortionary charity flows, important to recognize. Last, commerce is a proven tool to create jobs and
distribute goods in Africa—including "development."

My years of travel in Africa have revealed few true commonalities. The
languages, climate, and culture of towns vary as much as the smooth-
ness of roads that connect them. But there is only one exception: everything is negotiable.

This can't be taken for granted. Still jetlagged from a flight from Lagos to New York, I attended a friend's theater performance in Brook-
lyn. When I hit the concession stand during intermission, I was told
the theater had run out of a certain snack. I had spent months haggling
over everything from transport to textiles, and so I made the vendor a
counteroffer: substitute a bag of potato chips and slash 50 cents from

the price. In a lean economy, this would have been a perfectly reasonable proposition — fair, even — but the cashier's blank stare confirmed that, for the most part, Americans play by different rules.*

Of course I thought the cashier should have cut me a deal, but more importantly, I reflected on why I had made the offer. If formality and predictability define fat economies, Africa's commercial map is defined by great flexibility. Consumers in fat economies are used to accepting products as packaged and marketed, and paying fixed prices. Not so in Africa, where arbitrage and valuation are essential survival skills. Just ask the Ghanaian students crossing into Togo to buy cigarettes, or the man I saw in Dakar reselling airplane eye masks. The continent's malleable markets are impossible to define as legal or illegal, collective or independent, domestic or transnational. They just are. Unlike no other aspect of modern or ancient Africa, trade crosses political borders, religious and tribal lines, and the boundary between the formal and informal at will.

Just as I hadn't thought much about haggling while living in the United States, I had never given much thought to the bed supply chain. Yet finding a permanent place to rest my head in Kenya was an instructive introduction to the economics of sleep. My bed began as mahogany wood felled in forests in the DRC or, more likely, Uganda. Bought in bulk and piled roughly on a truck heading east, the logs came to a halt at the border at Busia, where massive trucks seek passage into Kenya. Thankfully, the cargo is not perishable. (At such checkpoints, some rent-seeking customs officials prefer to let bananas and tomatoes rot in the sun than to forgo a bribe they feel is their due.)

Across the border, the wood trucks along the path first leveled by the Imperial British East Africa Company (one of the continent's first formal multinational corporations). The climate dries as the cargo mounts the escarpment of the Great Rift Valley. Once in central

---

* As the US economy slowed in 2008, big-box and electronics retailers such as Home Depot and Best Buy embraced the "haggle economy" — consumers could name their price

Kenya, the hulking logs are released from their pen, thundering out onto the earth. In an industrial cluster in Nairobi, each log is sanded and split, divided physically and also commercially.

First-order processors sell planks to carpenters. Sprinkled with wood dust that resembles toasted coconut, these canny builders can fashion a double bed in less than three days. They then subcontract with entrepreneurs offering varnish to stain the wood, while other traders in the cluster sell foam mattresses, or access to a pickup truck for delivery. Though dozens of laborers conspired and negotiated to produce my bed, few of their enterprises are formally linked, or incorporated with government. Forget about intellectual property: furniture designs are stolen freely as tips and best practices circulate within the information neighborhood.

The carpentry economy helps to illustrate the complexity, scale, and flavor of commerce in Africa. In another place, one might expect this kind of manufacturing to involve vertically integrated brands backed by financial institutions. But in this cluster economy, margins are slim and the demand moves in fits and starts. Repeat players share clients without formally integrating. Bank loans are unheard of.

And so before building my bed, Emanuel, an eager twenty-something carpenter I hired for basic jobs, must puzzle over how many clients he is likely to serve that week, and what he will be able to negotiate with the local sawmill, including an extension of credit if needed. He must worry about when the rent is due at his home and at his shop, or how to manage if and when equipment breaks, or he is injured. And then he has to deal with my ruthless Nigerian haggling.

In the book *Portfolios of the Poor,* a team of economists led by Daryl Collins unpacks the behavioral watermarks of lean economies. They conclude that poverty produces incredible sophistication in money management. By virtue of being poor, low-income individuals and families must engage in a host of complex financial transactions, including rudimentary debt, equity, and insurance products. In their book *Poor Economics,* Esther Duflo and Abhijit Banerjee compare lean economy entrepreneurs and hedge fund managers: "No hedge-fund manager is liable for 100 percent of his losses, unlike almost every small business owner and small farmer. . . . For the poor, every year feels like being in the middle of a colossal financial crisis."

We've already seen community finance help Davis Karambi with school fees. In Cameroon, *tontines,* or social lending circles, have long met the capital needs of small businesses as well. Groups of men pool resources, meet regularly, and share the pot of savings on a predetermined basis. This "merry-go-round" arrangement, known academically as a rotating savings and credit association, keeps money from slipping through the fingers of those without banks. If a group member wants to finance a project or pay away an immediate problem, he or she can bid to win the entire pot, with interest rates determined by the group. This credit aspect adds a twist: "It's a common decision based on what they think your ability to repay is," says Rebecca Enonchong, the Cameroonian businesswoman. Among these informal networks of friendly borrowers, default rates are very low.

Access to any kind of finance can be the difference between subsistence and success. Jammed into a pickup truck with my bed, and Emanuel, I asked him why he didn't band together with other carpenters, buy a proper storefront, and start charging more. He told me he doesn't have the money to do so. The irony floored me: Emanuel sells his work just above cost, bearing all of the risk and hardship, because *he can't afford to make more money.* Still, even taking into account the flurry of arbitrage he must endure every day, business isn't so bad. His skill with construction makes him a decent living. And for the average customer, open-cluster prices (subject to negotiation) are more competitive than those of the imported products for sale at rarified big-city shopping malls. Thus the market clears, supporting the new boom in residential construction across cities in Africa.

While dynamic small-scale trade has supported generations of workers, larger commercial enterprises are now going after opportunities to serve Africa's emerging consumer class in growth sectors like real estate, telecommunications, and cosmetics. Basic goods are a good bet: Massmart, the big-box retailer operating in twelve African countries, was acquired by Wal-Mart in 2011 — evidence of a coming tsunami of high-volume, low-margin retail opportunities. Jumia, a Nigerian-grown e-commerce website, raised €20 million for its promise as the "Amazon of Africa." Where incumbents like Amazon, eBay, Alibaba, and Japan's Rakuten have steered clear of Africa's huge consumer market, Jumia's operations in Nigeria are a way to capture that value first. In each of these businesses, canny African entrepreneurs repurpose existing models and adapt them for local convenience.

Everywhere I have traveled, the writing is on the wall: storefronts and residences are often painted over as advertisements for products from diapers to razor blades. It's a fair trade: Homeowners gain the benefit of a fresh coat of paint, and corporate gets an ad hoc advertisement. The companies vary by region — in Ghana, MTN's signature yellow reigns, and in French-speaking countries, Telkom orange blankets the landscape. But everywhere, big-time brands — Coca-Cola, DSTV, Procter and Gamble — as well as more regional companies — Flamingo Tiles, Rhino Cement, animal feeds, hair products, or paint itself — rely on this alternative marketing system. It's evidence of both *kanju* commerce and new purchasing power.

Commerce has an unusually democratic footprint in Africa. Everyone participates. "The lifeblood of every Somali is trade," says Abdi Duale, the CEO of Dahabshiil. It's no surprise that his money transfer service began as an import-export service for traders, whose aptitude for business has kept the Horn of Africa afloat during two decades of war. Dahabshiil and M-Pesa are valuable commercial innovations because they are ubiquitous. You can find Dahabshiil kiosks in Columbus, Ohio, and Doha, Qatar, as well as across the African continent. Mobile money kiosks are now as common as coffee in east Africa. And, of course, these services rely on a widespread network of informal shopkeepers to build their business.

In the marketplace, social differences disappear. Yes, certain tribes, elites, and religious or other groups self-deal in parts of the region. But trade is perhaps Africa's only universal language. It creates and reinforces social ties and provides an alternative to state-citizen relationships. James Mwangi, head of Kenya's Equity Bank (focused on lower-income borrowers), notes that government is increasingly

In many towns, commercial advertising takes place
not on billboards, but on buildings themselves.

turning to the private sector for leadership and reform, that "entrepreneurial leaders are now as important as political leaders." And when
it comes to real development progress, the private sector is among
Africa's strongest existing networks.

The appeal of commerce in Africa also boils down to accountability. A long-running debate among development hands asks whether
less fortunate communities are better served by charity or by commercial products. Those who believe in giveaways argue that the poor
should spend their limited resources on food, shelter, or education
rather than, say, an antimalarial bed net. Strategic handouts, they argue, can offer a hand up. Those on the side of free markets claim that
free things are without value, to the poor or to anyone. Free bed nets
are doomed to be misused for fishing or as wedding veils, not used as
shrouds against disease.

While research on this issue supports both claims, markets have the
advantage of reflecting the real values of individuals and groups in a
way aid does not. Markets generate a built-in opportunity for ordinary

people to express choice. Consumers and producers are equal partners in transactions; as we've seen, donors and recipients are not. Free goods (shoes, laptops, or medicine) *may* be very important to their recipients. But without commercial agency, donees are subject to the well-intentioned guesses of outsiders.

What's more, markets solve the scalability problem. More often than not, a smart new practice stops at the clinic or farm level, bounded by an isolated information neighborhood, the equipment required, or the budget of the NGO that developed it. As we'll see, commercial viability is a proven path to scale.

At bottom, the argument for aid money rests on a kind of paternalism that is, in many cases, unnecessary: consumers in sub-Saharan Africa often choose to spend their money on goods that are "good." The biggest household expenditures on the continent are food, shelter, and transport. Health care is a frequent out-of-pocket expense. So is education. Generally, even the poorest in Africa are value rather than price sensitive. If consumers can see a product's benefit, they will buy it. The totally unsubsidized uptake of mobile phones in Africa is just one key proof.

Prahalad and Hart are respected business strategists precisely because they take poverty seriously. Granting that wealthy elites were already reliable customers for corporates, Prahalad and Hart argued that firms could access the massive collective purchasing power of the poor by developing unique strategies for the bottom-of-the-pyramid sales. The classic example is soap. The BOP needs fast-moving consumer goods, but they are typically sold in units too large for them to afford. A woman paid $5 daily may lack the cash for a big box of laundry soap to last a month or more. But she *can* find room in her budget for a small sachet that lasts a week. By mini-sizing products, from soaps to cooking oil to airtime and cigarettes, suppliers could capture tiny consumer outlays, at high volumes. In the process of making sales, corporations meet the demand for daily dignities.

A new wave of market-based innovations has evolved from the premise that you can sell development in a similar fashion. In fact, a radical and underreported trend is spreading across Africa: private school. This is counterintuitive; Millennium Development Goal 2 encourages the world to work toward free primary education for all. More than a decade later, many African governments (though not quite half) have abolished school fees. But the fix was often on paper only. Even when fees are lowered, many parents are still on the hook for uniforms, books, school feeding, and, sometimes, bribing administrators. Over six years in Moshi, Tanzania, the cost of "free" schooling rose by 64 percent — faster than inflation. These hidden costs put education out of reach for the poorest. What's more, as we'll see in Chapter 9, fail state schools are often terrible at preparing kids for the future.

African families have not stood idly by. In Kenya's slums, at least 40 percent of children are in private school. In Kinshasa, DRC, 71 percent of schools are private. In Lagos State, Nigeria, up to three in four schoolchildren attend private school. Uganda has 5,600 secondary schools, 4,000 of which are controlled by the private sector. South Africa's government schools are bleeding children as well; the Centre for Development and Enterprise found more than 100 private schools operating in Johannesburg and surrounding rural areas. Very few of these non-public schools are flashy or expensive; many are low-cost, mom-and-pop operations. South African children learn in empty warehouses and factories, or office parks. Enterprising churches, mosques, and ordinary, decently educated people create schools where the state does not reach. Almost one in four schools is unregistered — and thus technically illegal.

In some ways, this is an old story — independent missionary and community schools were a popular and productive option for families in the colonial era and the early years of African independence. In Botswana, many ordinary people contributed capital and labor to support the private offerings. If these cases are any indication, African parents are eager to exit the inefficient public system whenever possible — and they will pay to do it. "Parents have voted with their wallets," says Andrew Mwenda, a Ugandan journalist. "Students have voted with their feet. Most people have just walked out."

Bridge International Academies is leading this stampede. The network of low-cost private schools operates on an *über*-lean model: schoolhouses are usually made of plywood and corrugated tin, with neither plumbing nor electrification. Students use slates to write, and upcycled egg cartons, bottlecaps, and rubber-banded geometry boards to learn math. Though Bridge has opened 214 schools in Kenya since 2009, "we haven't found really compelling uses for electricity yet," says CEO Jay Kimmelman.

The Bridge philosophy is as basic as its classroom amenities: students in Africa are behind because their teachers are not teaching. In some cases, it's because the teachers aren't well trained— offering subpar instruction, or skipping their weaker subjects entirely. In other cases, it's because fail states don't pay well. The predatory governments that spirit away money earmarked for roads and other public services often do the same for education. For years in Uganda, just 13 percent of discretionary government funds reached the schools they were intended to support. Blessings, the teacher I met in Malawi, described unpredictable shortfalls in his salary, despite foreign aid earmarked as a hardship allowance for teachers.

Bridge actively rejects the public-sector approach and has tossed out most of the policy presumptions embedded in the MDGs. Where African governments have raced to abolish school fees, provide free uniforms, and build new buildings, Bridge doesn't even require uniforms, and its physical structures are an afterthought. "Kids sitting in a building that you call a school doesn't matter. Kids sitting under a tree getting educated — that matters," says Kimmelman, who founded the company with Phil Frei and his wife, Shannon May. "If you stick them in a school and the teacher doesn't show up . . . that's something, but it's not education."

More controversially, Bridge is not free. Tuition is bare-bones — something like $5 per pupil per month, and payable on flexible terms. But it presents a strong philosophical distinction from the fail state economy. "We are a retail service to our parents," says May, Bridge's CSO. "The definition of poverty is that there are things that you want that you can't buy — things that would make your life better or make it easier for you to survive, you don't have the ability to acquire. Often that's because of price points. We drive the price point low enough so [parents] can become a consumer of that product."

Bridge received early-stage equity funding from New Enterprise Associates, the philanthropic Omidyar Network, Khosla Ventures, and Learn Capital, and each school's customer base helps cover each school's operating costs. Running the schools for profit "is a direct shortcut to accountability," says Kimmelman. "If teachers don't show up, parents aren't going to pay. If they don't believe their kids are learning, they're not going to pay and the school's going to go out of business," he adds. "As a result you see much lower levels of absenteeism on average among these low-cost private schools, and on average you see higher performance in terms of the kids' academics." Indeed, privately schooled young Africans do better on average than peers on math and English tests. According to annual third party evaluations, even the lowest-performing Bridge students are beating out their peers at government and other private schools. In reading fluency, the gap is as high as 205 percent.

Bridge is an innovation for the bottom of the pyramid, responding to a market need with market forces. As such, it operates like a well-oiled education factory. The schools themselves are sited with corporate precision; before entering a given community, a team maps out competing schools, access to transport, and the maximal potential uptake in students and builds a school right in the crosshairs. Smartphones eliminate the need for secretaries, bursars, principals, and other administrators, and each academy runs with an average of three non-teaching staff members. Tuition is paid using mobile money, and staff salaries are, too.

Part of what makes Bridge possible is scripted instruction. Teachers are plucked from local communities and equipped with 350 hours of Bridge doctrine before beginning two-year contracts. In the classroom, they read from scripts containing instructions by the noun and by the minute. To relieve novice teachers of the burden of content expertise and lesson planning, Bridge focus-grouped the ideal methodology for teaching, say, fractions, or how to use *whom,* and deployed it in hundreds of classrooms.

To better understand how the model works, I dropped in — unannounced — at a Bridge school in Machakos, the original capital of Kenya. There, I met Teresia Jacob, the earnest, twenty-three-year-old principal of an eight-month-old school. One advantage to Bridge is the earning opportunity it provides for its several hundred employees: Jacob graduated from university and was unemployed for more than a year when she saw a Bridge job posting. Weeks later, she became the manager of forty-five students and four teachers.

When I met her, she relied on a six-inch binder on her desk that mandates how to interact with parents, when to monitor student attendance (every morning at 9:00 a.m.), and how and when to conduct teacher evaluations (once a week). "Without this book you can't work," she told me. "It keeps you on your toes." Since then, Bridge has replaced the binders with tablets running bespoke Android software. It's produced leaps forward in transparency and efficiency, says May. "I personally can see the reports we run on every teacher, every personnel, every financial transaction, every lesson that was supposed to be taught from 9:45 to 10:30 this morning — regardless of where in the world I am."

In a second-grade numeracy class, I watched as Miss Elizabeth, a willowy twenty-one-year-old teacher, drilled a room of seven-year-olds on double-digit subtraction. An acronym, SLANT, is posted in each classroom. It outlines expectations for students: "Sit up," "Listen," "Ask and answer questions," "Nod if you understand," "Track the teacher." A Pavlovian, singsong repetition strategy ensures that kids are never silent, but they are never talking out of turn.

Bridge thus leverages a typical corporate form: highly centralized and decentralized at once. The company can make the large-scale investments in training, testing, pedagogy, and day-to-day administration that mom-and-pop shops cannot. It can also expand rapidly; in winter 2013, Bridge opened fifty-one schools in one month. In fall 2013, it opened another eighty outposts, for a total of sixty-five thou-

sand students. Kimmelman, who previously built the education management company Edusoft* in America, uses the fitting analogy of a
Starbucks or McDonald's restaurant — eerily consistent across the
globe: "It's really weird and really amazing and it works."

The company won't be profitable until it's educating 500,000 students but intends to be serving 10 million children by 2025. The plan
isn't so far-fetched: nursery and primary education for families living
on less than $2 per day is a $51 billion market globally. "We're not trying to market some product no one's heard of, where they don't understand it or don't know why they want it," says May. "There's incredible
pent-up demand for what we're trying to provide, and it's about showing how we're providing the thing they want already." For parents who,
Jacob tells me, "do not have time or money" to supplement the public
school experience — or are poorly educated themselves — an affordable, reliable basic primary education for their children is a genuinely
attractive investment.

The agility of the Commercial Map helps Africans cope with processes
in the state's control — like school — as well as those out of state control — like rain. It's basic knowledge that farms need water. Fat economies have solved the problem with irrigation, but in Africa, most agriculture thrives or fails based solely on the whims of Mother Nature.
This has been so for much of human history, but climate change has
made things worse. Capricious weather patterns disrupt farm yields
and income. African crops may fail on a more frequent, yet still unpredictable basis. "Of all the bottlenecks and constraints, the tight-
est is the water one," says Nick Moon, who has been working on the
problem since 1991. "Water for most sub-Saharan African farmers has
never been considered as an agricultural input that they can control."

Improved water management has been an essential part of the
"green revolution" seen in Asia and Latin America that has been responsible for rising incomes and better nutrition and general health.
But without irrigation, African farmers can't get ahead. They plant

---

* Disclosure: Houghton Mifflin bought his company in 2003.

crops that arrive at local markets at the same time. Prices for oversupplied crops drop through the floor. Farmers take less cash home and can't buy airtime, education, health care, shelter, and food. They are excluded from the economy at large.

My father's father bought land in Oke-Igbo, Nigeria, at the kink of a highway connecting Ife, the great university town, and Akure, at the north end of Ondo State. When visiting, I enjoy strolling the stand of thick plantain trees outside the house, whose output ranks as my favorite food. We usually hack down a few bunches for the trunk, but there is nothing else to reap: the rest of the land is long fallow. I spoke with the woman who, with her husband and two children, ensures the property is not overrun or mismanaged. I gasped to see her son wielding a machete and toting plantains to our car. He was six years old (not a strange age to be running errands), but barely up to my knee. Despite living on a four-hectare plot of farmland, she's not able to feed him much more than plantains. I asked her why they weren't trying to grow more and better food. "No water," she said plainly.

Nick Moon's company, KickStart, proposes a market solution to this bottleneck. Beginning in 1998, KickStart began selling foot-powered pumps that draw water from deep beneath the ground, giving the smallholder farmer control over the heavens and the harvest. The company works in Tanzania, Mali, Kenya, and Burkina Faso and exports pumps to countries where it doesn't have full programs, including Ghana, Malawi, Rwanda, Uganda, and Zambia. The pump is guaranteed for one year and doesn't require maintenance or fuel that farmers can't afford. "You only need your energy," says Moon. "They are deliberately low-capital, labor-intensive technologies." Their distributed sales staff offers basic training on how to assemble and operate the pump and leaves the farmers with a tool to boost their income — hence the most popular model's name: the MoneyMaker Max.

I best understood the power of this innovation standing on a trellised farm in Musanze, Rwanda. The rolling landscape forces smallholders to build their crop rows high into the country's "thousand hills." After planting, getting enough water for thirsty seedlings would take several trips to the distant public well every day. While households frequently send a family member to fetch water, the bulk of what returns is reserved for cooking and washing. With KickStart's pump, even a child can "walk" the water up from the ground in large quantities — a lifeline to the season's potato crop.

KickStart has sold more than 200,000 pumps over the years, presumably impacting more than a million farmers. The company visits farmers up to three years after their purchase. After eighteen months, usage is between 80 and 90 percent (they've found some pumps nicely wrapped under the bed). Most of the customers are seeing better yields. "Our business is not selling pumps, it's creating successful rural enterprises," says Moon, who retired from the company in 2011. The MoneyMakers, which are manufactured in China, are distributed by private shippers and wholesalers and are also sold through private-sector retail outlets. The best-selling "Super" pump is about $100 and the smaller hip pump is $70. There are layaway plans for their cash-strapped clientele. "We're approaching these people as investors," says Regina Kamau, a development officer at KickStart. "We know that not everyone is going to buy the pump, but the majority will because they realize it's an opportunity."

Private solutions for education and agriculture are a huge opportunity in Africa — not least because so many millions depend on learning and farming to get by. Likewise, the most exciting innovations for health care are private.

At first glance, it would seem that market forces are unnecessary for the provision of health care in Africa. Between donors and governments, the basic health needs of Africans should be covered — like school fees. Foreign assistance now accounts for 10 percent of African health care expenditure on average but balloons above 50 percent in a few countries. Since 2007, Burundi, Ghana, Kenya, Lesotho, Liberia, Niger, Senegal, Sudan, and Zambia have moved to donor-subsidized free health care models, with a focus on pregnant women and young children.

This arrangement works, in some ways. After a dreadful delay, key childhood vaccinations and top-flight antiretrovirals are finally available at low cost to regions and individuals who need and can't afford them. When fees were abolished in Burundi, the birth rate at health facilities ballooned by 61 percent, and cesarean sections increased by 80 percent.

But even as donor governments and individual philanthropists send cash and medicines, poor people are still paying their own way. According to a report from the International Finance Corporation, the private-sector arm of the World Bank, an astonishing 50 percent of the total spent on health south of the Sahara is financed with "out-of-pocket payments from its largely impoverished population."

Public and private treatment centers I visited in Kenya, Uganda, and Malawi were strictly "pay as you go." It works a little bit like top-ups for cell phone airtime: pony up the fee for a consultation and only then can you see the doctor. If you're bleeding profusely, you still might have to stop to buy bandages, and in some government hospitals, blood transfusions are frequently the responsibility of the patient. It's not crazy to see a Facebook message announcing a same-day blood drive for a friend in need. Some pregnant women arrive at hospitals with "mommy kits" containing the bandages and syringes they suspect the clinic might lack. It's unlikely that a crowning baby would be shoved back inside an expectant mother, but health consumers know to come prepared.

The cash-first schemes are a way of dealing with the uninsured, who might not be traceable to an employer or even a fixed address. (It also has the effect of rationing care.) While plenty of Africans put up with the fees and poor treatment at "free" government hospitals, more than 40 percent of the poorest people in Ethiopia, Kenya, Nigeria, and Uganda now get their health care from for-profit providers. Infant checkups, broken limbs, suspicious headaches, and countless other nonemergencies are increasingly dealt with in the private sector.

As with private school administrators, private health providers can perform much better than their public counterparts in Africa. Not only are they directly accountable to patients, but the biggest for-profit hospitals are more likely to have the essential tools of quality care — MRIs, x-rays, and other imaging equipment; a well-stocked pharmacy;

and well-trained and well-paid doctors, including specialists (many of whom are double-dipping to supplement inadequate public-sector salaries). Lower traffic for such facilities can ensure more attention. But they are few and far between, and they're not cheap. Basic consultations can run $30 or $50 — a steal in a fat economy, but in Africa, out of reach for all but the upper middle class. Dr. Ismail's hospital in Somaliland charges $100 for a cesarean section. Even more complex problems can and do break the bank.

Juba Medical Complex is a private hospital in the "last born" African nation of South Sudan. In the garden, hawks are nesting in banana and eucalyptus trees. In the waiting area, a teenaged girl holding a plastic pail is trying to clear her chest of some hidden demon. Dr. Ronald Woro, the JMC's director, is enormously tall and walks enormously fast. In 2007, after twenty-three years in Kent, England, he returned to his newly independent homeland and built a sixty-bed hospital on what had been a local swamp. Today it operates completely for profit, and there is no donated equipment: Woro and his business partners bought every speculum and scanner in the place.

The tab was roughly $10 million, but its payoff seems worth it. South Sudan has virtually no medical care. Though its state is legitimate, it is horribly weak. In the public health sector, said one consultant for an international finance organization, "you have infrastructure and you don't have resources, or you have resources and not infrastructure, or when you have both, you don't have the road for people to get there." Another Juba resident panned Woro's competition, a government-run teaching hospital down the road: "People go there because they have no options," he said. "It's cheap but the doctors are not well trained."

The private clinic model offers a choice to families who otherwise would travel abroad for surgery or complex medical problems — or more likely, shell out for inferior care in the public sector. While Woro admits the price of most consultations is "still unaffordable for ordinary people," he likes to move fast: a building to house the country's only CT scanner was built (with Chinese labor) in six weeks. Patient fees support a budget to recruit and pay a dozen specialists from Uganda, Nigeria, and South Sudan. In part because it has more reliable imaging equipment, many public hospitals frequently refer pa-tients to the JMC. The presence of a private actor has improved the state of public health.

Lower-cost private options are also prevalent in Africa, but their services vary wildly in quality. Many facilities lack adequate staff and equipment, or staff are trained to handle common ailments that leave them at a loss when faced with the unexpected. Some of the remote diagnostic and task-shifting practices we've already encountered can help to close the human resource gap. But in many cases, private prac-titioners just aren't helping enough patients to make their business trusted and viable.

Some entrepreneurs have attempted Bridge-style models for private outpatient clinics. In South Africa, the Unjani clinic franchise follows surgeon Lynn Denny's lead, building facilities out of shipping contain ers (one way to save on overhead). Liza Kimbo, a one-time banker, founded a "hub-and-spoke" network of private health providers serv-ing lower- and middle-income Kenyans. The central hub organizes resources and takes the most complex cases, and satellite clinics try to handle incoming. Both models are designed to minimize costs and waiting times, but the economics are tough. (Unlike the schools-in-a-box, clinics tend to need electricity.)

Status quo challenges, however, make health care one of the better investment opportunities in Africa today. Open Capital Advisors, a financial advisory company that works with firms in east Africa, in-cluding health clinics, sees a high ceiling for investments in private health services. The demand is clear: remember that mothers clutch-ing babies, or men presenting for chest pains, are also forgoing a day of labor. Like parents picking schools, they are willing to spend more up-front to avoid pinballing between providers, or losing a child. Innova-tive suppliers could enjoy huge financial and social returns. (Kimbo's LiveWell clinics, for example, were recently acquired by Viva Health-care, a company in Singapore that runs clinics for profit across the developing world.)

The region's lack of access to health care is mirrored by a lack of health insurance. Coverage as a percentage of the continent's population is in the single digits. Rwanda, Ghana, and Tanzania have made the most significant strides in national insurance, now offering comprehensive outpatient and inpatient services to policyholders. But only 38 percent of the Ghanaian population is covered, and other national insurers have an even starker coverage gap, leaving out the most vulnerable. More serious medical problems almost always knock poor families to the ground financially.

According to a study of insurance providers in Ghana, Nigeria, Tanzania, Uganda, and Kenya, one in four of the poorest households in low-income countries is spending a "potentially catastrophic" proportion of its resources on health care; for 40 to 50 percent of households, all of the health care spending was on medicines. In fifteen African countries, roughly 30 percent of households financed health care spending by selling assets or borrowing from friends and family.

Insurance is particularly useful in African health systems because it pools financial risk and offers stopgap coverage for those with limited liquid income. Transferring these emergency investments into insurance premiums that cover medication makes sense for families in the emerging middle class. It's also good business: even the poorest quintile of Africans is willing to buy health services. Among the uninsured in Namibia, nearly nine in ten were willing to join a health insurance scheme — and pay up to 5 percent of their income for it.

Perhaps obviously, the sick in sub-Saharan Africa can't rely on "Obamacare" or other state-backed coverage common to wealthier countries. Health insurance plans run by African governments often find their tax base too small to properly fund an ambitious offering. Large private companies like Sanlam in South Africa and Resolution Insurance in Kenya are meeting demand effectively and structuring an often irregular industry. Dutch company PharmAccess partners with employers to provide insurance plans tailored for low-income workers in more than ten African countries. While these ventures don't typically cover the informally employed, six hundred additional local, community-based insurance schemes have been established in eleven countries.

Leaving aside diagnosis and payment, prescription drugs are the closest thing to a magic bullet in African public health. HIV treatment is basically HIV prevention — once patients are on antiretrovirals, the risk of transmission drops by 96 percent. Thus "drugs into bodies" — a rallying cry borrowed from AIDS activism in 1990s America — has driven the movement to bring cheap drugs to Africa — the cheaper, the better.

Big philanthropic players can negotiate prices downward and get more units to those in need. But many of the agreements among the Global Fund, America's President's Emergency Plan for AIDS Relief (PEPFAR), or African governments themselves are tied to purchases from the donor countries, in effect sending donated dollars or euros right back where they came from. And in many instances, drug companies have to be pelted with stones in order to reduce the cost of medication in Africa.

The ARV debates were a classic example. In 2001, brand-name AIDS treatment drugs cost $10,000 to $15,000 per patient per year — prohibitively expensive for any African buyer, public or private. To its discredit, PEPFAR refused to pay for generics (claiming that they hadn't been researched enough), and so its funding stretched to fewer patients. When Cipla, a market-leading Indian company, began making effective generic ARVs for less than a dollar a day, access skyrocketed — and even brand-name prices decreased, ultimately saving PEPFAR $300 million in three years (and countless lives to boot).

Even at low prices, government drug distribution networks sometimes fall short. I visited Hospice Africa Uganda in Kampala, where patients with terminal cancer are offered palliative treatments, including morphine. The center is calming and well-planted, awash in sunny paint to cheer the patients. But in a side room off the neat courtyard, a clinical worker has the unglamorous task of making morphine. For a facility that needs large quantities of pain medication to prevent suffering, the spate of government drug stockouts was a risk too high to bear. And so the technician I met painstakingly rehydrates independently sourced morphine powder that Hospice Africa in turn distributes to other clinics and health centers. It's a tedious but essential hedge.

Since 2005 in Uganda, Quality Chemical Industries Ltd. (QCIL) has been scaling up the private drug-making game. The for-profit venture emerged from a partnership between Cipla and a local chemical company. Logically, QCIL has focused its business on cranking out ARVs and antimalarials for local use, avoiding the need to buy everything or be handed everything from abroad. QCIL makes 100 million ARV doses per month, enough to serve three million patients in Uganda, Kenya, Tanzania, Rwanda, Burundi, the DRC, and South Sudan. It's one of only a handful of plants certified by the World Health Organization on the African continent.

Making drugs for Africa in Africa changes the game completely. Rather than allowing Indian or American drug makers to capture that value, QCIL replaces imports and creates local jobs so that ordinary people can finance their lives. As the health needs of the local population increase (Uganda's incidence of HIV has risen by 1 percent in the past five years), the ability to produce locally means fewer procurement headaches and more saved lives — a big sustainability advantage.

In private equity circles, QCIL was voted the small-cap deal of the decade in 2012, but like Good African coffee, it wasn't a go from the start. Even after the local Ugandan team had brokered the deal with Cipla, direct foreign investors and even the International Finance Corporation all backed away from the investment. "Institutions tend to focus on safe investments," says Zain Latif, the fund manager who sank his money into the plant. "People want to see the white face, not the black face." Against the grain, his firm put its faith in the local managers and the pent-up demand. QCIL made its investors $18 million in 2011 and $56 million in 2012.

Buying and selling human development in this way makes some people cringe. There are obvious drawbacks to inserting a profit motive into flows of local or global social democracy or humanitarianism. It's callous to withhold beneficial medication or nutritious food from the illiquid — which can sometimes include the continent's fledgling middle class. But where there is no official welfare or safety net, some of Africa's needs are exceptional business opportunities. Like it or not, the need for "mommy kits" has created an industry of mommy-kit vendors. State failures *are* market failures, and invitations to *kanju* thinking.

Fail states have enabled a new kind of start-up culture. "Social entrepreneurship" is now a term in vogue, particularly when it comes to Africa. There's no wholesale definition, but generally social entrepreneurship refers to the kind of market-based solutions to development problems that we've seen already — Bridge schools and QCIL manufacturing, KickStart, Solar Sister, Sproxil, and Virtual City. These ventures are plugging holes in the state safety net in a more literally accountable way. Networks like Ashoka, Enablis, the Aspen Institute, and Echoing Green flag and integrate social entrepreneurs operating across the world, helping them refine ideas, or scale them. For pay-toilet operators or solar lantern distributors, a community of like-minded adventurers accelerates the pace of change.

The boom and bust in fat economies are a reminder that the private sector is fallible as well. But the rise of social enterprise should undercut the ruse that Africa can thrive on charity alone. Distant donors and planners can't irrigate every farm, cure every patient, or educate every child in Africa. Private markets are innovating to maximize choice, and some of these new products for the poor are wonderful complements to the development agenda. Businesses let consumers decide what to do with limited resources. *Social* businesses empower the willing to buy a better life.

Sometimes, however, business isn't enough — and *kanju* kicks in. It's why the unfinished house is a common sight in sub-Saharan Africa. These structures are not on their way down, but on their way up. Without access to finance (there are only twenty-two thousand mortgages in all of Kenya, for example), millions of families build homes literally one brick at a time. It's a self-designed installment plan: when liquid, families invest in cement bricks, which, over years, will be sufficient to complete a modest home. Safer than cash, the "halfway house" is an unusual savings instrument.* Brick by brick, even the very poor are doing their level best to build assets.

If "Bangla-Pesa" tells us anything, it's that creative accounting and finance anchor the *kanju* economy. But human capital is also under-used. Unemployment in both the formal and informal sectors is a big problem in Africa (as everywhere). It's why the poor tend to articulate their desires not in terms of aid, GDP growth, or even cash at hand, but in terms of stability. More than a sturdy house, low-income house-holds prefer a steady job.

For all the *kanju* creativity in Africa's marginal economies, reliable income is uniformly coveted. The practical value of a job goes back to the Family Map — typically, a single wage earner in sub-Saharan Africa supports a household of half a dozen other people. But work is equally a matter of dignity and, as we'll discuss in Chapter 9, of youth empow-erment.

The most important fact about the Commercial Map in Africa is that it is very good at creating and sustaining such livelihoods. Private companies pay stable wages for skilled producers like my carpenter, Emanuel. They create profits for shareholders. Finance for businesses is a proven way to meet widespread demand for goods and services.

In their zeal to hang the bankers, Western progressives sometimes discount the social role of capital markets and financial institutions in an economy. This is an error of privilege: capital markets that are too weak, or just don't exist, can't finance efficient solutions to problems. And this is what we see across Africa. Emanuel suffers from the same species of short-term illiquidity that leads to an unfinished house. A farmer who can't afford the MoneyMaker pump makes less money and can't feed his children. A parent without a bank account lacks the cushion to pay a child's medical bill or school fees. Without finance, a good idea like QCIL will die on the vine.

Access to savings and credit is essential to building early-stage busi-

---

' The word *capital* comes from the heads of cattle that served as "mobile money" for pastoralists of bygone days.

nesses and helping mature businesses create reliable jobs. But these resources are much more likely to be found in a fat economy than in a lean one. In fat economies, high average incomes backstop savings and personal loans. And even among lean world regions, Africa is at a disadvantage. Husk Power Systems, one of the most innovative ideas for off-grid energy coming from India, burns biomass to make electricity. The social enterprise, which operates for profit, exists today only because the founders had banked $70,000 in savings to bootstrap their way toward a pilot and follow-on loans.

Among unbanked populations in Africa, it's nearly impossible to rely on that kind of financing. Without credit cards to max out, or rich relatives to shake down, African entrepreneurs begin businesses with one hand tied behind their backs. Moses Mwaura, who works with Enablis, an advisory network for small businesses around the world, says he was "shocked to realize that even small businesses that are structured, with an office, with three or four people, can also be in subsistence mode."

While cheap credit is a notable, even fundamental feature of fat economies, even commercial borrowing hasn't reached maturity in Africa. Some countries are worse off than others: Munya Chiura, a Zimbabwean investor, reminded me that following years of terrible economic management, "the reserve bank doesn't exist anymore; we don't print our own money. The central bank doesn't have a critical role." Even after the country abandoned its own currency and "dollarized" in 2009, a liquidity crisis persists. "There are not enough US dollars in circulation to lend to business."

The lack of capital put to work in Africa is surprising. After all, the marginal dollar goes much further in the region, where there is low-hanging investment opportunity. Rents, wages, and other labor inputs are much lower, and the markets are less saturated with competition. So what's the holdup?

Part of the problem is the image of instability and poverty that has nipped the wings of entrepreneurs for decades. Liza Kimbo left the world of banking to found a retail pharmaceutical company, and then the LiveWell health clinics eventually purchased and rebranded as

Viva Afya. She was astonished at how poorly capital markets worked to finance her ideas. "I left banking for a good idea. I wanted to bring health care to more people, and information. And I wasn't able to convince the market that there was a market," she says. Tech companies face similar obstacles. Even when we know what works in Africa, insufficient finance is a key driver of underdevelopment.

Where traditional finance has ignored the poor, microfinance — in which the poor are lent small sums, often in groups — has been seen as a magic bullet. Microfinance has been instrumental in removing the poor from the treadmill of moneylending and razor-thin margins for income. Though the model was pioneered in Bangladesh in the 1970s, it was not until Muhammad Yunus and his Grameen Bank, which has helped millions of borrowers, won the 2006 Nobel Peace Prize that the term became part of the global vernacular.

The movement began with good intentions and mutual respect. Lenders like Yunus saw the poor as competent financial actors arbitrarily excluded from the world of traditional finance. Like Prahalad and Hart's, his intervention bet on the fact that the poor are capable of using capital wisely. Since the start of the revolution, microfinance has built housing, started businesses, and covered the costs of health care and burials, weddings, and investments in needed items from sewing machines to motorcycles. In Africa since the 1990s, the uptake has been rapid. Targeted microlending, brokered through organizations like Kiva or MicroPlace, appeals to those who feel traditional charity is too detached — who support market-based solutions but dislike sending checks to industrial aid agencies. In 2011, 299 microfinance institutions (MFIs) funded over six million individuals in thirty-three African countries, with an average loan of $473 — a gross loan portfolio of $7.8 billion.

This general model of microfinance has advantages: it's fast, it's relatively cheap (compared with the expense of moneylenders, or making do without), and it offers self-determination to the poor. The group lending models also leverage community ties admirably. But the model has come into question as it has gained mainstream acceptance, and as large MFIs have become hugely profitable in Asia. The more relevant question is whether microfinance is truly tackling poverty at its roots.

On the ground, some complain that microfinance can't always bridge the gap between ambitions and outcomes. "If I hear one more time about women and microfinance I will puke," says Rebecca Enonchong, leaning forward over the conference table in her Douala office. "Why is it that when you're pretending to encourage woman entrepreneurs, the most you can give them is fifty dollars? You keep people just at the poverty line. They're not dying of hunger because they have fifty dollars to sell tomatoes — but you're keeping them poor."

Enonchong identifies the chief failing of African microfinance: it's too small. Even at today's scale and efficiency, it's clear that tiny loans are not enough to make poverty history. Emanuel could take out a microloan for a new set of tools, or a badly used delivery truck, but $473 would not help him invest in human capital to grow his business and his local economy. He could seek out a *tontine*-type credit circle, but that would require contributing more working capital than he has at his disposal. What is he to do?

Fledgling firms (often bigger and more organized than my carpenter Emanuel's) are known in development circles as small and medium-size enterprises (SMEs). They helped to build a middle class in fat economies and are having the same effect in lean ones. "I can create wealth because I employ people and pay them a thousand dollars per month and two thousand per month," says Enonchong, whose employees build specialized enterprise applications for clients around the world. "I don't want fifty dollars. I want five million dollars."

Unfortunately, even that may be a tough sell. Over the past decade, big banking has emerged as a profitable sector south of the Sahara. Citigroup, Barclays, J. P. Morgan, Société Générale, Banco do Brasil, Bank of China, and the like now play with African commercial banks such as Ecobank, UBA, Standard Chartered, and Absa Bank — not to mention the World Bank, the International Finance Corporation, the African Development Bank, and other development-focused lenders in the region. In 2009, the consortium of local and foreign banks made $2.6 billion south of the Sahara — *excluding* South Africa. By way of comparison, that's about as much as Western firms made in India and China.

Private equity firms are blooming everywhere; the accounting firm Deloitte determined that investors had raised about $630 million in private equity funding in 2011, mostly for SMEs in east Africa. Helios Investment Partners and African Capital Alliance are major funds with African ownership. Washington-based Emerging Capital Partners was an early foreign arrival. British private equity shop Actis has engaged in some thirty deals with African corporates. In 2011, the Carlyle Group launched its first fund directed at sub-Saharan Africa.

The interest is from all corners, not just the fat economies: Chinese, Turkish, and Indian banks have discovered the returns on investment in Africa as well. Brazilian megabank BTG Pactual launched a $1 billion fund for Africa in 2012, the biggest fund Brazil has raised for international investment, and the biggest targeting Africa. Announcing the move, CEO André Esteves said, "I want this to be taken as proof of the enormous potential that the private sector sees and its confidence in Africa, and show the enormous affinity that Brazil feels toward this important region of the world."

This updated "scramble for Africa" has been good to major businesses and industrial and infrastructure projects. Most investors have no difficulty sniffing out investments in more extractive sectors of the continent's economy. Global banks and funds have helped pay for roads, railways, refineries, heavy industry, real estate, and telecom infrastructure, satisfying the "trade, not aid" brigade and minimizing the need for government efforts. For example, SEACOM — the submarine cable operator that brought high-speed Internet to east Africa — is a syndicate of private investors, three-fourths of whom are African. In 2010, Nigeria's Fidelity Bank backed one of the region's most successful manufacturing investments: an aluminum can factory in the city of Agbara. In a country where 160 million consumers are still using glass bottles and steel cans to consume Coca-Cola and other beverages, supplying an obvious alternative proved to be a slam-dunk. (The factory employs 150 people directly, and another 2,000 as affiliated vendors and suppliers.)

In these growth sectors, the fruit could not be hanging lower. Call it *kanju* capitalism. "All sectors have great potential because Africa begins with such a low base," says Barbara James, longtime director of the African Venture Capital Association. "On the global level you look at other regions, and their growth is not that interesting. Even the wonderful China story is ending," she adds. "Africa has headroom."

Nevertheless, the governments of Africa have been accused of presiding over "jobless growth" — in which the all-hallowed GDP figure accelerates, but the people are left behind. Indeed, the exciting regional growth has yet to translate into daily bread for residents. The formal continent-wide unemployment rate is 9 percent, but the real story is that many millions more are out of work. Inequality is palpable — particularly when you contrast informal retail experiences with the gleaming shopping malls designed to serve Africa's "middle class." As we'll see in Chapter 9, African youth are less and less likely to find sustaining income.

"Macrofinance" is not trickling down to ordinary workers, in part because major multinational banks and institutional investors haven't figured out how to take smaller capital needs seriously. "If you want to build a bridge and you need three hundred million dollars, you'll get the money in no time," says Ashifi Gogo, who runs Sproxil, the mobile drug checker. Less than that is a hard sell, he says. For managers sitting on a $100 million fund (on the small side of the new boom), it's a headache to hand it out $1 million at a time.

Big banks tend to chase marquee projects with lower risk — aluminum factories and shopping malls. Most don't take chances on entrepreneurs like Emanuel. Even among formal-sector firms, risk aversion leads to lower access for borrowers. Banks prefer to lend based on short-term cash flow projections rather than innovation or social impact. What's more, banks provide capital alone, and no support in thinking about business strategy. Even some microfinance models backstop loans with training that encourages smart business, health, and environmental practices. But at commercial banks, as one review put it, "the availability and dedication of [staff] to spend time with SMEs, to fully understand their business and requirements, sadly is not always a priority."

Gogo's and Enonchong's ventures fall into what's now known in development circles as the "missing middle" between microfinance and traditional banking capital. Many promising SMEs are asking for investments of as low as $30,000 to get moving. These capital needs are tiny by global standards but stretch much further in Africa. Businesses at this size create jobs more consistently than the mega-infrastructure projects that have kept GDP growth rates so high this decade. But the prevailing culture of banking is depriving a key sector of the economy of the oxygen it needs to live.

As a result of this "missing middle" for finance, emerging market entrepreneurs rely disproportionately on informal finance, making up between 87 and 100 percent of outside capital raised. According to the United Kingdom's Department for International Development (DFID), approximately 80 percent of start-up capital for small and medium enterprises in Somalia was funded from remittances. Social networks in Africa have fueled the venture capital–style investments to date. Unfortunately, informal finance can't stretch as far as it needs to, in part because African lenders and borrowers are still poor. Even when a better-off "uncle" serves as an angel investor, small firms "don't have a growth vision," says Moses Mwaura of Enablis. "Your nieces grow up, and you employ them in the business. You humble along and bumble along. That's a big problem."

Taking the Commercial Map seriously means changing the way African ideas are financed. A number of innovative models have emerged to close the funding gap for job creators in Africa. Most prominent are organizations committed to "impact investing," or the deployment of capital to achieve not just financial but also social returns. The Rockefeller Foundation, with J. P. Morgan, has tried to define impact investing as a "new asset class." In Africa, there have been promising follow-on effects. Gogo's company received an investment of $1.8 million — squarely in the missing middle — from the Acumen Fund, an investment vehicle that calculates social benefits as part of its traditional return on investment.

Impact investing certainly has its pitfalls. If you're just trying to keep a business afloat, a requirement to measure impact — whether tons of carbon sequestered or children kept free from disease — can be burdensome. Measuring impact has generated superfluous meta-bureaucracies. And, of course, "impact" can vary wildly: Lonmin, the South African mining company thrust into global headlines for brutal conditions and unfair wages in its mines, is listed both on the Johannesburg Stock Exchange and at the *Financial Times* as a socially conscious investment. Other mangled incentives exist as well. But generally, the advent of social entrepreneurship and social investment is a good fit for African markets. Most entrepreneurship in Africa is inherently "social" in its downstream effects. For every job, several family or extended family members benefit.

The Gates Foundation and other huge philanthropies could spend their war chests on private enterprise far more frequently. In the United States, a funding mechanism known as a program-related investment (PRI) allows a nonprofit to invest its endowment as a loan or equity stake — and to earn a return. Few do so, however. For many philanthropies, and Gates in particular, the reluctance to support businesses is ironic, given the market-based success that fed the foundation itself.

But pure giving is not going away — in fact, it's a common way for African start-ups to get off the ground. A small grant can cover costs until "real" capital is available. Of the cases we've looked at, Baobab Health, FACE Africa, Solar Sister, KickStart, and others have been funded with grant capital. But it remains a fickle instrument. Regina Kamau joined KickStart over a decade ago, after working with an international NGO that provided heavily subsidized health care to poor women in Nairobi. It's part of why she believes in their for-profit, for-sale solution. "One of the questions I asked myself is that if these people leave, what next? When there is donor fatigue, what is going to happen to these poor urban women?" To her mind, selling tools and offering modest business advice are far more sustainable.

More troubling, aid money can have a chilling effect on private capital. "There's a lot of donor money, NGO money, and, less so, African government money," says Barbara James, who now runs Henshaw Capital Partners, a private equity fund of funds. "And sometimes these types of financing do not come and support what's already happening in Africa. They come and crowd it out."

James, a canny, crisply suited woman with a long history of investing in Nigeria, shared a personal example. Henshaw attempted to target the increasingly professionalized and strategic sovereign wealth funds around the world. Months into the venture, she heard the World Bank had set up its own, nearly identical fund. She approached the bank and said, "Just in case you don't know, there is this little African fund trying to target the space. This is what we do and it would be great if you didn't crowd us out." The bank didn't budge. Paula Goldman, a director at the philanthropic Omidyar Network, has described a similar experience: "Over the years, we've seen several strong for-profit enterprises serving the BOP that we were eager to invest in — but who ultimately found it too difficult to compete with other companies that had received large grant support from well-meaning philanthropists."

The past few years have seen hopeful points of convergence between better aid and better trade: the storied "public-private partnership." The uninspiring version of a PPP involves liquid Chinese banks financing mega-highways for shrugging African governments. A better version encourages local businesses to expand by accessing needed debt. This used to be (and remains) very difficult for the hiring class of SMEs. But in 2009, the Africa Commission (run by the Danish government) inaugurated a loan guarantee facility that would offer $3 billion to banks that lend to small businesses. USAID, the American aid agency, has also tried to nudge banks into taking more development-focused risks with their investments.

These public guarantees of private enterprise blunt the uncertainty of lending to an entrepreneur like Emanuel who lacks a credit history or guarantor. They're a welcome hint of support for the informal in Africa, and a good way to lower the risk involved in market-based solutions. Importantly, these transactions are neither charity nor equity

— merely a recognition that financing a small-scale business in, say, Accra, can and should look different from funding a mature company in Amsterdam.

In addition to encouraging investment, perhaps the most important prescription for markets in Africa is to provide support for the informal sector — for workers like Emanuel. "Governments have never tried to find ways of making them grow," says Aleke Dondo. "Given that the informal sector is so large in Africa, why do we pretend by continuing to support the formal sector? Let us put in resources, budget for it, and try to promote it. Because it's a big sector in terms of employment creation."

The nimbler African banks are specifically reaching out to untraditional borrowers. In east Africa, James Mwangi's Equity Bank, Kenya Commercial Bank (KCB), and Cooperative Bank all have created particular loan services and officers to handle small-scale agribusiness needs. Juhudi Kilimo, which is affiliated with Kenya's K-Rep Bank, finances agriculture inputs like cows or plows by using the inputs themselves as collateral. Rather than keeping savings in cash (or cement bricks), many millions of mobile money users treat their phones as quasi bank accounts. M-Kesho (the word for "tomorrow") already offers M-Pesa users savings accounts with Equity Bank. M-Shwari, a new entrant, allows users to build credit, despite informal addresses and nonexistent pay stubs.

Some of the most innovative work in philanthropy today cuts out the middlemen entirely. Professor of development studies David Hulme, with others, has lobbed out a fairly radical but simple argument: "Just give money to the poor." Recipients of micro-welfare payments, donated with no strings attached, are free to choose the best investments for their lives. At least a few may choose to fund health, education, water, and other once-donated goods and services. Related organizations like GiveDirectly also channel cash directly to those who need help. Mobile money now enables "conditional cash transfers," a more structured form of this direct subsidy. Parents who, for example, send their children to school are paid for it — no questions asked. The program has been an overwhelming success in Mexico, where mobile money is *less* developed. Africa's advanced m-payments ecosystem could handle the same task — though it bears the risk of depending on corruptible government and fickle foreign aid.

Another way to skirt the bottleneck in financing is to rely on the African diaspora — knowledgeable and engaged potential investors. Diaspora finance comes equipped with a built-in understanding of high-context investing environments. Abdi Duale, who runs Dahabshiil, has seen it firsthand: whereas an investor in New York or in Tokyo might be scared off by "political risk" calculations — or simple ignorance — "migrant investors are not only well informed about the opportunities existing in their communities of origin, they are willing to invest in fragile markets when others won't."

Diaspora bonds are one way to formalize the family relationship in private markets and make existing micro-investments macro. Governments in Israel and India have successfully marketed retail savings instruments to members of their communities abroad in order to fund national development. The idea was first floated for Africa by Nigerian finance minister Ngozi Okonjo-Iweala and her World Bank colleague Dilip Ratha:

> Through retailing diaspora bonds at small denominations ranging from $100 to $1,000, a developing country government or a reputable private corporation in a developing country can tap into the wealth of relatively poor migrants. . . . The money could then be used to finance projects that interest overseas migrants — such as housing, schooling, hospitals and infrastructure projects with a concrete benefit to their families, or the community back home.

The idea has some *kanju* creativity to it — why not organize the informal flows of money? African diaspora savings are estimated by the World Bank at more than $52 billion annually. Mobilizing this money could be a coup for the ventures locked out from conventional finance. Former Liberian foreign minister Olubanke King-Akerele has suggested a special diaspora investment office in Liberia that could help connect diasporas to opportunities at home.

One drawback of a government-floated bond is, well, government.

While transparency has improved by leaps and bounds in recent years, the bond has the effect of funding institutions that are still not credibly accountable for such earmarks. In fail states, who is to say housing and roads will actually be built? Ethiopia's recent diaspora bond flopped in part because of lingering animosity toward a repressive state. Dambisa Moyo's big plan to supplant aid to Africa with international credit financing flopped as well, in part because government bonds are still comparatively unattractive to global creditors.

Siobhan Cleary, an economist who works with the Johannesburg Stock Exchange, identifies African public markets as a way to finance growth and ease state influence in key industries like power. Unfortunately, some stock exchanges have suffered from mismanagement, and the consequent reputational harm. In Nigeria, she says, "it was discovered that the head of the exchange who is also the chair of the list was running it as a private piggy bank." More basically, trading and settlement are still done on paper, and some exchanges are open only half the day (imagine if London or New York tried this). Others are just too small to make a splash in global markets. The Bombay Stock Exchange has over five thousand companies listed, both large and quite small. While exchanges in Rwanda, Côte d'Ivoire, Kenya, Nigeria, and South Africa perform respectably well, they list just a few hundred companies. There are days that go by without a trade in Cameroon, for one example. "It's hard to privatize if you have no market to privatize to," says Cleary.

In order to show up on the global financial radar, Cleary advocates African integration. "Rather than each country having its own exchange, there should be regional ones," she says. A single set of rules, a single currency for trading, and automated cross-listing present a number of advantages — strength in numbers, essentially. While some markets (east Africa, for example) already operate this way, the idea of pan-African listing often runs aground on sovereignty concerns. "People think about exchanges the way they think about national airlines," she says. "You should have one, and it's important for nationalistic purposes." This focus on symbolism over substance might be the most direct way in which African formality bias hurts African business.

Crowdfunding is a less formal, less bureaucratic way to leverage local wealth for more distributed growth. Munya Chiura, the venture capitalist who returned to Zimbabwe after eighteen years away, says it's a win-win for Africans who have yet to come home. "We understand and know that every single Zimbabwean or diasporan may not have the opportunity and desire. How do you get them to participate in the marketplace?" His firm, Grow VC, solicits plans for investment from businesses in Africa and submits the proposals to a group of pre-approved investors. The small amounts required diffuse the burden, and the process can be cheaper, faster, and more accessible than bank finance, grant money, or the like. There is a more structured diligence process and a focus on exchanging equity that is missing with Kiva, Kickstarter, and other incumbent crowdfunding sources. The hands-on process produces more active investors. "We want to push Africans investing in Africans," says Chiura.

Whether embraced or held at arm's length, commercial solutions will support an increasing share of regional development. The dollar amounts aren't as important as the structural changes under way. As Barbara James puts it, "The government isn't set up to have enough money to solve social problems." Neither is aid money likely to address the various pain points for increasingly sophisticated consumers on the African continent. African capitalists are building platforms that give more businesses a break, and better choices to consumers.

As Africa's commercial century continues, fewer good ideas will die for lack of finance. Ventures of all sizes and persuasions will continue to experiment with both funding and business models unique to Africa's challenges. They may not fit our existing labels — public-private partnerships, IPOs, or impact investing — but are more exciting for their novelty.

8

The Nature Map

To Feed, Fuel, and Build the Future

I N LATE 2012, Hurricane Sandy slammed into the US Atlantic coast. The tragic storm killed dozens, froze commerce and transportation in the busy northeast United States, and wiped out power to eight million homes and businesses. In New York City, aggrieved, disconnected residents clustered around any live wall socket available, charging their fancy devices, cursing the falling of the sun, dreading the bathing they would have to do in the dark.

Aerial photographs of the city captured the scale of the blackout, the bright lights of midtown contrasting sharply with the darkness of lower Manhattan. For me, the surreal images evoked another aerial shot, of the whole Earth at night. Viewed from outer space, fat economies and their major metropolises are ablaze with light. In the same photographs, sub-Saharan Africa is painfully dark.

The African continent has a power problem. Only one in every three people has access to reliable electricity. Often, there just isn't enough to go around: total generation capacity for the forty-eight sub-Saharan countries is roughly equal to that of Spain annually. State distribution lines, if they exist at all, are notoriously fickle. Never mind

Compared to the rest of the globe, sub-Saharan Africa has a big electricity deficit.

the "last mile" of distribution: in too many places, light never makes it
to the first.

Over the years, I've run into blackouts in hospitals, airports, shopping malls, conference halls, and in nightclubs, right in the middle of
my favorite song. The radio snaps off over morning coffee. Internet
access comes and goes with the raindrops. We groan and adapt. We
buy candles and lanterns, flashlights and surge protectors. We boil and
bathe. We take the stairs. Those who can afford to exit the system do
so by purchasing a generator, and the diesel gasoline to run it. (An acquaintance told me he spends $20,000 annually just to keep his home
electrified.) During the hours when the power is working, I, too, rush
to plug in my fancy devices. The vast majority of Africans respond by
doing what they have always done: burning local carbon for heat and
light, or doing without.

Photographer Peter DiCampo's "Life Without Lights" project documents the world's mundane responses to commonplace blackouts.
In Ghana, children study the Koran by candlelight, vendors light tiny
flashlights and wood fires to stay in business, community members
gather around televisions powered by generators. The scenes are
charming, in a way, but belie a situation deeply corrosive to progress.

In Voggu, a rural settlement in the northern region of Ghana, Di-
Campo captured a head teacher at a local high school grading papers

with a flashlight. He's found a way to do his job, but many teachers in rural areas prefer to commute back to homes in the city, where power is more constant. It's common for them to skip one or two days of school each week.

Thus energy poverty in Africa traps the region in real poverty. Students who can't do their homework after sunset don't do well in school. Mothers who cook with dirty charcoal expose themselves to worrying indoor air pollution, the equivalent of smoking packs of cigarettes daily. Children — often young girls — who fetch firewood across long distances do so at the risk of being attacked on their way. Kerosene lamps account for an alarming number of burns and fires. In urban areas without reliable power, the building blocks of business — a tailor's sewing machine, a contractor's bandsaw — depend on access to a generator. When available resources can't cover the cost, business stops entirely. We sit in the dark. It's a breathtaking drain on productivity — a forgone loss of 2.2 percent of GDP growth annually. It's a *kanju* miracle that anything happens at all.

It should be no surprise to learn that sub-Saharan Africa has the lowest carbon footprint in the world. World Bank figures suggest that the average use of basic electricity in high-income countries is over 10,000 kilowatt-hours per person per year. The average African uses about twenty times less. The energy New York's 19.5 million people consume every year covers nearly 800 million on the continent. Excluding South Africa, the region is the only part of the world where per capita consumption of electricity is *decreasing*.

The differential in consumption goes beyond energy. On average, North Americans use 400 liters of water per day to drink, cook, and clean themselves — in part because they can. William Rees, who coined the term *ecological footprint*, explains that humans are "K-strategists" predisposed to consume maximally. The species lacks an "off" switch. As we consume more, he says, our level of satisfaction diminishes, and "the tendency to consume and accumulate ratchets up."

In lean economies, however, the "off" switch is imposed — often quite literally. As a result, African households operate with radically different capacities and expectations for consumption. Resource scarcity affects electricity and gas, food, water, and shelter. In rural out-posts and proliferating slums alike, housing is ad hoc and unreliable. Bucket baths are a way of life (from a relatively early age, I learned to get squeaky clean with a gallon or two of water). The pop-up device-charging enterprises that graced Manhattan after Sandy are a standard business model in virtually every village and city center in sub-Saharan Africa. For many millions, every day is the day after the storm.

Of course, the problem is not that Africa lacks energy. A large and growing share of the petroleum and natural gas that keep the lights on and the cars running in fat economies comes from African pro-ducers. The land beneath Nigeria, Gabon, Angola and South Sudan, Ghana, Kenya, and Uganda is laced with oil. What's more, a genuinely new oil boom is under way: half a dozen other countries have begun exploration in earnest. Coal deposits line Ethiopia, Sudan, Tanzania, Zambia, Botswana, South Africa, and other pockets of the continent. The Nile, Senegal, Zambezi, and Congo rivers provide ample force to create hydroelectric power. The Congo is certainly the biggest wasted opportunity; thoroughly dammed, it could become the world's biggest power plant — providing up to 40 percent of the continent's electricity needs.

Unfortunately, national governments have failed to pass on the ben-efits of energy wealth. Monopolistic utilities don't provide electricity. Decades of power sector subsidies have gone mainly to the wealthiest and best connected (literally), without making light more affordable. Crude-rich Nigeria still imports refined petroleum. In the DRC, half the year is spent in darkness. In Guinea-Bissau, it's the equivalent of one in three days. In Tanzania, which has a projected $150 billion in natural gas reserves, 86 percent of residents have absolutely no access to electricity. In rural areas it's 10 percent higher, with the same ava-lanche of negative development consequences.

State investments in energy have been shortsighted. The very last Portuguese colonial project in Africa, for example, is the Cahora Bassa Dam in Mozambique. The high-modernist hydroelectric dam, fin-ished in the early 1970s, has been celebrated equally by fascist coloniz-ers, the Marxist independent government, and the neoliberal leaders who emerged after Mozambique's protracted civil war. The leaders loved the dam because it was a source of cheap foreign exchange — 1,000 miles away, South Africa buys two-thirds of the electricity produced. But not only did construction interrupt the Zambezi River's flooding and farming cycle, it displaced forty thousand people — none of whom benefit from the harnessed resource. While the energy sent abroad would more than power the entirety of Mozambique, the Cahora Bassa pylons and power lines cut through local villages left in the dark. The ham-handed execution is perhaps understandable — the overseeing Ministry of Natural Resources has only fifteen employees.

Hydropower represents just one type of overlooked natural resource in Africa. (Indeed, rivers are natural highways, having connected civilizations and directed continental traffic for centuries.) A thermal map of Africa, depicting temperature and sunlight, confirms that the continent is *literally* bright. While the nations of the OECD appear largely in cool tones of blue and green, Africa glows red and orange. Its solar resource is greater than anywhere else in the world. The region starved for electricity is spoiled for sun.

The Nature Map presents huge advantages for Africa. Too often, buried metal and mineral wealth steals the limelight. Starting with the old names for west Africa ("Gold Coast," "Tooth Coast"), natural resources have made the region a dartboard for extractive foreign interventions. For more than a century, colonizer-, state-, and corporate-led mismanagement of copper, cobalt, coltan, gold, platinum, oil, and gas reserves has produced labor and environmental woes both too banal and too broad to recite here. Fortunately, however, Africa's fortunes are beginning to revolve around more creative, generative uses of this terrestrial birthright.

As I amble through Dar es Salaam after dark, the motivations for new methods are obvious. Every third storefront is lit with a naked incandescent bulb, the next with a kerosene lamp, and the next lit not at all. A dozen young men play football in an open lot on the edge of the city. A dozen more watch perched atop a half-hewn concrete wall, cheering until it is too dim to see the ball.

The Tanzanian company EGG-energy has given itself a simple job: bringing electricity to the country's doorstep. Subscribers pay EGG to install electric wiring in their homes, and for access to rechargeable batteries needed to power the same. The batteries are charged centrally and plug right into the newly wired households. When the old battery wears out, subscribers return it to one of EGG's depots in exchange for a new one. Founder Jamie Yang likes to describe the model, which has also seen success in India, as "Netflix for energy."

EGG operates for profit, which "enforces a certain discipline," says Yang. Like other *kanju* solutions, Tanzanians are willing to pay for the system because they are already paying a price. Energy poverty isn't cheap; stakeholder surveys estimate that families in Tanzania spend $125 annually — almost 40 percent of household income — on one-and-done batteries and piecemeal access to power for charging cell phones. Like their counterparts in the rest of Africa, most Tanzanians also buy charcoal or kerosene to light and cook after dark. Second, they realize no cavalry is coming: TANESCO, the Tanzanian power authority, has privatized electricity generation, but not distribution — which is still atrocious. Seventy percent of residents don't have electricity but live within three miles of a cable. "A lot of areas you will see power lines running overhead but they have no access," says Yang. "You find people who live within spitting distance of a transmission line. Ask when they think they'll get power and they'll laugh in your face."

By contrast, EGG is a convenient alternative — with a sense of comparative permanence. Once the household has paid for installation, the home is wired, with real overhead sockets and wall switches (in case TANESCO ever gets it together). The batteries are imported from China, but the other inputs come from local markets and are installed by local employees. To a bystander, EGG-energy appears no different from grid energy, at roughly half the cost.

Most importantly, the informal economy does EGG's legwork. The company runs central charging and swapping stations but also enlists kiosk owners to stock its batteries alongside the soaps, chocolates, and mobile airtime typically for sale. When a subscriber swaps out a battery, the kiosk owner gets a cut.

"We're trying to use the same distribution networks that already exist," says Yang, "people who go around selling produce on motorbikes, who walk eggs on bicycles or use wheelbarrows." These extended networks enable EGG to reach ordinary people 30 or 40 kilometers outside the biggest city. It's a marriage of high and low technology that solves the last-mile problem with feet.

EGG is just one of dozens of examples. In addition to Solar Sister, firms like Nuru Energy, d.light Design, Sunny Money, Mobisol, and Fenix International have similar schemes for distributing low-cost, off-grid energy solutions to those who need them most. Nuru solar lamps, sold for profit mostly in Rwanda, can be charged from the sun or by pedaling a bicycle. Mobisol sells solar panels via layaway payments made by mobile phone. D.light, which designs and sells lamps rugged and cheap enough for the bottom of the pyramid, sold lamps to 30 percent of Tanzania's Mafia Island in less than a week by making the basic argument that it would help children learn. Where the current model is grounded in central monopolies, these smaller businesses compete to help illuminate that which the state does not reach.

Fenix International deploys the most explicitly market-based model for both the sale and the design of a renewable energy product. The company, which has partnered with the Grameen Foundation and the telecom MTN, created a product specifically for Ugandan entrepreneurs. Its solar lantern, the ReadySet, provides light but also powers up to ten cell phones at once. This functionality—deliberately built into the design scheme—can help to seed small-scale mobile-charging businesses. Fenix is notable for actually doing research and design for a local product, rather than simply buying a product designed for someone else. The company realized that African consumers are not American, Indian, Chinese, or Latin American. The design takes into account a preexisting business model and profit motive. Like Solar Sister, the model works well for Ugandans who are seeking not simply to light their lives, but to generate income as well.

Of course, Africa still uses its dirty energy—in 2010, oil-import bills in Africa went up by $2.2 billion. But fail state capacity is so degraded that Nigeria, a major oil producer and member of OPEC, exports crude oil and then reimports it as refined petroleum. The bottom-of-the-pyramid alternative energy sources like wood, dung, and kerosene are in wide use — and produce more greenhouse gases than more efficient technologies. The widespread use of charcoal is a devastating driver of deforestation. Still, Africa has only 4 percent of the world's coal reserves, concentrated in South Africa. Botswana, Malawi, Niger, and Zambia operate only a single coal mine each.

These solar ventures are just a sliver of a growing off-grid market. Bloomberg reports that developing countries as a whole spent $72 billion on new renewable energy investments in 2010, more than developed countries invested. The African solar market is set to double each year to two million lamps sold annually by 2015. Even for the sixty million African households that *do* have electricity, these solutions help plug the holes when state-run utilities are offline. In the same way that Africa has leapfrogged the landline telephone infrastructure that evolved in fat economies, solar allows the continent to leapfrog the mediocre stopgap of coal-fired power plants and evolve to a cleaner, more individually controlled paradigm. In that sense, the lack of effective organization at the state level may be the best thing that ever happened to Africa.

The power pinch affects big businesses, too; manufacturing plants with machinery or ordinary businesses with IT equipment suffer from electricity failures. Mobile network operators gnash their teeth at the cost of maintaining power to the wireless towers that connect their exploding customer base. Over drinks in Lagos, Kwabena Smith does the math for me. MTN spends $5.5 million a month powering six thousand base stations for nineteen hours a day — in Nigeria alone. I gawked at the statistic. "On maintaining the cell site infrastructure and everything, they spend about one hundred eighty million dollars a year," he says. "It's a massive pain point."

Smith, who grew up pinballing between Sierra Leone, Ghana, and Nigeria, saw this failure as a huge opportunity. "You are always looking at it from a point of deficit," he says. "You are already conscious and aware that energy is a vital resource and you can't take it for granted." Watching the second Gulf War unfold, and taking "peak oil" theories seriously, he became transfixed by the idea of distributed generation — meeting power requirements locally, rather than waiting for transmission lines to arrive from the government. "I look at it from an opportunity standpoint: How do we create innovative ways to bring energy to people who are on the wrong side of what I call the energy divide?"

His company, Orun Energy, developed a clever hack: a generator and batteries that could hook up to cell phone towers that were running on diesel. Power flows from the grid when it is available, but when the state "takes light," the system cuts to a backup supply that doesn't rely on diesel inputs. During the pilot in Ghana, Smith held his breath that it would work. When Orun reviewed the data from control towers, they found a 72 percent reduction in diesel use. It wasn't totally clean energy, but it was cleaner. Smith spent the better part of three years getting Orun's efficiency to a self-reported 90 percent. Now he is offering large corporates relief from the expense of private, dirty energy.

He's not the first to work with telecoms on targeted energy efficiency. As in the exploding market for individual solar solutions, dozens of African companies are building businesses that fix the power problem for corporations. In 2012, the Nigerian company IHS, which runs four thousand wireless towers in five countries, launched the continent's largest solar-powered "cell site." The mini solar farm keeps local lines of communication humming and will reduce carbon dioxide outputs by 24,000 tons a year.

Smith rubbed his palms as he detailed the familiar docket of fail state problems that have frustrated Orun in the short term. By dramatically reducing fuel consumption, the company is also challenging what Smith calls the "diesel mafia." It's a consortium of private thugs and well-connected civil servants who capitalize on public rationing and subsidies for petrol. Millions of residents depend utterly on diesel generators for comfort and livelihoods — a rent-seeking opportunity that no one cedes without a struggle. When in early 2012 Nigeria ended (and then partially reinstated) its longtime fuel subsidy, it was to arrest the $6 billion flow of "diesel mafia" graft.

Crooks and profiteers aside, most people in Africa hope that national electric grids improve, and soon. But *kanju* lessons learned in their absence are crucial for the local and global energy innovation ecosystem. Retail alternative energy products are much more prevalent in lean economies than in fat ones. It's a corollary to marketing theory: the best customers are those who are pushed rather than pulled into using new products. The technologies are far from native to sub-Saharan Africa. But the general dysfunction in large-scale production, distribution, and consumption of energy serves as an aggressive "push" to adopt alternatives.

Take William Kamkwamba, the Malawian boy who became a global celebrity in 2007. After reading a local library book on wind power, fourteen-year-old William fashioned a working windmill using a tractor belt, plastic scraps, and bike parts. His incredible story landed him a mention in Oprah's Book Club and a spot at Dartmouth College. Like the Yahoo Boys, living on the margins of African economies, he saw within the raw materials of his life in Malawi the ingredients of a richer future.

I traveled to Wimbe, William's hometown — a tiny community at the end of a road washed bald by recent rain. The road is flanked by acres of newly picked tobacco, drying in fat fans before sale. Volcanic rock formations are scattered like giant footfalls in the distance. It's some of the most beautiful country I've ever seen. In Wimbe, his windmill still stands. Instead of buying paraffin and kerosene to light their home, the family uses the 18 to 30 volts of electricity generated with each windmill revolution to live free from darkness.

William's curiosity and drive allowed his family to leap completely off the grid — no state power cuts interfere with their way of life. Just as importantly, his invention overhauled his family's farming practice. The windmill is helping to irrigate the Kamkwamba crops: peanuts, tobacco, maize, sweet potatoes, and beans. His father told me that before the windmill, the family could harvest some twenty bags of maize annually. With wind-powered pump irrigation, the farm produces more than a hundred.

William's solution is unusual but the problem is not. Agriculture continues to be the most common use of sub-Saharan land — the beating heart of the region's past, present, and future. All told, agriculture makes up nearly two-thirds of employment, one-third of GDP, and more than one in five businesses. Africa is the second-largest landmass in the world, with more potential farmland than Latin America or Asia. Soil, not oil, is its most abundant natural resource. Diverse climates across the continent can support cash crops like cocoa, tea, and coffee, basic cereals like wheat, sorghum, and barley, pulses and legumes, sweet potatoes and cassava, exotic fruit, fish and livestock, and virtually all of the vegetables we know about.

Growing up in the United States, I never experienced that level of bounty firsthand. But while reporting for this book, I saw pineapples tumbling on vines, communal avocado trees dropping fruit onto the roadside, and wild coffee plants pop out of nowhere. Returning from shopping at Kenyan markets, I happily faced the culinary puzzles I'd created — how to combine watermelon, avocado, and okra; carrots, kale, and mango; peas and papaya. The abundance amazed me.

On paper, Africa's farm production is growing at a rate of 12 percent — about double that of other economic sectors— in the past decade. This should be a huge boon to the population. Unfortunately, real income from farming is hard to come by. At planting time, many smallholder farmers are stuck with Stone Age tools, unimproved seeds, and inadequate fertilizer. At harvest, many more lack storage to house or roads to distribute their crops. Though arable land in Africa is abundant, only 4 percent of it is irrigated (compared with 58 percent in India and 55 percent in China). Not all farmers have formal rights to profit from property. Some land is state owned, some is communal, and much is expensive. Most small-scale agriculture in Africa has faltered.

This wasn't always the case. My mother's grandfather, from south-central Nigeria, was a very ordinary farmer, and so was everyone he knew. Somehow, growing cocoa was enough to scrape by in the early twentieth century. Today, however, cocoa production in the same geography has atrophied.

We already know the logjams for farmers. Many — like water access — are environmental. Climate shocks and rising global temperatures are beginning to hobble production. The region is particularly vulnerable to climate change and the accompanying desertification, pests, invasive species, floods, frost, heat waves, food price volatility, and famine. Some of the decline is due to impenetrable markets. My Nairobi neighbors were lucky to have a built-in urban market for their maize. Without training, finance, and market access, ordinary farmers have a terrible time making ends meet.

The remaining cocoa farmers in my great-grandfather's home region are tentatively organized into a cooperative that bundles their harvest to sell to one of several middlemen. Dead poor and mostly illiterate, they're not able to leverage prices or trends in commodities markets and are often cheated as a result. They've pooled funds to build a storehouse for cocoa — one of the big bottlenecks to making a profit. But they aren't always able to finance the seeds, fertilizer, and pesticides they might need to expand capacity. Their rudimentary on-site processing is inadequate to global standards. Thus, even as large developing countries like China develop a taste for chocolate, the African smallholders are shut out from the value chain.

Some of the underperformance is a result of state action. Though farm owners in Nigeria are eligible for low-interest government loans to buy fertilizer or equipment, funds are often embezzled. In the 1980s and 1990s, World Bank–led structural adjustment programs starved many local agricultural schools, research institutions, and extension services that had distributed advice and technology to farmers. Marketing and commodity boards often wangled the price of crops, under the guise of creating markets for farmers and keeping food cheap for citizens, but as often a way to siphon profits from forward sales.*

As of 2008, 80 percent of African countries spent less than 10 per-

---

* In Ghana, the state-run Cocoa Board still organizes and negotiates sales of its product and takes a Shylockian 30 percent cut. Farmers are unable to opt out of the system.

cent of their budgets on agricultural development. What is spent is intended to cheapen inputs like seeds, rather than to train farmers in how to cultivate them. More consequential is the lack of substantive land reforms across Africa. States play an inherent and important role in supporting and enforcing land tenure, property rights, and title deeds. The absence of focused policies crafted to support smallholders without formal ownership rights has created an unstable, ad hoc framework for families like Gladys's and has reduced incentives to invest in land. And, of course, agriculture was excluded from the MDG framework.

Some of the crisis is due to troubling demographic trends. My great-grandmother had six children, only one of whom took up the agricultural mantle. The women married away, and their children's children took to school rather than the plow. Gradually, our land, once swollen with cocoa plants and oil palm, turned fallow. The same rural-to-urban transition that has made more than half the world into city dwellers has undercut agricultural expertise. Millions of young potential farmers would rather head for the nearest urban center — to sell airtime if nothing better presents itself. In the span of three generations, I'm embarrassed to say the closest my family comes to proper farming is the view from my Nairobi window.

Across Africa, agriculture needs a champion. The combination of state failures, uncertain markets, and a fickle climate has made the livelihoods of ordinary farmers in Africa increasingly unstable and unpleasant. While there are 883 tractors per thousand farmers in the United Kingdom, Africa averages only 2. Families with fertile land may be sitting on a gold mine but lack the pick to dig. The grim side effect is that just about every African nation has remained food insecure. Africa has 20 percent fewer people than India and similar land quality but somehow does not manage to feed itself. Nigeria spends over $8.2 billion annually importing basic food items like fish, rice, and sugar. Sporadic famine in places like Niger and Somalia is only the most obvious case in which food supply is mismatched to demand.

Without so much as an *oops*, major donor countries and multilateral institutions have reversed course and begun to prioritize farming in

Africa. It's telling that, immediately after leaving the United Nations, Ghanaian former secretary-general Kofi Annan started a foundation committed to investing in the Nature Map. His Alliance for a Green Revolution in Africa (AGRA) recognizes that smart growing practices will produce cascading benefits.

Beyond the nutritional and employment dividends of a strong farm sector, African growers can help balance global consumption. Today, 1.5 billion people overeat (and waste 1.3 billion tons of food in the process), while 1 billion people go hungry. Food demand globally is on the uptick as once-poor consumers shift their diets to include meat, dairy, and processed foods like chocolate. All told, the planet needs 70 percent more food for a projected 9 billion inhabitants by 2050. Current production and distribution aren't even close to that capacity. Even heavily agrarian India recently experienced a run on the supply of onions — what had once been a cheap, staple crop. African agriculture holds an obvious value proposition for the rest of the world — one that can defeat local poverty and hunger at once.

There's still a robust debate about how to take advantage of the land dividend. Some development economists are encouraging small-scale farms to give up the hardscrabble routine of hoe, plant, pray — and embrace the large-scale industrial farming that has allowed countries like the United States, Australia, and Brazil to feed themselves and export cash crops. Others advocate an aggressive focus on the "one acre" plots that are so prevalent in Africa and other developing parts of the world.

For the mega-farming enthusiasts, Fitsum Hagos is a perfect poster child. In Mojo, about 70 kilometers outside of Addis Ababa, Luna Farm Export and Slaughterhouse PLC is bulk-growing bell peppers, chilies, onions, potatoes, maize, beans, and tomatoes, among other crops. The compound is stacked with piles of tef, a notoriously hard-to-harvest grain favored in Ethiopian cuisine. On neat trellises, table grapes hang firm and heavy. In the shipping warehouse, crates of tomatoes make the weigh scales moan. Luna, run by Hagos and his brothers, also raises pigs and cattle in stables on the grounds (a handy

*Fitsum Hagos employs close to four hundred people to
produce food for Ethiopia and its less fertile neighbors.*

source of fertilizer) and buys goats and sheep from local shepherds to
slaughter in a state-of-the-art abattoir.

Luna has close to four hundred employees, earning a living wage
producing food for Ethiopia and its less fertile neighbors — Somalia,
Djibouti, and Sudan. The region's need for fresh fruits and vegetables
is Hagos's gain. The dire lack of grassland in the Middle East supports
the same logic: the Luna slaughterhouse — run to exacting *halal* standards — feeds the vast meat markets in Saudi Arabia. Every day, Arab
buyers bypass traditional meat markets from Australia and the United
States and pay Hagos to send thousands of kilos of butchered livestock across the Red Sea. Pork is not readily consumed in Ethiopia,
but Luna's pigs, which have multiplied (as livestock will) in the short
while he's raised them, are a steady source of meat for hungry Chinese
laborers swarming the region — some of whom work for Luna.

Hagos, trim and perpetually grinning, makes a surprising farmhand. He was born in the Tigray region of Ethiopia but went to graduate school in biochemistry and molecular biology in Germany and what was then Czechoslovakia. For twelve years afterward, he enjoyed a position at one of the premier research hospitals in the United States, working on cancer genetics and saving lives. In 2005, however, Hagos traded American medicine for African farming, exchanging his lab coat for coveralls. Driving his gleaming new pickup truck across a riverbed in the hills outside Addis, he tells me the exact moment he determined to head back to Africa: "When Bush beat Kerry!" He guffaws. "That was the time that I decided: this is not for me."

Like other diaspora Africans, Hagos had left home in body only. In America, he was living the life of a medical professional, while Ethiopia struggled to break the cycle of poverty and autocratic government that had haunted the nation since he and 2.5 million others fled in the 1980s. Though he was practicing at the cutting edge of Western medicine, he felt a responsibility to the taxpayers in Ethiopia. To peers who so often discount farming in favor of the professions (many parents push their sons to become doctors, and their daughters to marry them), he's setting a fascinating example.

He's also building a new narrative for Ethiopia, a nation that may be hard to imagine feeding others. At times, the country's hunger has been its primary cultural export. In 1985, the mega-hit "We Are the World" and global Live Aid concerts spotlighted starving, wide-eyed Ethiopian children with arms outstretched and anchored the largest, most astonishing flow of private charity in history. In the end, that famine killed hundreds of thousands of Ethiopians — but not because the region couldn't grow food. Rather, institutions and markets, both foreign and local, could not and would not distribute it.

For several seasons preceding the Live Aid moment, crops had failed in the northern Ethiopian regions of Tigray and Eritrea — which happened to be the center of clashes related to a decade of civil war. In response to the protracted insurgency, Ethiopia's autocratic Marxist government was spending nearly half of its budget on Africa's then-largest standing army. As food aid arrived, supplies were diverted to troops instead of the malnourished.

Choosing gamesmanship over guardianship, the government with-held shipments from rebel areas, leaving more civilians in peril. While rhetorically supporting aid efforts, the government opted also to relo-cate some half a million Ethiopians from the areas where hunger was worst. The forced relocations were an attempt to streamline food and services distribution, but the tactic failed miserably, forcing millions into exile and leaving farmland abandoned.

The two-year crisis and the aid that followed it is a high-profile case study in misinformation, uncritical interventionism, and callous gov-ernment priorities. There have been a total of forty-two droughts in the Horn since 1980, and food aid continues to arrive — most recently in the summer of 2011. It's frustrating to see how, more than twenty-five years after Live Aid, the same bureaucratic institutions and mar-kets are still working badly.

While the land that Hagos farms belongs to the government (all land in Ethiopia belongs to the government), the Luna project is a pri-vate-sector rebuke to food aid and proof of organized, efficient indus-trial farming — managed locally to boot. I'm convinced that with best practices on irrigation (the rubber tubes he uses to water his crops come from Israel), storage, and distribution, Africa could easily feed local and global populations.

Hagos and his family are not the only ones to see the extraordinary financial upside of agriculture. The pan-African food market is set to grow from $50 billion to $150 billion by 2030. And global demand has yet to peak. Across the world, urban populations are expanding faster than rural ones, and the ratio of growers to consumers is fall-ing as quickly. The United States, Australia, Europe, and Brazil have responded with specialized, capital-intensive growing practices that lean heavily on biotechnology, chemicals, expensive farming equip-ment, and irrational subsidies.

Other fat economies are turning to Africa. Surplus labor, organic growing conditions, and vast quantities of arable land are the sub-ject of envy and interest in land-poor Japan, South Korea, and Saudi Arabia. The European Union, Canada, Turkey, and China have all cut deals to provide what they can't grow. The African continent hosts large-scale, private industrial farms — many times bigger than Luna — in Ethiopia, Zambia, Zimbabwe, Mozambique, and Madagascar, to start. Congo-Brazzaville has leased 80,000 hectares of land for commercial farming to a gaggle of homesteading, white South Africans. Across the board, yields are spectacular, and mostly for export.

It doesn't take much time in Africa to see the vast distance between traditional agriculture and Western mega-farming, aided by gene science. The strawberries I'd regularly eaten in Nairobi were a quarter of the size normalized in the United States. The plantations and commercial greenhouses I've driven by in Malawi, Kenya, and Cameroon looked like kitchen gardens compared to the miles of meticulously sown corn I've seen framing highways in the American Midwest.

A rush to expand the intensive, expensive model to Africa will change the landscape entirely. It may also expose the region to the downside of centralized food production. Monocultures — in which a single crop is grown — are vulnerable to disease and fickle weather. Breeding livestock in huge feedlots requires antibiotics, hormones, and feed production that inevitably suffuse the final output. Processed foods of the kind growing in popularity in wealthy pockets of African cities carry the same health risks as they do in literally fat economies. And the farther produce and livestock travel to their point of consumption, the more vulnerable the supply chain is to disruption, and the more distressing the environmental impact.

Perhaps most importantly, the mega-farm model leaves out the majority of farmers in Africa — smallholders who could never dream of hiring four hundred workers, importing irrigation tubes, using a tractor, or buying a refrigerated truck. They range from my neighbors in Nairobi to the Kamkwamba farm in Malawi. To move from subsistence to prosperity in this century, they need training, finance, markets, and, in many countries, a cultural overhaul. Nick Moon, founder of the Kick-Start water pump company, names smallholders "a massive, unrecognized, immobile reservoir of human and social capital which is crying out for some representation."

Nigerian Nnaemeka Ikegwuonu is calling right back. After seeing the steady slide in farm outputs in his home state, he devised a plan to give many thousands of smallholder farmers a fighting chance. He offers neither tractors, nor pesticides, nor fancy genetic hybrid seeds. Ten hours a day, on radio waves across southwest Nigeria, he broadcasts information on "what to produce, how to produce, when to produce, and for whom to produce." His innovation is clever for its simplicity: across rural Africa, where even print newspapers don't reach, radio is still the killer app.

Ikegwuonu has a wicked sense of humor and a chatterbox persona. Most of his broadcasts are hyperlocal dramedies, with an educational twist. The radio show highlights elements of climate change that will adversely impact Igbo farmers, new practices in pest management, or stories of great success at market. The characters are immediately recognizable (following the Nigerian tradition, "Mama Emeka," the female protagonist, is known by the name of her first child). And so are their problems: in one episode, the elders of the area have invited an environmental specialist to explain why the seawater is rising, causing their low-altitude crops to fail.

Thinly disguised as characters in the drama, Ikegwuonu and his colleagues provide solutions (in that case, pre-irrigating the soil, or using salt-tolerant crops). Their knowledge is encyclopedic: To stop soil erosion, plant vetiver grass. To protect new seedlings, cover them with leaves. If birds are wise to your scarecrows, switch to careful application of herbicides. But their methods are comic: the banter among villagers is reminiscent of Nollywood at its best.

Like Anas, Ikegwuonu has pioneered a new kind of development journalism: by scouring the region for tricks, tips, and success stories in the Igbo language, Ikegwuonu is serving the role of master farmer and expanding the information neighborhood of 250,000 listeners in Nigeria's rural Imo State. In a collaborative twist on the model, he's also disbursed interactive mobile radios (powered by the sun, naturally) that allow farmers to send their own free voice messages on farming back to a central broadcaster. While such advice is vital for commercial farmers, those who grow part-time greens gardens or subsistence crops also derive the benefits.

A number of Africa-based mobile ventures have also tried to cut down on the information asymmetries that keep farmers from maximizing income. Farmer's Friend, an app created with Busoga Rural Open Source and Development Initiative in Uganda, is a mobile database farmers can search for all kinds of agricultural information, from types of weevils to (increasingly variable) seasonal rainfall patterns. MFarm in Kenya and AGRO-HUB in Cameroon are similar apps for agriculture. Esoko in Mauritius and Ghana, one of the earliest and most successful mobile apps, deploys a similar strategy to help farmers, who can use the app to check crop prices as well as place buy and sell orders from their mobiles. Esoko is now in sixteen countries across the African continent.

These supplements are a lifeline to farmers laboring without access to the extension schooling that backstopped earlier generations of growers. But even with their expanded reach, the apps and broadcasts can't replicate a dirt-under-the-fingernails training experience. A firm adherent of John Dewey's pedagogy of "learning by doing," I put on my high boots and headed for the fields in Kenya's fertile Rift Valley, to try my hand at a technique that promises to put more money in farmers' pockets and more fruit on their vines.

I had company in my lessons: Daniel Gai, Peter Aguto, and David Akech — three lanky, weathered young men from South Sudan's fledgling Department of Agriculture. While their country has incredibly fertile lands, naturally irrigated by the Nile River, the population scattered by war has virtually no experience growing their own food. It's a liability. "You go to the market and you come back with nothing," says Gai, a bit mournfully. "Things are quite different."

We're here to learn from Samuel Nderitu, the director of Grow Bio-intensive Agriculture Center, an organization that commits to teaching organic farming practices. In contrast with the new recruits, Nderitu is wonderfully earnest and voluble and has spent the better part of five years preaching "food sovereignty": not just access to food, but ownership of the food production pipeline.

We learn that the first step is improving the land — without tractors, of course. Across the roughly two-acre plot, metal hoes rise and fall in silence. Nderitu demonstrates the best way to form raised beds in the aftermath: layering stones beneath the topsoil. He plants crops in a jumble, and quite close together. It seems disorganized to me, but there is logic to it: "Weeds won't be able to breathe this way," he says. Intercropping with pungent onions helps to repel insects. He shows me a burlap sack brimming with soil and kale shoots. Slashing holes into the sides of the sack allows crops to grow vertically — a work-around for farmers with limited land. I'm taking notes for my hypothetical apartment garden.

In keeping with *kanju*, Nderitu fixates on intelligent recycling. "Grow your own seeds, grow your own food, grow your own fertilizer, grow your own money, grow your own everything." He beams. He believes farmers can reduce dependence on inorganic inputs while still providing healthy yields.

The imposed frugality can help farmers eke out larger profits.

Planting vertically in burlap sacks helps to save space and improve yields for one-acre smallholder farms in Africa.

Chemical fertilizer, for example, is costly and, with overuse, toxic to soil. As an alternative, the farm's detritus is neatly stacked and composted just next to the planted beds. A few tosses with a pitchfork reveal a beautifully loamy fertilizer that is chemical free.

Seeds are also a big expense. Many genetically improved seed varieties — salt or drought resistant, for example — have spread across Africa, but the current model requires an annual or semiannual purchase. This nets a tidy profit for seed companies like Monsanto but is a financial blow to buyers, even at subsidized prices. Instead, Nderitu keeps all the seeds left behind at harvest — amaranth, soybeans, climbing beans, pigeon peas, sorghum, wheat, and coriander. His community seed banks disburse handfuls at planting time and expect the harvest to replenish their stores, like an interest-bearing loan, months later. He shakes a bucket of pearl millet seeds that have grown exponentially with every season.

Nderitu and his staff train thousands of farmers a year. He and his colleagues have spent weeks in the Yei and Bor areas of South Sudan already. Daniel, Peter, and David are training to become trainers themselves. Nderitu distinguishes their decentralized model from the Kenyan Ministry of Agriculture, whose staff tend to stay in their offices, waiting for farmers to make appointments. "They call it 'demand-driven assistance,'" he says. "But I don't think a farmer can stop what they're doing and go twenty kilometers to find them."

The One Acre Fund, as the name suggests, also addresses the small scale of most farming in Africa. The organization provides finance, guidance, and raw materials to farmers in Kenya, Rwanda, and Burundi. Their mission is to ensure smallholders are no more than 3 kilometers from these key inputs.

Both firms remind me of the community health worker model that has been transformative for African health outcomes. Biointensive trainers live together with farmers and maintain engagements for up to three years, training the early adopters and convincing the "laggards." One Acre field workers, says the group's government relations analyst, Nick Daniels, "can actually explain in familiar terms, check up and follow up, have a proactive relationship with the farmers, and are prepared to visit everybody every week." While their field officers are not always expert practitioners like Nderitu, their blanket coverage is impressive. Since 2006, the American nonprofit claims to have touched more than 135,000 farmers.

As we've seen in other chapters, predictable support from familiar faces makes a difference. One Acre's running comparison with non-participating farmers in east Africa suggests that its vigorous technical assistance doubles grower yields.

Though both organizations run as nonprofits, they seem to have bested the existing bureaucracy of food aid and government subsidies. Daniels explained the cacophony of "solutions" at the district level in western Kenya. "A lot of initiatives come from donors. USAID says, 'You need to be doing this,' DFID comes in and says, 'Do this.' The World Bank, Sweden, Denmark are all doing all kinds of initiatives. They lack resources, there's a lack of focus. You have these poor extension workers who are being pulled in every direction."

The rise of alternative agricultural support structures is a classic *kanju* response to institutional failure. And despite its nonprofit status, One Acre's chief innovation has been financial. Farmers can pay One Acre 5 percent down for seeds and fertilizer and return the balance in installments over time. In the case of a major crop failure, the farmers' debts are usually forgiven. Swimming in the uncertainty of modern farming, smallholders welcome a loan that is tied to effort rather than fate.

Against the fates, there are also guarantees. Crop insurance is a growing industry — policymakers sell the insurance at harvest, when farmers are flush, and pay out in case of a major failure, whether disease or drought. Another product being developed for farmers in the private market is index insurance, a kind of protection against changing weather patterns. The scheme is novel in that it doesn't require a farm visit from auditors or inspections for flood damage, which are logistically complex and can distort a farmer's incentive to grow well. Rather, insurance policies are "indexed" to climate indicators. If the rain falls short of a benchmark for a given season, farmers who have bought the insurance see a payout.

These are important solutions for entrepreneurs trying to backstop a livelihood without a true social safety net. Insurance, while an unfamiliar product in many parts of Africa, decreases uncertainty — the terrible thing about poverty and one of the chief concerns of farmers deciding what, when, and for whom to plant. Marketed effectively, such products can be an extension of the horizontal safety net. And they help take the edge off of the unevenly distributed effects of destructive environmental practices.

Such painstaking plot-by-plot retraining and support help smallholders enormously, especially where government encouragement hasn't materialized. But there is always the problem of market access. My neighbors had a captive audience on a busy Nairobi road, but without a sense of who will buy their crops, other farmers lose the incentive to grow at peak efficiency, and at harvest, many tons of food simply rot.

Cooperative farming can smooth risk, minimize waste, and help farmers get paid. In western Uganda, a region made lush by the nearby Nile and colloquially known as the "Garden of Eden," a family of seven owned title to 1,000 acres of prime farmland. But because they didn't have a tractor, the family settled for farming a small corner for their own subsistence and dispatched one of the sons to earn a living selling mobile phone airtime by the side of the road. Their plight is typical, and part of why agricultural knowledge is fading from some areas where farming was once central.

UNACOFF, a collective of experienced farmers in Uganda, has established a novel business model for such families. UNACOFF will clear and plow land and enlist the landholder (or other local workers) as a member of a collective for growing cotton and other crops. UNACOFF encourages best practices for fertilizer, crop rotation, and irrigation. The farm enjoys invaluable technical assistance and a guaranteed buyer for its output, and UNACOFF gets a steady stream of valuable export commodities. Plot by plot, the "Garden of Eden" is becoming a cash cow.

Cooperative farming is an unusually popular model in Africa — the Family Map applied to land. Collectives operate as information neighborhoods; farmers share tips, practices, and profits. UNACOFF's version works well because it guarantees Ugandan farmers a buyer for their crops. The established supply chain has given laborers on the outskirts of landlocked Uganda a straight line to world cotton markets — an enviable achievement. Collectives bundle the single digits of African smallholders into a fist to be reckoned with.

While the jury is still out on organic versus chemical and industrial versus smallholder farming techniques, one fact is obvious: bringing agricultural systems into balance presents the flip side of the power problem. Profligate energy usage has contributed to climate change, which in turn prevents farmers from growing crops consistently and well. Better outcomes for farmers will increase purchasing power for products that improve lives — and perhaps permanently reorganize the way Africa uses land.

The distance from Ire-Ekiti to Ado-Ekiti is about 30 kilometers. The journey, however, may as well be fifty years in time. Ire is a cluster of modest homes built from locally made cement blocks, with others hanging together in wood and tin. Social life revolves around the (small, somewhat empty) churches and the (small, somewhat empty) market. What cars there are have settled under a thin layer of red dust. Families share intertwined histories, child-rearing and livestock-minding duties, and food.

My grandfather is buried in Ire, and my aging grandmother is among its best-known residents. Remittances and regular visits have kept her standard of living high, but most of the population is quite poor. The soil is bursting with yams, the tuber held most responsible for my tribe's high rate of twin births. Some residents also farm cocoa or maize, to little profit. Everyone else freelances as day laborers, cooks, contractors, and artisans. No one is starving, but few are doing more than getting by.

Twenty minutes down a winding, sporadically paved road, Ado is booming. The state capital is five hours from Lagos, at the center of a cluster of seven townships like Ire. In the shadow of massive, pleasing rock formations, sloping avenues and roundabouts shape the surpris-

ingly dense and sprawling city. While my grandmother's village stag-
nates, Ado is fully urban, and growing fast. Half a million people live
here, roasting corn, hauling cement, pumping gas, subdividing meat
for sale. There are few telltale construction cranes, but plenty of make-
shift wooden scaffolds prop up ambitious, multistory concrete buildings. The surest sign of Ado's future fortunes is the parade of billboard
advertisements that validate the town as a proper market for Bourn-
vita drinking chocolate and Star beer.

In Ado, I met a cluster of teenagers celebrating a seventeenth birth-
day. They speak English, peppered with mouthy Yoruba. A trio of
boys pester a slim girl in Costello-style glasses. One boy is wearing
skinny trousers and a T-shirt that reads "I Heart Crap." The majority of them are also seventeen, and from Ado-Ekiti and environs. The
demographic that once spent their days as farm laborers is fresh from
secondary school. A few of them have already started university. They
have saved for or been given mobile phones, used primarily to snap
endless group shots of themselves — presumably for Facebook. The
entire scene is set to a score of throbbing west African pop, of the sort
you would hear in interchangeable nightspots from Calabar to Dakar.

The exuberance belies a distressing reality. In general, teenagers are
barely committed to anything — but those I speak with are committed
to leaving Ado ASAP. "This place is not attractive," drawls Abiodun
Williams, also seventeen. He's wearing a hat praising Texas. He wants
to be a lawyer. "If you're born, raised, work, and live in Ado, you won't
know anything outside the place." His lament is consonant with that of
teen residents of provincial towns the world over. After all, my grandfather walked straight out of Ekiti when he was about the same age as
Abiodun, in search of education and exposure.

But the story of Ekiti State is a story of modern Africa. Rural populations are streaming into African mega-cities faster than in almost any
other part of the world. If the traditional vision of Africa is windswept
savannah or quiet forest, the new one is of urban jungle. All in all, Africa will surge from under 500,000 city dwellers in 1950 to 750 million
by midcentury. As migrants flock to the jobs and services and to the
networks we've discussed, over 40 million will live in Lagos, Kinshasa,

and Johannesburg — the club of mega-cities famous for their Hobbesian density. Likewise, the continent's commercial and political capitals — think Accra, Abidjan, and Addis — will each house millions more.

The scale of urbanization in the continent's major cities is breathtaking. It's no surprise at all that Africa's richest man, Aliko Dangote, should have made his fortune with cement. Behind the sterile statistics on African GDP growth is a fact visible to anyone on the ground: the continent is under construction. Every road, bridge, roundabout, and shopping mall in the increasingly metropolitan region depends on cement as a foundation.

The major boomtowns capture the cacophonic, vibrant, and at times exhausting urbanism particular to Africa. In the past ten years, Accra — a stately coastal town in Ghana — has bred a previously unknown scourge: traffic. The city's fortunes follow the country's growth trajectory — gold, cocoa, banking and services, and new oil finds have expanded the city's "middle class." The associated demand for processed food, electronics, and the like has led to gleaming new megamalls financed by foreign private equity funds. To reach the malls, and expanding formal-sector or professional work, Accra's upper-middle class has begun to buy cars. Putting thousands of new cars on roads built for a previous generation has an obvious outcome: road snarls that last for hours daily. The novelty of Accra's traffic jams makes them no less obnoxious.

In Johannesburg, easily the most Western of cities on the continent, huge retail and office parks overtake the skyline in the central business district and commercial suburbs like Sandton and Randburg. Residential areas near Rosebank and Auckland Park offer stylish apartments and vegan brunches for increasingly wealthy locals — black and white alike. High-speed rail service connects Johannesburg with the capital, Pretoria, swelling the peri-urban population of both cities to twenty million by 2020.

The overcrowding of Africa's biggest cities is a drain on resources, public and personal. The truism of global urbanization seems to be the coexistence of slum areas hobbled by limited public services and shelter and boundless disease and crime. In sub-Saharan Africa, the number of slum dwellers hit 200 million in 2010. Nairobi has Kibera, Baba Ndogo, Kawangware, and Mathare. Lagos has Makoko, the stilt city floating inches above the lagoon for which the city is named. Johannesburg has Hillbrow and Alexandra — crowded, dangerous, and omitted from the continent-leading formal economy.

Outsiders tend to overlook the continent's second-tier cities, which are as dynamic but less discordant. The population of Ougadougou, the capital of Burkina Faso, will explode by 80 percent in the next decade. Likewise, Yamoussoukro in Côte d'Ivoire, Nakuru in west-central Kenya, Goma in eastern DRC, Durban in South Africa, and a smaller tier of cities like Ado-Ekiti. These fast-growing cities in Africa are far from the largest but may prove more important.

By virtue of their youth, cities at this scale can be built better, out of firmer, more efficient materials. Likewise, these cities can *be* better, offering residents more than a hardscrabble slum existence. Seen in this light, the extraordinary realignment of Africa's booming population is an opportunity like no other.

The controversial "charter cities" movement, championed by economist Paul Romer, advocates a fundamental renaissance in global urbanism. He dreamed up charter cities as a mirror to the concept of charter schools — independent incubators of smart ideas in urban planning. They are a bit of an homage to the successful city-states of history: Singapore, Hong Kong, even Athens. In Romer's modern formulation, a willing sovereign will bestow virgin land for the purpose of building a kind of "urban free enterprise zone," run according to rules and practices that economists and sociologists believe work best.

In the charter city, blackouts, bucket baths, begging, and crime will be no more. There will be no *Système D* of workarounds and scofflaws. Romer imagines location-appropriate industry, mixed-use neighborhoods, ultramodern buildings, and effective utilities for water and electricity. Like a charter school, his metropolis will offer a gradual set of changes to serve as a counterpoint to the disorganized or corrupt status quo. If young people like Abiodun opt into the charter city, it's an instant leap to a better life. "Choice and the potential to copy existing ideas are a powerful combination," says Romer. "All that's holding

us back from making full use of these mechanisms is a failure of imagination."

Some charter-style ventures already exist. Sixty kilometers outside
Nairobi, ground has broken at Konza, what's being billed as Africa's
first "technopolis." Homes and offices will dot a currently unoccupied,
5,000-acre slice of the savannah. Global firms like Samsung, Huawei,
and Toyota will set up offices there. Upwardly mobile Kenyans will
buy homes built to their specifications. Water, electricity, high-speed
rail — all of the goods of which the government has deprived ordinary
Kenyans — will be diverted into the twenty-year, $10 billion project.
As a "special economic zone," Konza will enjoy preferential tax and
zoning treatment.

The itch to start from scratch is understandable, given the sense-
less privation and disorder that plague cities the world over. The sagging architecture and relentless crowding of many African towns and
cities perpetually let down my spirits. But charter cities and planned
satellites offer a basically pessimistic view of what existing society has
achieved. Starting over erases any talents, habits, and competencies
that predate the central planners.

Put another way, charter cities are the high-water mark of formality bias. It's the bias that led colonial powers to draw borders for ease
of management. It's the bias that has since led countries like Nigeria
and Equatorial Guinea to abandon their cacophonic capitals in favor
of sterile, planned cities in the hinterlands. In Oyala, the capital built
by Teodoro Obiang Nguema Mbasogo, Guinea's self-styled "Guarantor of Peace and Propeller of Development," every brick is imported.
Glorifying the blank slate is a sublimated wish for millions of people to
just go away.

What's more, it's easy to imagine the wealthy buying their way out
of existing cities, while individuals and families with high switching
costs — employment, kinship circles, and housing — lack the means to
do so. Such an exodus may resemble the "white flight" from America's
inner cities and reify the inequalities that are already so damaging to
Africa's progress.

Rather than drawing a brand-new urban map, Moladi is improving the old one in South Africa. The company builds dignified, modular family homes in under a week. Its engineering innovation is a simple plastic skeleton — one bedroom, two bedrooms, three bedrooms — to fit residential and commercial needs. Trained contractors hew a foundation, set up the housing mold to accommodate plumbing and wiring, and fill it with a concretelike mixture. After two days, the walls are dried and done, and the plastic, vanished. Moladi is a genuine disruption: no more will unfinished homes be saved for, brick by brick. No more will porous scrap and mud walls put families at the mercy of flooding, collapse, or otherwise.

Moladi is another example of innovative consumer product development besting government provision. In a country where housing is a state-sanctioned right, South Africa's government has fallen far short of its constitutional aspirations. When Nelson Mandela came to power, there was but one formal brick home for every forty-three black residents. Miserable tracts of government housing line the outer rings of Johannesburg and the Cape flats. In Cape Town, as of 2009, some 400,000 people were on waiting lists for public housing and would have little choice about where they eventually settled. Moladi — privately run — puts affordable housing, with access to water, electricity, and choice, within the reach of millions of those in South Africa's striving class.

Such improvements to the built environment are fundamental for evolving cities. But the bigger riddle for African urbanization is convincing a kid like Abiodun to stay put in Ado-Ekiti, rather than turning to the crush of Lagos or economic flight out of Africa. He told me there is no "atmosphere" in Ado. He craves the whiff of cosmopolitanism that is, as of now, absent from his hardworking home state. When pressed, however, he notes that his real quibble is economic: he can see that "some graduates are still driving *okada* because they can't have jobs."

Joyce, a moon-faced friend of Abiodun, doling out cake, was the only one of the teens I met who is committed to coming home. Not incidentally, both of her parents are stably employed — her mother as an accountant and her father as a contractor. For her part, she intends to be a politician. "I really want Nigeria to be a better place," she says. "I'll be married by then — age twenty-four at least — and I want to be the governor of Ekiti State."

The current man in the job is Kayode Fayemi, a young, progressive leader who succeeded a hysterically corrupt former governor in 2010 (who, among other follies, helped himself to millions of taxpayer *naira* to fund a chicken farm that produced nary a chicken). In his short tenure, Fayemi has improved roads and paid for solar streetlights in Ado to keep them safe at night. Despite high enrollment in public primary schools and a shocking number of advanced degrees per capita, Ekiti is among the poorest states in Nigeria, with a 21 percent (official) unemployment rate. Like most leaders the world over, Fayemi is most concerned with luring employers to his constituency. In conversation at his Ekiti office, he reminded me that "the devil makes work out of idle hands."

If Joyce is a true believer in political power, even Fayemi realizes that the public sector can only do so much. "I don't know that government can always be in charge," he says. "My job is to create an enabling environment." In proof of ideology, he bought Samsung laptops to reach about thirty thousand pupils and eighteen thousand teachers — a show of demand that ultimately convinced Samsung to create a training center for local workers.

Samsung is not the only multinational to contemplate investing in Ekiti. British Petroleum is considering Ekiti as the site of its first forays into west Africa since the 1950s. Its investment won't be at the shores of the Niger Delta where crude oil flows and natural gas flares. Rather, the company is hoping to manufacture ethanol out of the area's abundant yam and cassava crops.

The big uptake in biofuel production is an increasingly important innovation for Africa. Plants with high oil content can be processed into fuel that, like traditional diesel gasoline, can be pumped into a car or any electricity generator. The emissions impact of biofuels is marginally better than that of fossil fuels but does not require tapping into dwindling global reserves. Whether you believe in theories of "peak oil" or not, planting energy is a tantalizing prospect.

Ethanol produced from local sugar is already added to petroleum coming into Ethiopia. The process, much simplified, is rather like adding water to soup or soap to make it stretch further — something simple most Africans intuitively understand. About 18.5 million liters of ethanol can be refined locally, and when blended in this fashion, it puts the price per liter at Ethiopian pumps below the price in Kenya — a country that doesn't have to pay for expensive petroleum transport. Ethiopia now has more than 200,000 hectares committed to growing power. Senegal, Mali, and Tanzania — with similarly vast reserves of nonarable land — have also jumped aboard the biofuel bandwagon.

Most experts agree that a large-scale rush to produce biofuels is a dangerous game to play with farmland currently in use. Trade-offs with food production are a huge concern in this emerging global industry. Common "first-generation" biofuels include sugar and corn, which farmers around the world are growing with the same intensive inputs of water and nitrogen fertilizer — but not for us to eat. This means less food for a planet poised to gain more people: bad news. Other trends — the increasing global consumption of meat, for example — are also reducing the supply of food available. Plenty of American corn is fed to animals that are then fed to people; more than 80 percent of US agricultural production goes into livestock feed.

Second-generation biofuels, however, are not food. Agave and palm oil, which belong to this category, have byproducts (tequila!) that humans consume. Jatropha and castor plants, whose seeds are oil rich and also inedible, are two of the promising new plants. Elephant grasses, switchgrass, and fast-growing willow trees are similarly unsuitable for human consumption but better for fuel production. Because they use little water and store nutrients in their roots, they may even leave soil richer than it was when the seeds were planted.

Non-food fuels do require fertilizer, water, and the labor inputs of any other crop but, with the exception of palm oil, have a higher potential upside in climatic outcomes. Some can be grown on polluted soil or "marginal land" — which is, of course, a designation in the eye of the beholder. Scientists in the West are tying themselves in knots to determine how to sidestep the food-versus-fuel issue — enzymes that break down the inedible parts of corn, for example, are currently too expensive to compete with traditional ethanol being grown in the American Midwest. But, at least in Africa, these "oil plants" are not yet in immediate conflict with food production.

The triplet issue of energy poverty, environmental change, and agriculture-based prosperity finds a natural meeting point in biofuel production. Growing power becomes profitable when oil goes above $100 a barrel — which has been the case for much of the new decade. As a result, most of the biofuel exploration in Africa is coming at the hands of large foreign companies worried about fat economy energy costs; the *Guardian* counted one hundred projects and fifty companies in over twenty countries in sub-Saharan Africa. Many buy up land (the Tanzanian government provided Sun Biofuels a ninety-nine-year lease for more than 20,000 acres in Kisarawe District, free of charge) and promise to build roads and supply other public goods in the sparsely populated areas where they set up operations.

But some areas have yet to see results. What's more, there is no guarantee that biofuels won't be shipped off to European markets where greener fuels may soon be required by EU and UK law. African participation in the biofuel supply chain should be predicated on local availability — importing oil to the continent is a miserable drain on national foreign exchange reserves. Ethiopia spends 10 billion *birr* (about $800 million) on petroleum annually.

Fairly traded, second generation biofuels could jump-start income and reduce local energy costs in Africa. The production side still contains many avenues for small-scale farmers to benefit. Growing these second-generation plants is not capital intensive, and as with other cash crops, cooperatives can aggregate the seeds and sell them to the refiners for a profit. Processing, storage, distribution, and providing associated services are other industries that could provide jobs.

Aside from the Ekiti plan, JMI, an initiative in Mali, involves 1,300 smallholder farmers in just such a scheme. Diligent Tanzania Ltd, headquartered in Holland, contracts with four thousand suppliers of jatropha. In Mozambique, "outgrowers," as they are called, can make more producing sugar for the big biofuel plants than those working in the factory that refines it. This could be welcome economic news for Abiodun and his peers.

African leadership in the production and sale of alternatives to fossil fuels is a rich irony, considering how little Africa has contributed to climate change. But with the right mix of supports, Africa's natural assets can solve the world's looming consumption problems and build livelihoods for a new generation of workers.

The momentary rift between the haves and have-nots during Sandy's blackout replicated the everyday divide between fat and lean on environmental issues. The Atlantic storm launched a justified wave of hand wringing about food, energy, and infrastructure — the interlocking environmental challenges of the twenty-first century. The disaster exposed a humbling dependence on power that never fails, food grown far away, water piped from the ground, and buildings assumed to be tough enough. The same vulnerability exists in other fat economies, where advanced development has actually *decreased* resilience.

From flooding to drought, more upheavals are in store for all economies, and especially sub-Saharan Africa. But however counterintuitive it may seem, the region is well prepared to confront these challenges. Lean economies have had to learn restraint at a microscopic level: how to balance food production and consumption, how to live without fossil fuels, how to build cities from scratch — all without entrenching the behaviors that may create future weather crises. The challenge for all societies is how to pivot from greedy K-strategy to *kanju* — and develop adaptive practices that can scale.

9

The Youth Map
Africa's Demographic Dividend

SOMETIMES WE FORGET how young Africa is. Not in terms of civilization — most schoolchildren learn that the continent is where humans first began. Nor in terms of its states — which took their modern shape roughly fifty years ago. But in terms of its people. Indeed, the quality most widely shared — across the Sahel and through dense forests to the southern Cape of Good Hope — is youth. The eldest competitor in the 2012 Olympic Games was a seventy-one-year-old from Japan. The youngest entrant was a thirteen-year-old from Togo. Increasingly, this is the way the world looks. As the average age of fat economies like Japan, Italy, and the United States creeps up (adding to anxiety about a coming tsunami of retirees), Africa is enjoying a demographic dividend. The median age is nineteen. Seventy percent of sub-Saharan Africa's population is less than thirty years old — the highest proportion in the world.

Africa's youth recalls an old saw about population in China and India: any action, however small, becomes a large one when multiplied by a billion. Africa's force multiplier is nearly 600 million youth between the ages of fifteen and twenty-four, with another 182 million joining the ranks by 2050. This century, these African children are living past childbirth and stepping into adulthood. They are an untapped source of pure potential energy.

Contrast the regional youth bubble with the powers that be. In many African countries, the recycled representatives of the state are long in the tooth. Kenya's 2007 election pitted a seventy-six-year-old against a sixty-two-year-old as though the latter were fresh blood. Liberia's Ellen Johnson Sirleaf is seventy-five — during her presidential reelection campaign, I saw countless fliers flogging the slogan "Too old to hold" (she held). Robert Mugabe, once a youthful liberation activist, is now a withered octogenarian crank, angling to keep power from Prime Minister Morgan Tsvangirai — himself over sixty years old. Yoweri Museveni in Uganda has been in power since 1986, well before the majority of his population were even born. Paul Biya in Cameroon is eighty-one and has led since 1982.

It's easy to cherry-pick examples of this generational disconnect; sub-Saharan Africa has the biggest gap between the median age of the public and the age of its leaders — a whopping forty-three years. By contrast, Europe and North America have an average age gap of sixteen years. Twenty of the top thirty such gaps worldwide are in sub-

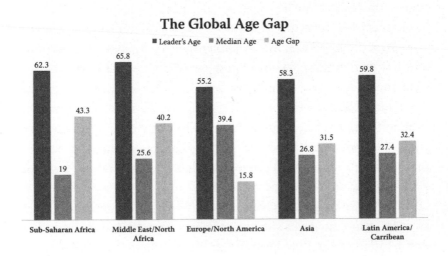

Sub-Saharan Africa has the biggest gap between the median age of the public and the age of its leaders — a whopping forty-three years.

Saharan Africa. And, whereas the average age of African heads of state is around seventy, the average life expectancy on the continent is fifty-six. (This makes a twenty-eight-year-old middle-aged!)

The formal political economy operates with the assumption that power and influence accrue with age. Even the lower ranks of civil servants and deputies responsible for representing regional and local interests are often generationally skewed. In South Sudan, where government is the largest employer, military officers born in the 1950s, and who led the twenty-two-year struggle for independence, have been rewarded with ministerial positions for which few are genuinely equipped. Ghanaian academic George Ayittey calls this class of elders — lying leaden atop African bureaucracies — the "hippo generation."

The effect is to exclude youth from state decisions and planning that will affect them long after the hippos are gone. In Cameroon, says Rebecca Enonchong, elder statesmen (and they are almost all men) lack the most basic understanding of fast-moving spaces like technology policy. "The man in charge of physical mail is the man who sets the price on our Internet connection — and uses Yahoo! to e-mail," she says. In countless other ways, the silent majority of young people in Africa confront a statist political arrangement that looks nothing like and cares little for them.

Some leaders like Obiageli Ezekwesili, the one-time education minister of Nigeria, are keenly aware of the gulf between a generation stumbling along with old habits and a new one poised to take power. Generally, she says, "[youth] does not carry the albatross of failure. They don't. The youthful population in Africa today had no idea of colonialism — it's story to them. They didn't know military rule — it's strange to them. They are intolerant of poor performance — they don't understand why that should be their lot."

At the same time, the International Labor Organization reported in 2010 the highest global youth unemployment rate since it began collecting statistics. In sub-Saharan Africa, young people make up 37 percent of the working-age population, but 60 percent of the unemployed — at least in the formal sector. Rote memorization is still the preferred pedagogy in public high schools and universities. Few institutions help young people navigate career choices, and labor markets offer no clear staircase to income security.

While the booming GDP growth rates for African economies this decade are certainly cause for celebration, the youth of Africa have remained mostly untouched. Ezekwesili described a young man asking her why the region's massive growth hadn't reached him in the form of a job. She cringed and called the failure to translate paper prosperity into tangible opportunities "the policymaker's nightmare."

For an ordinary civilian such as myself, it's equally distressing. Over the course of a month living in Kampala, Uganda, I wore out many days in reliably electrified cafés and canteens, pounding away at this manuscript. One afternoon, a girl approached me with a large manila envelope. "Can you give me a job?" she asked. I was startled — my writer's uniform of T-shirt and jeans didn't seem indicative of hiring and firing ability. "Come again?"

A young woman I'll call Sarah, wearing neat braids and a neater collared blouse, had graduated six months earlier with a BST in chemistry from Makerere University, once considered among the best in east Africa. Her marks and graduation certificate, which she had apparently been toting around Kampala ever since, showed a respectable B average in pharmaceutical medicine and biochemistry. But she couldn't find work and apparently had resorted to approaching complete strangers with her creased envelope of earthly qualifications.

Sarah wrote her contact information down in the tidy script of generations of African students without such easy access to a MacBook Air. I felt compelled to honor her boldness, e-mailing contacts from a previous visit to the local hospital. The response I got pretty much tells the story of the young and hungry in Africa today: "She is welcome to send me her CV, though I have to be honest and tell you that I receive about one such CV each week and don't actually have any open positions at the moment."

Even as hierarchical societies insist that the young defer to elders and wait their turn, they also fail to provide adequate support, training, and engagement for eventual leadership. It's a recipe for frustration among the youth cohort, of whom 2.2 million reach working age every year. Nosarieme Garrick, a young Nigerian activist, points out the distress among her peers. "Kids know that they're not getting a proper education," she says. "You can have someone who's gone to school, did everything right, has taken the right steps, graduated from university — and there's no jobs for them."

Thus the prevailing state for youth in sub-Saharan Africa is "waithood." Dr. Alcinda Honwana, a Mozambican anthropologist, describes waithood as a kind of purgatory, for young people who are "no longer children in need of care, but . . . still unable to become independent adults." Notably, Honwana rejects an age-based definition of youth and instead discusses anyone who has not yet reached "social adulthood," a stable moment associated with jobs, marriage, civic engagement, and children of one's own. Of the features of adulthood, a job may be the most significant. While unemployment is brutal at any stage of life, its damage is gravest when it hits at the beginning of one's career. According to the International Labor Organization, "This is tantamount to a denial of economic citizenship and gives rise to despair and resentment."

What happens to these youth matters — mischief and misfortune often occupy the space left by lack of work and structure for young men in particular. With millions of Africans stalling in the march from youth to adulthood, figuring out how to harness their potential energy is the most urgent task of the next decade in Africa.

The Youth Map offers three paths forward. One is to give young Africans relevant experience, moving from the memorization-based schooling system to more practical and even income-generating education. Another is to reach young people through more creative channels. Public schooling does not cover those who have dropped out of school, or emerged "half baked." Last, the young people who will assume leadership from the "hippo generation" must be encouraged in a spirit of responsibility that could transform the very fail states that have disappointed their parents. If the shift from public failure to public success is to occur, their grass-roots leadership and role modeling will be instrumental. But it won't happen if we don't pay closer attention.

· · ·

Elizabeth Skosana grew up in a tough neighborhood in Johannesburg, South Africa, deeply damaged by the apartheid system that ended when she was just a baby. Before 1994, black South Africans were constrained to the periphery of the city and the country's continent-leading economic growth. Today, "there's an atmosphere of teenage pregnancy, severe drug abuse, and alcohol abuse from a really young age," she says, with uncommon seriousness. Fifty percent of young people in South Africa are unemployed, and "there's also the attitude that after the twelfth grade, there's no need to go to university. Through cronyism and nepotism, I'll just go to where my dad works and stay there the rest of my life. That's the highlight of teenage lives where I come from."

When I met Lizzy, she was just eighteen and a bubbly second-year student at the African Leadership Academy. Set in a leafy suburb amid the sprawl of Johannesburg, ALA hosts roughly two hundred students from across the continent, in a setting reminiscent of the tony boarding schools of America's East Coast. The interior culture, however, is quite different. Ninety percent of the kids are on financial aid. Many of them come from difficult neighborhoods like Lizzy's — yet as the school's name suggests, all of them are being trained to sit at the top of Africa's future hierarchies, private and public. "Some will be central bank governors, some will be running their own nonprofits, some will be university professors," says Fred Swaniker, a spry Ghanaian who cofounded the school in 2008, when he was just thirty-one years old. "It's crucial that we nurture and develop young people so they can become leaders ten, fifteen, twenty years from now."

ALA's campus is full of sensible prodigies like Lizzy. It's where William Kamkwamba went to school after harnessing the wind — preparing him for a degree at Dartmouth and an engineering career. At age thirteen, Trevor Kibet wrote a letter to his minister of finance, laying out a complaint about national underdevelopment, rationally and with economic statistics. He was promptly paraded around Parliament as an example of Kenya's promising next generation and later admitted to ALA. Joel Mwale started a clean-water company in Uganda and

Kenya. Brian Waweru, a young Kenyan I met in his final semester, had recently been awarded a prestigious Huntsman scholarship to study at the Wharton School of the University of Pennsylvania.

ALA teaches everything you might learn in an American high school—Rwandan first-year Janine Muganza is taking physics, math, history, geography, and English. Where ALA departs dramatically from the curriculum at virtually every other school in the world is a two-year emphasis on entrepreneurship and leadership. In an act of unusual pedagogical daring, Swaniker believes he can distill *kanju* and teach it.

"The best way to develop as an entrepreneur is through practice and experience, not through theory," he says. Thus, his students are required to "major" in one of three areas: a long-term social service venture, an original idea that is developed by students and nurtured throughout the year, or a student-run business. One popular student business was to supplement the school's cold breakfast offerings with hot eggs and bacon. Spencer Horne, a recent graduate, devised a compost machine for when the kids are done. "It breaks down waste and turns it into methane gas, along with other by-products which can be used as fertilizer afterwards," he told reporter Kyle Brown. "Once it's complete we'd like to see [the school] cutting down the cost they're currently spending on gas for cooking."

The ALA program, intended as a supplement to local secondary schools, lasts two years, and students range in age from fifteen to nineteen. Students like Lizzy completed public high school in their home countries. Others leap from inadequate domestic educational systems to join the elite team. Still others are already the best-educated young people in their home nation. Whatever their background—and students hail from forty-some countries—the students understand intuitively that this place is different.

Like any boarding school community, its members are not from the same hometown. Thus ALA is slowly and surely building a network of powerhouse pan-Africanists whose internal connections will serve the continent well in the future. Any high school experience will seed important memories and relationships. At ALA, they have the handy and humorous effect of blasting down internal African stereotypes.

New students come armed with assumptions: Nigerians argue furiously. Ghanaians are loud. The francophone students want only to be French. AIDS is airborne in South Africa. Kenyans party a lot. As students cross paths, they cross borders, leaving a healthy network of respect and mutual reliance (and some unusual young romances). "You have all these people you can draw from, anytime, anywhere," says Jenneh Jah, a student from Sierra Leone. "You have people to talk to and can get advice." ALA, says Swaniker, expects to build robust collaborative networks that will last a lifetime.

On some level, ALA offers vocational training, but the vocation is independent thinking and enterprise development. "I have been at ALA for a year and a half, and I've been operations manager of a student-run business. I'm currently COO of a community service organization. I've made balance sheets. I've had board meetings. I've faced audits — and I'm just seventeen, recently," says Akan Nelson, another second-year student from Lagos. "These are things that I'm going to be encountering in my future life and that's really what makes it different. You can be taught about how to do a balance sheet or a profit-loss account in any other high school. Very few schools give you the opportunity to make it where it counts — not for a grade, but for your own credibility."

This belief in practicality, risk taking at an early age, and self-reliant bootstrapping is a key distinction between Africa's *kanju* culture and other societies. Remember the trail of young students walking to class every day? Many millions more African students leave home by age twelve for boarding schools like ALA. Though the experience is far less grand, independence is normalized. "This situation in Africa is one that teaches us risk taking and risk management," says Emanuel Feruzi, then the managing director at Tanzanian Tri Labs Limited. "They don't teach us this in university, but we learn it every day." At ALA, the classroom is treated as the ideal safe space in which to understand how the world really works and establish adaptive habits early on.

Take, for example, ALA's obsessive focus on time management. Students, like so many of the most "well-rounded" teens breaking into elite universities, are overscheduled, with sports, community service, student businesses, and a taxing workload designed to prepare them for SATs and International Baccalaureate exams. Rather than expecting the best and brightest to swim through the sea, ALA begins each year with an extended boot camp on scheduling. Students are assigned a journal in which they must allocate every waking moment — class time, free time, meals, meetings at meals, and everything else. The schedules are homework assignments to be submitted to a teacher at the end of the week. "It's forcing you to get used to the idea of not just wallowing time away, but maximizing time," says Lizzy, whose easy charm belies an obviously high grit quotient. "You don't have time to be sitting on your bed trying to remember what your chemistry teacher said was your homework."

The regimen works in multiple ways. It can be a grounding experience for students on their first sojourn away from home (and, for those from francophone Africa, learning in English for the first time). "At first I said, 'Why would I do this?' and now I can't stop," says Lizzy. "When I feel overwhelmed by schoolwork, looking at my diary and planning what I am going to do actually calms me down."

It is also an essential counterbalance to the endemic disorder jokingly known as "African time." In general, time in the region is rather cheap — there seems to be an unending surplus — and as a result life is often running behind. I've both given and received enough grinning apologies for tardiness to last a lifetime. "You don't see your parents managing their time, you don't see anybody in your life being as focused or dependent on time management," says Lizzy.

ALA refuses to tolerate the inefficiency. It's a smart way to introduce students to something ALA calls "deliberate practice," drawing on the research of the Florida State University psychology professor Anders Ericsson. This is the principle that classroom lessons — framed in units about self, team, and community — must be applied and internalized.*

Deliberate practice is only part of what makes ALA one of the best high schools I've ever seen. Students enjoy red-brick buildings, cushy dorms, and global visitors like Carly Fiorina, Michelle Obama, and Teach for America founder Wendy Kopp. They are confident. They are articulate. They seem bound to succeed. Over a lunch of pasta and potatoes, I found students ready to debate everything from regional economic integration to the pitfalls of foreign aid. Like many tony boarding schools, ALA offers liberal arts at a junior level — an incubator for excellence where a lucky few are taught with care and encouraged to think outside the box.

ALA is not alone at the top of the heap; other African countries have long educated the elite in similar fashion. Kamuzu Academy in Malawi, Hillcrest in Kenya, and a flight of Zimbabwe schools named for British princes and Catholic saints have long traditions of competitive education. Ashesi University in Berekuso, Ghana, is an upstart offering at the undergraduate level, founded by Patrick Awuah, another young Ghanaian returnee. St. Francis College, a lower-cost independent school in Benoni, South Africa, keeps classes to thirty students each and had a 100 percent pass rate for national secondary exams in 2010. Like Bridge Academies, their existence is a lifeline to the families who crave a higher-quality product than the free state schools.

But in contrast with Bridge, the elite schools cannot reach as far as Africa needs. Even with the increase in mom-and-pop independent offerings, demand for private schooling far outstrips supply. Millions of the less fortunate — those who have yet to hear of ALA, or find a way to crack its rigorous admissions process — are left to the whims of the fail state education system.

In leadership class, most ALA students read W.E.B. Du Bois's landmark essay "The Talented Tenth." As an elite school founded on the

---

* The behavioral focus contrasts with what Paulo Freire, a Brazilian pedagogist, calls the "banking concept of education," in which information is deposited and withdrawn at a later date.

premise that individual excellence can trickle down to the less privileged, ALA seems to recapitulate Du Bois's message for black Americans.

Jitegemee does the opposite. The nonprofit youth center, whose name means "self-reliance," has mastered ways of supporting kids who have fallen through the cracks of educational and other safety nets in Kenya. Like many of the cases we've seen, the program was born out of multiple institutional failures. When the UN-backed free educational regime hit Kenya in 2003, it left secondary damage: community centers and shelters for street children began to close, penalized for not being formal schools. The children themselves had been orphaned, abandoned, or had fled from abusive or unlucky homes. Once on the streets, they became reviled by virtually all of society. In the city of Machakos, Jitegemee is pioneering a system to straighten them out and equip them for life.

Jitegemee's program has two tracks: one of formal schooling and one of vocational training. The younger kids who haven't missed as much school are prepared for and then reintroduced into the primary schooling system, with all of the nutrition, tutoring, and financial support the organization can offer. For those in their late teens, who are unlikely to or simply don't want to conquer the curriculum they missed, Jitegemee offers skills training in a craft or trade — tailoring, welding, carpentry, hairdressing, auto repair, and the like. The students are paired with master craftspeople to learn the ropes.

So-called tracking is highly controversial in the United States. Parents dislike their children being placed in remedial mathematics, or in special behavioral environments, instead of in mainstream classrooms. Children are said to understand they are being demoted and by their performance reinforce the lower aspirations that the system holds for them.

The inverse appears to be true at Jitegemee — perhaps because of the dire straits from which the kids have come. Their mentors pay them, occupy them, and offer another form of adult supervision that strengthens their gathering confidence. Forty-year-old Wilson

Musembi, for example, has taken in Jitegemee interns for several years. After two years of training and nominal pay, he hopes to hire Patrick, a retiring seventeen-year-old, into the workshop of half a dozen mechanics he operates in central Machakos.

The teens I spoke with take pride in achieving "reform" — but there's nothing sentimental about their evolution. Patrick left home and school when he was in his early teens. Ostensibly, he was collecting charcoal and eking out a living, but he admits that, then, "my job was sniffing glue." Tracey, an observant eighteen-year-old, will tell you, in smooth English, that she was also an addict. Ronald, one of the oldest youths in the program, slept on the street for ten years. Today, he and the dozen other vocational students I met fairly boast about what they can do.

"If I get work I can just build my house," says Ronald. It's something his parents were never able to do. "I will have my work," says Patrick. "I will be helping [my family] with whatever they need. We will have enough to eat." Jitegemee cofounder Farah Stockman points out that 80 percent of the program's vocational graduates have jobs and are earning money, and 60 percent are the primary breadwinners in their household.

Jitegemee makes a clear-eyed push for this empowerment, with respect for the particular needs of kids living mostly on their own. "We teach living values, we teach life skills, we teach things like development," says Alex Mutiso, a director of the vocational program. The administrators' local sensitivity has helped: an early class of rescued girls dropped out of tailoring training, one by one, because they hadn't learned to interact in an organized, traditionally educated environment. "They were feeling belittled," says Mutiso. "They were in the same place with people who finished class eight, or form four; they thought because they were from the street they were despised." Like the ALA scheduling diaries, building their skills and confidence with a positive narrative of honest work has made the difference.

Africa-based outsourcing ventures — such as Samasource, KenCall, and Digital Divide Data — have also launched vocational schemes that

give young people marketable skills and pocket money. Like the clusters in Bangalore and Manila that provide similar services, they engage
young part-time or full-time employees to work with private clients in
real-time, accountable fashion.

Cheerleaders for vocational programs explain that not everyone is
born to be a minister or manager. Sometimes young people thrive,
given a concrete skill. In *Up From Slavery,* Booker T. Washington offers a pre-buttal of Du Bois's "Talented Tenth" thesis: "One man may
go into a community prepared to supply the people there with an analysis of Greek sentences," he writes. "The community may not at that
time be prepared for, or feel the need of, Greek analysis, but it may feel
its need of bricks and houses and wagons." Prince Kludjeson, a Ghanaian parent who has sent children to school abroad, sees practical skills
— not oil or mineral wealth — as the continent's ticket to prosperity.
"The economies in Africa are all about the development of human
capital and knowledge-based capital. We should forget about all these
natural resources. The people of today aren't interested in this. I am
not interested in this and my kids are not."

On the African continent, few state-run systems contemplate practical education. Jenerali Ulimwengu, a Tanzanian journalist, recalled
his ninth-grade curriculum: "I learned a great deal of the paddocks in
East Anglia, animal husbandry, the freezing temperature of the Kam-
chatka, the height of Mount Everest, and the impressive features of the
Great Barrier Reef of Australia. I have been asking myself since if there
was any relevance." Now he believes "we need to be teaching masonry,
ironmongery, mechanics, handcrafts, commerce and bookkeeping,
artistic and creative endeavors."

In Africa, the best economic and educational opportunities for
youth may lie in the informal economy discussed in Chapter 2. Informal "attachment" employment has been a long-standing means of
passing on technical expertise and earning opportunity in Africa and
elsewhere. Ever-greater numbers of young people — fully 99 percent of
working youth in Zambia, for example — are employed in the informal
economy. Despite being separate from the formal schooling regime,

Wilson Musembi trains street children in his workshop. Apprenticeships like this are a proven way to equip young people with practical skills and earning potential.

informal-sector apprenticeships can be very organized, grounded in local social norms that are a useful skeleton on which young people can build practical skills.

Jitegemee's practices also conform to our best knowledge about getting cash into the hands of young people. The International Labor Organization notes that vocational schools work best when they offer a job placement component as well. The apprentices are initiated into a business culture and network of practitioners — a way to build not only skills, but extended professional relationships that will matter for future job prospects.

Trusting and engaging the informal sector as a training partner allows Jitegemee to make more effective interventions than its competitors — underfunded public polytechnical schools that offer few employment guarantees. In Jitegemee's model, Musembi and other mentors get a helping hand that amplifies their earning potential, an incentive that needs no justification or subsidy. The program is grounded in the same practice-makes-perfect logic as ALA — or any summer internship around the world — but accomplishes its objective in careful and realistic ways.

Unfortunately, "when African countries are designing [vocational] programs, they tend to focus more on the formal sector," says Abiodun Alao, a research fellow at King's College London who has studied such efforts in Nigeria. Given the disregard for informality we've seen over and over, this is an understandable oversight. But gradually, in many countries, the education marketplace has become divorced from practical skills. The shift has come at the expense of young people beginning their careers. Muganza, the ALA first-year from Rwanda, had no firm plans for a career but sees the need for entrepreneurial education. "You get out of college and . . . you get a job and they ask you for experience. You don't have experience. When are you going to get that experience?"

In the mid-1990s, the global education community turned away from measuring inputs (spending on schools, for example) to measuring outputs (student performance). Unfortunately, the development community did not adopt similar best practices. MDG 3 flagged enrollment as the way to measure progress. Thus, since 2000, African schools are increasingly well attended. Free schooling schemes swept the continent in the early part of the millennium. Between 2002 and 2007, 2.1 million children flooded classrooms in Kenya. Sub-Saharan enrollment leaped from 58 percent in 1999 to 76 percent by 2010. Today, Togo, Malawi, Madagascar, Uganda, and Rwanda are at near-universal enrollment in primary school.*

But enrollment doesn't mean education. Malawi enacted its free school reforms in 1994, well before the rest of the continent — and promptly felt the pain of overcrowding. The average first-grade classroom size in Malawi is one hundred students, and only three in ten

---

* The boom in private, less documented schools contributes but, like other informal arrangements, is overlooked. In Lagos State, for one example, including mom-and-pop alternative schools would reduce the number of out-of-school children by half.

students will complete primary school. Overcrowding can lead to less personal attention, and less absorption of material. To wit: About three in ten Kenyan third-graders cannot read a second-grade-level story. In Ghana, only one in four fifteen- to nineteen-year-olds scored over 50 percent on a test of one- and two-digit math problems of the kind Miss Elizabeth was drilling into Bridge's seven-year-olds. Not one student passed the 2013 entrance examination for Liberia's flagship public university.

Jonathan Starr, who cofounded and ran Abaarso Tech, an independent high school in Somaliland, says the smartest eleventh-grade girls in his school are taking calculus but also working on long division from a fourth-grade math textbook. "They're doing both because they still need to fill in all these other holes," he says. "You know math, but not some parts of math; you know fractions and you don't know what a fraction is. There is no handbook that says what you should do."

But there is *Shujaaz*. It's neither school nor teacher. It's a comic book. The Kenyan magazine stars Boyie, a high school graduate who, in *kanju* style, has built an FM radio station in his mother's basement. Broadcasting in secret, "DJ B" befriends a diverse crew of youth, with whom he trades advice on how to make money and improve their lives. Malkia is a punkish teen living in an unnamed city on the coast, drawn in a slashing anime style. Charlie Pele is a football-obsessed boy living in an unidentified slum area in central Kenya. Maria Kim is a sensible, studious teen taking care of her younger brother. Their surnames and cities are purposely vague; fans are free to project their reality (and tribe) onto the characters.

Shujaaz means "heroes." Instead of battling traditional baddies with superpowers, the kids deploy common sense and homegrown innovations to win moral victories and sometimes cash. The first issue of *Shujaaz* urged readers to dye their chickens pink. The practice, piloted in west Africa, prevents baby chicks from being taken by birds of prey. As it turns out, between 50 and 80 percent of chickens are snatched by hawks while they are running around the farm. The bright dye confuses the predators and helps farmers to keep their investment. In the comic, Charlie Pele's mischievous brother dyes the family poultry—

but when the hawks show up, his angry father has to acknowledge the benefit.

These and similar stories are simple and splashy, told in a pitch-perfect fusion of Swahili and English known only to the young as Sheng. The subject matter might appear to be banal — seed soaking, alcoholism, "national cohesion" — and the mandate a bit sentimental. But the aesthetic is effortlessly hip, and in the hands of the very capable young illustrators, writers, actors, and producers, the ideas come alive.

Some of its most daring issues urged young voters not to be intimidated during the 2010 referendum on Kenya's new constitution. They've taken on corruption: *Shujaaz* producers profiled a man from Kisumu, a town on Kenya's western border with Lake Victoria, who had uncovered theft and injustice within a government program seeking to help parents cover secondary school fees. "We pointed people at a website where you could find out more information," says Bridget Deacon, head of production. The story went live on a Saturday, and four days later, twelve thousand people had clicked on the link — many times the normal traffic for an obscure government website.

"You'd think [readers] would go '*Boooooring*,'" says Fatimah, the twenty-six-year-old director of art at *Shujaaz*. "But they like that they're all just practical, responsible, moral, constructive, proactive citizens. Maria Kim is a no-nonsense young girl with practically no social life as such, and she's our most popular character."

Shujaaz is not the first media project to use entertainment to get audiences to eat their figurative vegetables. In addition to Smallholders Radio in Nigeria, soap operas that sprinkle in life lessons are common in Africa. More than thirty-four million South Africans watch the local soap *Soul City*. It's as popular as Coca-Cola among black South Africans, and regular viewers are almost four times as likely to use condoms as non-watchers. Deacon and Rob Burnet, another director, are alumni of *Makutano Junction*, a *telenovela* that also dramatizes social issues in Kenya. There, they discovered the authentic imprint is key. "If you give people a choice between a very high-quality imported program and a low-quality local program, they'll still watch the very low-quality local program," says Burnet.

Nollywood proves that point. But few media incumbents are exclusively targeting young people. In fact, youth media in Africa consists of little more than brow-raising music videos. And, aside from scarce textbooks, reading material is hard to come by. According to Starr, his Somali students tackled *To Kill a Mockingbird* but with little preparation. "If you're reading on a second-grade level and you pick up a book that's a high school book, you're going to understand half the words —that's torture. No human being can deal with that. And if they read *Go Dog Go,* it's like, 'That's beneath me.' What you need is something that very clearly progresses you."

A graphic novel is an ideal solution. *Shujaaz* can be shared until it falls apart, pinned on a wall, passed around a schoolyard, read and reread for its gorgeous drawings and its boring informatics. And, adds Burnet, "it is an enormous amount cheaper to produce than these very expensive television shows which are gone in an instant."

The offices of Shujaaz, *which produces a graphic novel and radio program aimed at educating Kenyan youth.*

The potential to get sound moneymaking advice to millions of children is tantalizing. On a patio just off the *Shujaaz* war room, Burnet did some cocktail napkin math on the pink-chicken solution. "You start adding up the value of a chicken which isn't taken: three hundred shillings, one hen at home, thirty-six eggs a year, of which eighteen, maybe sixteen eggs are taken by birds of prey. Each egg is worth five dollars if it grows up to be a full chicken. That's eighty bucks per chicken." If only 1 percent of the comic's five million readers take the advice, it is worth about $4 million. "That was one of our key objectives — it's got to be massive. We cannot muck about with another micro-project."

Circulation for *Shujaaz* (supported by philanthropic funding) is at 600,000 monthly, but the project reaches 10 million with its clever, 360-degree approach to connecting with its audience. DJ B's fictional radio show is also a real-life broadcast featuring some of the same material as in the comic strip, as well as interviews and bonus tips. The live show, aired every day on twenty-six stations in Kenya, follows the form of the fiction: "DJ B," played by a twenty-five-year-old actor, will greet listeners and then say, "I got a text from my girl Maria Kim — I'm going to call her; she had an amazing story to tell me . . ." Then the drama begins.

A live SMS interface and well-trafficked Facebook and Twitter accounts — which are sometimes used to solicit material for future print issues — also maintain the elaborate fiction. This dance between reality and fantasy can be confusing; listeners have called the Well Told Story offices asking for the real DJ B. "Once a week," says Deacon, "we get a call saying, 'Can I have Maria Kim's telephone number?'"

Shujaaz, which won an Emmy Award in 2012, makes an important educational intervention into the sixteen-to-twenty-six-year-old demographic that is more likely to be out of school than in it. Many countries in the region suffer dropout rates to spin your head. Ghana serves 5.4 million kids in 14,000 primary schools, 1.34 million kids in 8,000 junior high schools, and only 730,000 students in 510 public senior high schools. In South Africa, 66 percent of first-graders in 2001 didn't make it to their high school certification in 2012. And only 12 percent of those who made it tested well enough to try for a university

degree. Few official statistics exist, but at crucial inflection points—
between primary and secondary school, and then again on the road to
college—millions of African schoolchildren are left behind. By blur-
ring the lines between education and media, *Shujaaz* offers a continu-
um of learning for those who need it. By putting the classroom in the
popular press and on air, says Burnet, "we ignore the local education
system completely."

Obami, a South African social network designed specifically for education, likewise tries to meet young people where they are—but also
involve their parents. Not unlike Facebook or Mxit, Obami networks
schools, students, and parents in a slick and open way. In partnership with school administrators, the company uploads all education
materials, schedules, and parent-teacher feedback mechanisms online
and lets the existing network effects take over. Parents can log on and
meet their child's biology teacher, and students can seek out informal
feedback on scheduling or specific assignments, from both teachers
and other students.

The secure system has been introduced in three hundred schools
in South Africa, mostly private, but serves an increasing number of
township and rural schools and has the potential to add many thousands more. While not all families in the region have consistent access
to online interfaces, Obami helps to fix the system that tends to keep
overwhelmed parents out of the loop. It also forces more accountability and personalization into the educational experience. "Teachers
are very technophobic and very complacent," says Barbara Mallinson,
Obami's creator. In an unusual inversion of authority, students now
drive usage. "We don't even have to tell them what it's about; they get
it right away."

An education-focused social network makes sense, particularly in a
region where limited transparency allows teachers to check out of their
core duties. And like other technology innovations for development in
Africa, Obami amplifies what already exists. "There are such apparent
networks in the real world—subcommunities that emerge and communities that emerge between schools," says Mallinson. "Nothing was
really reflecting this very effectively online."

Digital education is a global growth industry; the Khan Academy and other "MOOCS" (massively open online colleges) offer lessons in an enormous variety of subjects. Likewise, programs like One Laptop Per Child have attempted to introduce digital literacy to young people in lean economies. Tools to connect and learn are revered among youth, especially in Africa. But Mallinson believes building new media tools that are grounded in existing relationships is a better way to improve outcomes.

Education innovations more than pull their weight in Africa. Better education leads to better health outcomes for all children, delayed childbirth for young African women, and more robust economies of skilled workers with greater opportunities for self-improvement and earning. Physical schools are the front lines for numerous social benefits including feeding and medical care. More schooling certainly checks the spread of mischief and idleness, and improves income stability for families. And it is generative: the longer a mother attends school, the better her children do on exams.

But demand for schooling still substantially exceeds supply, and millions of youth in Africa cannot afford to depend solely on the status quo. Promoting innovation within (and not just access to) education is essential.

Jitegemee, *Shujaaz*, ALA, Obami, and Bridge Academies carve pedagogical freedom from the obvious lack of alternatives — *kanju* logic in service of Africa's youth bubble. This climate of adventurism is not unlike the charter school movement in America. David Aylward, who works with the UN Foundation, laments fat economy gridlock. "At this point, we have some combination of teachers, unions, and school boards, state boundaries and others that defend this ridiculous status quo. But at some point, in a country where you have no education system . . . you don't have a barrier. It's more likely that you'll see this kind of experimentation early on." With shrinking opportunity costs for access to ever-greater amounts of information, the whole world is liberated to pay similar attention to curriculum and processes of learning. Taking a page from Africa's education innovators makes good sense.

• • •

Proscovia Alengot Oromait was sworn in as a member of Uganda's parliament in September 2012. She was just nineteen years old — the youngest elected official in Africa. Sixty-eight-year-old Yoweri Museveni, her president and party leader, has been in office eight years longer than she has lived.

That Alengot is young and hungry for political power should be comforting. That she is female should be even more so. Globally, there are precious few women in higher office — though six African countries top the world in their proportion of female representatives. Alengot represents a district in eastern Uganda with only one functioning public high school.

Alengot proved, however, a visible target for criticism. One of her new male colleagues, Barnabas Tinkasiimire, called her election a national shame. "This is unbelievable," he said. "When you analyse that baby, what kind of knowledge and experience does she have?" The grenades were not limited to men. Angeline Osege, a female MP from Soroti, slammed Alengot as well. "Parliament is not a daycare centre," she said. "This is somebody who has never bought for herself salt or a dress. What do you expect her to do in Parliament?"

Alengot is hardly running national policy. She will be enrolled in a local Christian college while serving her term in office and is expected to vote mostly in lockstep with the longtime ruling party that helped her win. In fact, her rise to comparative power reveals an unfortunate set of problems with politics for the young. Her election was a fluke exception to the traditional barriers to entry for new-generation activists. She coasted to election on the name of her father, who died in office just two months prior. Her education left her truly inexperienced — no "deliberate practice" has or could prepare her to lobby against seasoned and protectionist lawmakers.

Perhaps worse, there is no indication that she represents a new wave of political movers from a younger generation. While government jobs are still a steady lure for the risk averse and well connected, very few young Africans are following Alengot's path. For a generation steeped in fail state dysfunction, the public sector is unattractive. In the iHubs, university pool halls, or the open-air industrial clusters of the African continent, the importance of politics ranks well behind start-up woes, idle entertainment, and the struggle for daily bread.

Part of the indifference stems from a sense that other avenues are more exciting, less corrupt, and potentially more effective. "If politics is trying to win by making the other person look worse off, then I will never be a politician," says Davis Karambi, the young Kenyan who helped his village build a sustainable education fund. "But if politics is building schools, if politics is setting up infrastructures getting to make sure that everybody has certain rights like education and health — if politics is trying to optimize what you have in the system in terms of public resources, then that's the kind of politics I would like to do. And I am already a politician in that sense."

Karambi's framing — that social progress is more than politics — is a partial response to decades of disinvestment and dysfunction in state-run institutions. Importantly, it is not an abdication of interest in progress. It's a restatement of what we already know — that central processes relying on official hierarchies miss the good that ordinary people can do and are doing right now.

Still, for all the problems with Africa's formal institutions, their best hope is the young people who are poised to inherit them. The movement includes the Kenyan graffiti artists painting the truth about the country's "vulture" political class. Likewise, the most encouraging signal in the runup to Senegal's elections in 2012 was the youth rap slogan *y'en a marre* — "had enough." And for changes to take root in both the public and private sectors, encouraging a climate of accountability and duty among young people is a must. The question is just how to engineer new commitments among the disillusioned.

In some cases, youth alone is doing half the work. Compared with their parents — and even those a generation older — the younger Africans I've encountered are delighted to be approaching their moment of social empowerment. Olamide Aladesuru, a second-year ALA student from Nigeria, wears pink stud earrings to accompany the slouchy track pants that appear to be the unofficial school uniform. "My parents don't believe in change; they believe it's just [about] dealing. Well, me, I have more hope in changing, changing systems, changing political systems, changing family systems," she says. Lizzy, the ALA student from Johannesburg, likewise lacks the "hangover" of bitterness from the humiliation of apartheid. She is clear-eyed about the need for a social and educational revolution. "I don't see why you would want to settle for that much when you have potential," she says. "I want to change that mentality."

I trace their unusual optimism to the third ALA subject that is alien to most schools worldwide: African Studies. The first class of teachers at ALA, who set the curriculum, determined that a sense of history and place matters greatly to confidence and success. Thus tales of the Kingdom of Axum, now Ethiopia, and its protracted resistance to colonization are taught alongside calculus and chemistry. "Some schools in Africa don't really teach about the history of the continent as a whole. You know your national history, and maybe the regional history and biggish events on the continent," says Nolizwe Mhlaba, an African Studies teacher from Zimbabwe. "We're trying to help them to think up ideas for moving the continent as a whole forward, and to do that you obviously need to know what challenges you have in common but then also how other countries and leaders in other parts of the continent are dealing with these different issues."

This approach helps to confront a particular problem of the Youth Map: apathy. Many cultures grapple with a steady erosion of decency — the texting and the music videos and the lack of respect for tradition, and elders. Sub-Saharan Africa is no different. In its extreme forms, boredom and disillusion generate destructive behaviors. The easily swayed young suicide bombers of Boko Haram in the Sahel and Al Shabaab in the Horn illustrate the dangers of disrespecting political hierarchy and civic culture. Teaching uplifting regional history is a potential counterweight — and at ALA, it has become a pillar of its education philosophy.

"We talk about Africa as the entrepreneur's paradise," says Segun Olagunju, head of the school's leadership and entrepreneurship department. "You can be at the forefront of something — you can start a company that can be the J. P. Morgan of Africa in ten, twenty years. You can't do that in the US — they're already there. You are uniquely advantaged to take these opportunities and do it where others cannot." This attitude is codified in ALA enrollment policies: students on financial aid must make a commitment to return to Africa after age twenty-five and stay for ten years. The expectation is that they will "pay it forward," making positive change in an area of their developed expertise. This is not a hard sell. Jah, the ALA first-year from Sierra Leone, says she'd prefer coming back to Africa to work. "These days you hear about this potential in Africa, if only people knew how to explore it," she said. "That has me interested."

The emphasis on Afro-optimism — independent of politics — makes a difference. Olamide wants to study international affairs, or become a lawyer, maybe. But she is sure she wants to work for something bigger than herself. "Before coming here I thought I would get a normal job, get a banking job, have a stable life, and that's what a lot of my friends want to do with their lives," she told me. "But that's not enough for me. I want to start something and do something and help my community. That's the most important thing."

Formal institutions in Africa have been ill equipped to take on battles that build for the long term. Coherence and commitment among youth can challenge that past and fill the void of "waithood." Honwana, who developed the term, hopes that youth in developing countries will "no longer allow themselves to be manipulated by the elites into fighting ethnic and religious conflicts but instead choose the fight for their own socioeconomic and political rights." Real skills, better engagement, and cross-culture and cross-class consciousness will raise the ceiling for Africa's youth to do better — in or out of government.

Africa's youth are ignored at everyone's peril. Rather than reinforcing the systems that have left millions behind, the Youth Map must remain grounded in risk taking and rejection of conventional pedagogy. Emanuel Feruzi, speaking to a crowd of educators in Tanzania, explained the generational divide: "I think for many of us there are two teams — one that says no, no, no, this is too risky, you're not ready. The other says go for it." According to him, African youth are ready to go. "The uneducated of the twenty-first century are not those that can't read and write. The uneducated of this century are those that cannot unlearn their old lessons and learn the new ones to adapt to this age."

10

Two Publics

Who's in Charge?

A
FRICA IS AT a crossroads. Millions share a vision of *what* needs doing — that is, social, economic, and civic empowerment for the historically marginalized. This includes women's rights, fair trade, modern education, balanced consumption, and issue based politics — as well as good roads, and rules for them. But it's not always clear *how* to get from today to tomorrow, from point A to point B.

The late economist Albert Hirschman identified three possible responses to systems in turmoil. Members of a group can signal their opinion with disengagement ("exit"), with expression ("voice"), or with obedience ("loyalty"). The framework is easily applied to sub-Saharan states.

As the preceding chapters make clear, exit is a popular choice. A preference for extralegal systems makes sense, especially in low-legitimacy environments. Where the fail state has been a predator, individuals and businesses have adopted a libertarian posture to counteract its worst practices. Millions like Gladys, Bridge Academies parents, or Somaliland patriots exit the formal system to pursue their goals.

Voice, too, can help to improve development prospects: from Villages in Action to mPedigree to the night artists painting murals in Nairobi, and new whistleblowing initiatives like "I Paid a Bribe," some activists attempt to amplify the voices of ordinary people. But civil society in Africa is everywhere embattled. Freedom House, which tracks human rights around the world, finds the countries in sub-Saharan Africa woefully unfree. This means that groups focusing on human rights, free expression, and gender-based empowerment — among other political aims — are often an afterthought.

In most countries, the press is just as sickly. Freedom House finds only 3 percent of African media environments to be "free." I've seen stenography, misinformation, and harassment firsthand. A culture of deference and fear of reprisal lead many reporters to file "who stories" (rather than "what stories"). Even liberal darlings like Liberian president Ellen Johnson Sirleaf are guilty of enabling repressive media environments. The passage of African laws against hate speech suggests

*A sign in Kigali, Rwanda, outlining the rules of the road
for a state that is rebranding itself after genocide.*

a narrowing environment for expression — even as technological tools of dissent grow more accessible.

On some level, this is an argument for protecting and strengthening the media in Africa. As a proxy for the public to which they belong, free and fair local coverage can help to keep institutions honest and break down the information asymmetries that perpetuate the fail state. Foreign correspondents, of whom I count myself a representative, are simply not capable of illuminating the depth and breadth of information across the continent. Happily, modern discourse now includes citizens, wielding twenty-first-century tools to tell stories better, longer, and with greater reach.

But voice itself is often a petition to power — dependent on the same systems that persistently fail ordinary people. And so it can fall short of our aspirations. The vulture mural, for one example, changed nothing about the practices of the powerful; just two months after inauguration, Kenyan MPs voted to give themselves a 60 percent salary hike — to roughly $10,000 a month. Many African civil society groups depend on external grant funding or compete with foreign NGOs that supplant their work. Jamillah Mwanjisi, head of State of the Union, a pan-African NGO consortium, now worries about the "shrinking space" for non-state voices.

Even where local NGOs have devised an agenda for change, formal institutions still drive action. When the African Union convened a gathering to celebrate fifty years of regional independence and map a plan for the next fifty, civil society groups were banned outright. The official rationale: outside voices presented a distraction from the high-level gatherings of diplomats. Nkosazana Dlamini-Zuma, the new head of the AU from South Africa, offered a with-us-or-against-us frame for the meetings: "We decide which ones are closed . . . we decide which sessions are open. And if you are not going to be participating in the discussion, why do you want to be here?"

Loyalty — belief in, rather than critiques of, authority — is a third way. It's also counterintuitive; few people outside the continent's myriad bureaucracies argue for more concentrated power in African politics. Even fewer actively rely on government to improve their lives. But establishing loyalty is a tantalizing prospect. It suggests some measure of legitimacy, and the social progress that comes with it. And while my arguments cheer on those working around distortive or extractive institutions, one need only look at the high turnout rates for some recent African elections to see that many people still hold on to the dream of competent, representative government.

The real question for Africa's future may be: Loyalty to *whom*? Or *what*? The basic tension in development practice runs between inductive and deductive processes. The "stuff we don't want" approach is overly deductive. Such solutions begin with external priorities and remain inflexible as they move from elite conference halls and parliaments to the population at large. At the same time, inductive, grassroots processes struggle to be recognized and to scale up.

In her office in Lagos, activist Ngozi Iwere described these "two publics" in the region today. One is "the public of the community, which is the governance at the community level that works for the people. They set it up themselves, they have their sanctions, they have their boundaries, your rights, my rights." The other public, she says, is "modern-day Western government that pretends that this other governance does not exist."

She's observing a phenomenon known as legal pluralism. Systems of dueling legitimacy and authority aren't limited to Africa; informal laws, whether customary, mercantile, religious, or clan determined, coexist with formal law in many parts of the world.* In Africa, one "public" is decidedly Western — oriented around states and bureaucracies, parliamentary democracy and the administrative state, international trade and human rights laws and GDP-centric calculations. The other public is far more decentralized and less culturally determined, comprising family hierarchies, tribal or religious laws, or even

---

* One merchant may offer fixed prices with tax; another may embrace the haggle economy. One family may condone alcohol consumption before the legal age, just as another may forbid drinking, even when it's legally permitted. Islamic banking law, for another example, governs many transactions that take place in the Arab Middle East

informal contract norms like the *lex mercatoria* that for centuries governed trade around the Indian Ocean, and inland from Asia to Europe.

Iwere is right that rule of law acolytes have repeatedly overlooked the existence, strength, and utility of the latter category in Africa. Indeed, the chief failing of development practice has been to presume loyalty to the African state or nation rather than to the shifting tools, tricks, and affiliations that make life in the other "public" viable.

But acknowledging dual norms is just the first step. Both publics have strengths and both carry dangers. At one end of the spectrum is the *kanju* spirit I've cheered throughout this book — playing naughty, bending rules, and devising new games entirely. At the other end of the spectrum is the strong and functional state — still rare in modern Africa.

The closest thing I found was in Rwanda, which everybody remembers for its 1994 genocide. Today, the country is among Africa's leaders in the ease of doing business, and roads that were once littered with bodies are now butter smooth, from the cities to the hinterlands. The economy continues to grow at a substantial pace — about 7.5 percent in 2010, 2 percent higher than the East African Community and more than sub-Saharan Africa at large.

I wasn't prepared for the charming calm of the aptly named "Land of a Thousand Hills." The country looks like a Cézanne landscape, a stark contrast to its sinister history of violence. And after months of sifting through white papers on bad bureaucracy, I also wasn't prepared to see a government eager to please. But just as Somaliland is doggedly building institutions from destruction, the Rwandan nation is clambering out from the civil conflict that once defined it.

Since reconstituting itself in the early 2000s, the Rwandan state has enacted a series of innovative reforms. As a push to integrate the nation into the global economy, the official language of instruction and business was changed from French to English. Children are required to attend three additional years of school, and a universal health insurance scheme is in its first stages. In response to a threat of environmental damage, no plastic bags are allowed in the country. An enormous international airport is under construction, as a way of leapfrogging Rwanda's isolated central African geography. Fiber-optic data cables are being laid for the same purpose.

Also at the behest of the state, neatly uniformed women daily sweep the streets of the capital, Kigali, just as they might sweep the dust from their own homes. Even the informal-sector industries that are the backbone of African economies have been brought under the reins of the state. Motorcycle taxi drivers wear reflective vests, and they carry identification cards and a spare helmet for their passenger. Crime is nonexistent.

The level of organization and control is audacious — and even more so given the country's brutal history and particularly forsaken real estate. Rwanda is landlocked and poor, with no natural resources to speak of. Ten percent of the country was killed in the genocide, hundreds of thousands more people were forced into refugee camps, and those who were left were barely alive, inside and out. An entire generation of orphans needed homes. There was no central bank, no auditor general, and no school syllabus. Archives and documents were irretrievably destroyed, and there was no institutional memory. The fleeing Hutu militias crouched on the Congolese border threatened to return and finish what they had started.

But as with other appearances of *kanju,* the devastation and uncertainty produced a significant upside. Today, for example, the country has the highest proportion of female lawmakers in the world. Women run the ministries of foreign affairs, agriculture, and health. The same goes for the speaker of Parliament, the vice president of the Senate, and the president's chief of staff. This is one positive aspect of the genocide, after which female survivors found themselves alone, with a country to rebuild — and skills to contribute. "That's the secret of the nation building in Rwanda; it's the women, it's the youth, it's the marginalized groups," said Aloysia Inyumba, the loyalist, no-nonsense gender minister who passed away in 2012. While Rwandan society is still deeply bound up in the genocide, the destruction of 1994 allowed for a partial "reset" of the social compact. It allowed Rwanda to start from scratch.

In all of my travels in the region, government has been seen as an ambiguous, often mistrusted, and mostly irrelevant participant in everyday life. By contrast, the Rwandans I spoke with — CEOs and farmers, government ministers and expatriate missionaries — are relentlessly upbeat. Many are eager to shape a new reputation for Rwanda. Few expressed anger or bitterness about the past. Somewhat eerily, multiple people told me that "the best revenge is success." "They're doing all these kinds of things that are extremely unusual," says Manzi Kayihura, the one-time head of Rwandair, the national airline. "I traveled over Christmas. There's a card that comes back from the immigration guy: 'We wish you a joyous festive season and we hope to see you soon.' It's just so different."

In Kigali, I stopped by the Rwanda Development Board, the government agency responsible for building Rwanda's private sector. Its claim to fame is the ability to register a business in twenty-four hours or less. (In fail states, the process can take up to a year or more.) At the RDB, I met Pasquale Karambisi, a lanky Congolese trader who was registering his export-import business — thereby committing himself to paying taxes in Rwanda. This was novel; Karambisi was swimming against the flow of most small firms in Africa. He justified it as good business: "Here there is security — even if there are taxes. In Congo, there is not."

This gets at one of the key justifications for loyalty to a central government: stability. Compared with the DRC, where tribalism, nepotism, patronage, and rent seeking pervade the political parties and the bureaucracy, and bursts of violence toss refugees across borders with galling frequency, Rwanda's bland competence is a virtue. Betty Mutesi, who works with the finance ministry on the MDGs, drew a direct link between a bleak past and a bright future: "If you are running away from something, will you run faster? I think so."

Whatever the causation, power and legitimacy are combined in an unusual way in Rwanda. For all of its scrappy successes, Somaliland is still not a state. For its hard-won partition and new nationhood, South Sudan is still years away from a stable, prosperous existence. Even South Africa, following the triumph of its liberation struggle, has deep developmental problems and still-damning racial divisions.

Today, Rwandan people want their government to work and, more importantly, trust that it will. "Government is to serve the people. The people now know that and they demand it," says Clare Akamanzi, head of the Rwanda Development Board. At thirty-two years old, she is emblematic of the new boss — responsive, eager, and sharp. On occasion, she has been personally called out of her office by constituents with complaints. "When they see that you're consistent about corruption, when they see you're consistent about economic development, when they see they have more to eat than they have ever had, when you see all this construction happening, when you see more houses in Kigali, that hope makes everybody energetic," she says.

The most energetic of all Rwandans may be Paul Kagame, the rebel leader who stopped the genocide and now serves as president. He was first elected in 2003 with a reported 95 percent of the vote. Previously, he had been a kind of shadow CEO, first as national liberator, then vice president, and then, beginning in 2000, unelected president. His personality casts the longest shadow in Rwanda. Locals joke that he is treated as George Washington, Abraham Lincoln, and Barack Obama rolled into one. His critics would point to flashes of Mugabe and Mussolini, too.

The reputation is not unwarranted — since marching his guerrillas from Uganda into the Rwandan capital, Kagame has been exceptionally canny and nimble in his reconstruction efforts. He's a magpie for innovation — he was one of the first lean economy leaders to bite at the controversial One Laptop Per Child program. He takes to the hustings regularly to explain and defend novel national policies like One Cow Per Poor Family. He is a vociferous user of Twitter and is also easily spotted at global events like the World Economic Forum at Davos or the Clinton Global Initiative in New York. He is the only African head of state with a personal website. "He is very committed and serious, very unlike the traditional leaders who are in Africa," said Inyumba.

"This is a president who will challenge you, who will demand accountability, who will emphasize doing things right."

Thus, the banned plastic bags are screened for at the airport as
though they were shipments of cocaine. The government mandates
umuganda — a ritual monthly cleaning of public streets and construction of homes. To prevent a *Système D* from evolving, the imposing
Rwanda Revenue Authority is among the largest, most visible buildings in Kigali, and the fines for shirking tax payments are fierce — 10
percent of the bill if it's a day late. Like Akamanzi, the bureaucracy
is impossibly young, bright-eyed, and hardworking, showing up to
their offices seven days a week. Contrary to the fail state tradition of
recycling familiar political dynasties and repeat players, turnover in
the ministries is high. Rwandan bureaucrats "don't confuse their positions with their persons," says Kayihura. "Six months down the road,
if you're not performing, you're out." Massive billboards remind the
population that there will be "zero tolerance" for corruption.

Over time, the Rwandan state has provided an unexpected disruption to stale development habits — often deploying *kanju* logic within
the state itself. Kiosks in Kigali offer free Internet access for any resident. A Ministry of Health program called Rapid SMS enables monitoring of maternal health from pregnancy until fourteen days after
birth. Community health workers gather text messages from families
in labor and pass word of the most urgent cases directly to district
hospitals. According to Denis Murenzi, director of information and
communications technology for the Ministry of Health, the deployment worked all the better after the government gave every community health worker a mobile phone.

Rwanda used the Family Map to dispense justice in the wake of
the genocide. In the days of cleanup in 1994 through 2000, the gutted judicial system had processed only 3,500 out of some 130,000 accused criminals. The international tribunals that have since built cases
against the worst of the *génocidaires* could not have handled the burden of prosecution for the tens of thousands of small-scale murderers.
Into the breach came *gacaca*, a traditional system of dispute resolution
in which elders resolve conflicts "on the grass." There was no impunity:

criminals confessed in exchange for more lenient sentencing, and survivors received a modicum of catharsis. The docket was cleared in ten
years. While the controversial system has provoked criticism from advocates for more traditional Western justice, to Akamanzi the calculus
was obvious: "Do we innovate with what we have or do we risk never
having justice?"

It was jarring to hear this call to *kanju* from the mouth of government. But Kagame has justifiable suspicions about the official global
institutions and protocols that, in 1994, left Rwanda to die. While he
has sent bureaucratic envoys abroad to see how other systems solve
problems, his government has also rejected the basic power disparities
in the donor economy. Kagame has started a domestic development
fund to get Rwandan individuals and companies to fund Rwanda's social needs. Though almost half of the budget still comes from foreign
donations, today, Kayihura says, "the smart thing Rwanda is doing is
saying, 'If you give us aid, we want to do this with it.' Traditionally they
come to you and say, 'We want to build you a bridge.' And they say, 'No,
we don't want a bridge, we want a school.'"

Alongside Rwanda's unusual stance on aid and public service provision comes an unusual focus on private-sector development. A sign
at the RDB offices promotes the corporate mentality in government:
"Welcome to Rwanda: We value our customers." The analogy is not
so far-fetched. Just as the consumer relationship promotes accountability, Rwanda sees its citizens and investors as clients and prides itself enormously on its performance in the World Bank's "ease of doing
business" rankings. In 2013, the government successfully issued a $400
million bond to international investors at an enviably low interest rate.
While the population and capital needs are too small to register on the
radar of multinationals, the RDB greases the wheels for any company
that does choose to play in Rwanda.

Perhaps obviously, dealing with the psychological fallout from the
genocide has been the trickiest part of governing post-conflict Rwanda. National unification has required actively considered deracination
— something other political systems in Africa still struggle to promote.
Today, even mentioning the two dominant "ethnic groups," Hutu and

Tutsi, is a major taboo. The best trained call the cleavages "divisions," not ethnicities. This is a reversion to proper form — Belgian ethnographic scientists arbitrarily assigned Rwandans to the groups based on superficialities like height and skin color. But it is also a shrewd way of cementing the national identity. A well-placed diplomatic observer told me that hypersensitivity to ethnic favoritism has made Rwanda's government nominally more inclusive.

To speed Rwanda's process of reinvention, Kagame has adopted a philosophy of *agaciro*, a Kinyarwanda word for self-reliance and dignity. "The *agaciro* I often talk of is about fighting for our integrity and our future," he said at a leadership retreat in 2010. At a regional youth development conference in Kampala, he pronounced, "It is when you have that dignity and are prepared to protect it that you will make inventions that answer our circumstances."

The hospital-corners approach has had mixed results. Rwanda has made comparative gains in traditional MDG indicators like maternal mortality, HIV prevalence, and primary school enrollment (for whatever it's worth), as well as private metrics like banking services and the number of days it takes to enforce a contract. But clean water and sanitation still elude four in ten rural Rwandans, and the nation has miles to go before its stated goal of "middle-income" status (per capita income is about $1,200 a year).

The loyalty model carries promises and pitfalls, and Rwanda's political culture is a good example of both. Reporters like to call tiny Rwanda "the Singapore of Africa." The country has indeed aped east Asian "tigers" that have surged from poverty to prosperity. But the real similarities are less flattering: the state is heavily involved in all walks of Rwandan life, with harsh controls over public behavior and information flows. Political institutions are weak, and a growing autocracy and a cult of personality swirl around Kagame.

The president who trained as an intelligence officer in the Ugandan army, in Cuba, and in the United States before leading the Rwandan Patriotic Front from guerrilla status to ruling party is, to be blunt, paranoid. Speaking ill of Kagame has been punished with arrests among local journalists — among the least free on the continent. Rwanda has jailed individuals for failing to attend national days of remembrance. Since Kagame's first election, anti-opposition crackdowns and allegations of vote rigging and vote suppression have been whispered and sometimes shouted. His military adventurism in Africa's Great Lakes region is directly responsible for toppling Mobutu in 1997, and special forces under his command have destabilized the neighboring DRC ever since. The UN has released a series of damning reports about Kagame's long-running inflammation of regional armed conflict.

As much as he represents the visionary leadership of which so many in the region have felt starved, Kagame also embodies the dangers of earlier strongmen in Africa. A young lawyer who travels between Rwanda and Uganda (where Kagame's old friend Yoweri Museveni has been in power since 1986) reminded me that "in Kampala, people can criticize the president on the radio. Here, you get to the airport and people just stop talking."

Despite underlying frailties, loyalty persists — Kagame was re-elected in 2010 with 93 percent of the vote. (In 2017, term limits will force the first real test of this remarkable do-over.) In Rwanda as in Somaliland, the specter of vulnerability in a bad neighborhood produces a strong urge for stability at all costs. Stephen Kinzer's excellent book on Kagame and the genocide helps to explain why few Rwandans have contested the growing autocracy. Pre-1994, "organizations of civil society in Rwanda were deeply compliant with the authoritarian, centralized system, with seemingly little capacity to question Government decisions and directives." Outside of a gutted civil society, "most are miserably poor agro-pastoralists whose hopes are concentrated on essentials like security, work, and food. Many find the idea of competitive politics terrifying. Their only experience of it was during the final period of the Habyarimana dictatorship, and it brought catastrophe. Few are eager to try again."

Of course, fearful acceptance is a far cry from true loyalty. Durable trust in any form of authority is best earned and driven by social norms first. Individuals must identify with rules and believe them worthy of collective obedience. In this conception of loyalty, the people wield power. Mahmood Mamdani, the Ugandan academic, puts it thus: "The real custodian of democratic order was never the state but society."

But local social norms are hard to pin down. Formal and informal frameworks present complex codes and languages that most people in Africa toggle between daily. In an effort to answer the question, researchers from Stanford and the Center for Global Development constructed a market test.

The experiment began because there are technically two legal systems in Liberia. The end of its civil war saw a host of new formal laws and statutes passed. At the same time, the country's "Hinterland Regulations" recognize the continuing existence and influence of customary courts that empower community leaders to act as judges. (Plural regimes also exist in Uganda, where "resistance councils" have had the right to manage police, health, justice, education, and other public services since 1986, and in South Africa, where local tribal and community courts handle disputes in a similar fashion. Somaliland's unusual parliamentary arrangement adopts voting and bicameral legislation but also uses traditional clan structures of conflict resolution.)

Between filing and lawyers' fees, petty bribes, transportation to and from remote courts, and even food for the incarcerated awaiting a hearing, formal justice in Liberia is costly. But informal legal fixes aren't necessarily any better. The study architects determined that customary courts in Liberia and elsewhere in Africa can be "expensive, corrupted, discriminatory, and administered by local judges who have poor knowledge of the law." As Mamdani notes, customary authorities may care more about enforcing traditions than supporting rights.

This dual arrangement enabled the researchers to track the choices of parties to more than 4,500 conflicts in Liberia, using interviews with six hundred community-based paralegals who mediated between the two systems.* Like nurse practitioners who "task shift" to cover

---

* The participants with paralegals were much happier with the outcome of their disputes, and more likely to choose the dual system over the customary system alone. There's some indication that the paralegals decreased incidences of bribery.

more rural patients, the paralegals made counsel accessible across the hinterland — reaching their destinations on motorbikes at times.

Faced with land and debt disputes, petty and serious crimes, or family disagreements, some parties chose customary law, and others chose to pursue recourse in the official judicial system. Mostly, everybody valued expedience over ideology. Liberians chose the system they believed would produce a more favorable judgment. It's why some socially powerless women chose the formal system when pursuing cases against men. Those without status thought the formal law would be more objective.

But the final tally showed *in*formality bias: 38 percent of disputes were taken to the customary system, but just 4 percent ended up in the formal system. Another whopping 58 percent of disputes went unreported entirely, resolved by the parties to the dispute themselves. Just as many Africans choose private health care or "private school," many Liberians opted for private law.

Many more people chose the informal system because it better reflected abstract social priorities. Where formal legal systems are designed for punishment that "provides little or no material or social gain," the customary courts emphasize restitution, flexibility, and the well-being of a broader community. Victims turned out to be less interested in discipline than in being made whole for the crime. This pragmatism favored the customary courts. In one illustrative case, a young man killed another in a hunting accident; rather than sending him to jail and rupturing the social bonds of the community, the uncle of the deceased ended up convincing both families to settle for a sacrifice of livestock and a solemn toast.

What's remarkable about the two Liberian "publics" is their interchangeability. At any given time, people can leap from one system to another. If a customary judgment is ignored, parties can pursue formal — and presumably more enforceable — remedies. Official disputes that become financially or socially costly can likewise exit the formal framework and return to community courts.

Around the world, these "two publics" are more than simultaneous — they are fundamentally codependent. The one requires the other.

Some social or market-based norms, or what economist Avinash Dixit calls "private government," depend on the existence of laws, from
import restrictions to license plates to a stable currency. Likewise,
some laws, like the Bretton Woods agreement that stabilized global
exchange rates (for a time), or the municipal regulations that fix the
price of a taxi, derive from pragmatic, informal trade practices. Both
laws and norms inform everyday decision making.

But this reliance varies greatly by world region. Fat economies tend
toward greater formality and stronger laws. A German car maker, for
example, relies on contract laws and powerful courts that ensure investments will be executed. Customers rely on safety and emissions
regulations to protect passengers and reduce energy consumption,
and public-sector roads to drive on. In Africa, reliance on the fail state
is weaker. In fact, some ventures need only the loosest of rules and
thinnest of supports. "It's not about direct intervention and regulation
— you will remove all their creativity," says Obiageli Ezekwesili, the
former Nigerian education minister who now leads an institute committed to building private-sector capacity. "For some of these transport or retail ventures, all you need is a good road for them. Their
productivity will skyrocket."

This perspective joins an ongoing debate over the proper role and
reach of government the world over. It has been nearly twenty years
since *The End of the Nation-State*, in which Jean-Marie Guéhenno
proclaimed it "time to realize that the idea of the nation that Europe
gave to the world is perhaps only an ephemeral political form, a European exception, a precarious transition between the age of kings and
the 'neoimperial' age." He argued that economic modernity and previously unthinkable mobility trump political modernity, that "the nation
appears increasingly like a straitjacket, poorly adapted to the growing
integration of the world."

He made the point well before the juggernaut of globalization
brought Latin America, Asia, and now Africa into a moment of simul-
taneity (if not equality) with fat economies. Since then, legacy monopolies on force and influence — cultural, military, and economic — have

largely evaporated. A glance about contemporary Africa captures the shift: Turkish airliners, French telecoms, and Brazilian private equity funds find as much relevance in the region as American Peace Corps volunteers or Chinese day laborers.

It may be easy to read this book as a libertarian celebration of hustling, hacking, and free-form development in sub-Saharan Africa. And it is. Rwanda's strong state is the exception, and not the rule. Public institutions are not maturing at the pace that the region deserves. Some goods, like safety and security, justice and rights to land and water, are the traditional domain of state actors. But development necessities such as health care, electricity, and education flourish outside the reach of the African state — and even roads and sanitation are increasingly the province of private ambition. There is a pronounced gap between smaller forms of organization that provide structure, finance, and services, and the political institutions that frequently fail to do the same.

The region desperately needs recognition and support for the role of informal ties, between families, businesses, landholders, young people, and information neighborhoods on- and offline. These powerful forms of affiliation have been marvelously resistant to the state cartography and bureaucracy that grid and divide the world. Understanding and accepting *kanju* will be exciting and transformative for global decision making.

But closing the gap also depends on hybrid commitments, from both "publics." The Liberia study concludes that incorporating elements of formal law into informal structures, and vice versa, is a low-cost alternative to rigid formalism, with far greater potential for legitimacy. The same "open-source" mentality can be applied to other areas of development practice. Achille Mbembe calls for an "entanglement," an effort "to account for time *as lived* . . . in its multiplicity and simultaneities, its presences and absences, beyond the lazy categories of permanence and change." Innovations that build on both institutional and informal frameworks may be doubly effective.

The United Nations, for an unexpected example, has launched a project called Global Pulse that seeks to mine data in order to predict economic shocks. If, for example, an individual has been purchasing mobile phone airtime in denominations of $10 every month and suddenly begins to purchase denominations of $1 every week, the Global Pulse model might treat the shift as a sign of pinched income and step up a local school feeding program. If cattle begin showing up on markets (live or virtual) several weeks ahead of the season — and for below-market rates — it's another sign of stress. Online searches for "banana rot" or "jobs in France" are similar canaries in the mine.

The program is grounded in a recognition of past malpractice. In 2008 — at the height of the food, fuel, and financial crisis — governments and development agencies around the world stood flat-footed as millions of people slipped back below the poverty line. Instead of sending bureaucrats to compile interviews with select households, or waiting for local governments to spit out household income, rainfall, or maternal death statistics, Global Pulse tries to read between the lines and act fast. By mining ambient data and passing on what is learned, the team seeks to strengthen development responses. The first of the "Pulse Labs" will be in Kampala, Uganda.

While limited in scope, similar open government and transparency movements have emerged to insist that basic information be shared among the center and the periphery. The governments of Kenya, Liberia, South Africa, Tanzania, and Ghana have committed to posting full government data sets online. The initiatives work better with an assist from civil society. Uwezo, an east African transparency organization, has been conducting a national education survey that goes beyond schools and into homes where some students had been left behind.

Some aid agencies and philanthropies leverage their grants as startup capital for market solutions. New "public-private partnerships" fund products and processes rather than handing out basic necessities. USAID's pilot policy of loan guarantees, for example, looks more like the vision for capital discussed in Chapter 7. The World Bank, which generally sees more balance between markets and states, has created a "development marketplace" that solicits ideas through competition. The ten-year-old project is global, but in Africa it has funded projects like Seeds for Needs, designed to match female farmers in

Ethiopia with locally adapted seed varieties that can improve yields and bolster traditional efforts to mitigate the effects of climate change. In contrast to the mega-millions disbursed to governments (in 2011, Ethiopia received some $3.8 billion in official assistance), this grant was just $200,000.

Slowly, some of the biggest battleships in global philanthropy are trying to turn things around. Jim Yong Kim, the newest World Bank president, was plucked from Partners in Health, one of the least deductive and most effective global charities in operation. Shanta Devarajan, chief Africa economist at the World Bank, argues that in an age of "Development 3.0," we must see the poor "as monitors and analysts as well as recipients of government assistance." A recent, anonymous World Bank report noted that "creative thinking is needed to find alternatives to nation states, that can incorporate indigenous African forms and traditions of governance." The writer's recommendation? "Looser political arrangements, to enable greater autonomy in divided societies."

While the World Bank and other institutions haven't always followed through on the suggestion, these looser arrangements have the virtue of reverting to a less determined map of Africa. In the future, regional political bodies like the African Union may enforce common rules of the road for transport, trade, technology, and security without strangling innovation, or enabling the tribal, issue-free politics of the present. AU reform will require an overhaul of Dlamini-Zuma's closed-off approach. But past diplomatic successes — the quashing of an attempted power grab in Togo, for example — offer a template for a lean, inclusive, pan-African framework, perhaps like the Schengen zone established in Europe.

Smaller bodies such as the Southern African Development Community, the Economic Community of West African States, and the East African Community can also give shape to norms, duties, and affiliations that have always been transnational. The principle of strength in numbers applies: more expansive borders allow for wider migration and capital flows. Regional stock exchanges may strengthen the commercial viability of emerging businesses. More African workers can determine their own path of best opportunity.

W. B. Yeats wrote in his poem "The Second Coming" that "the centre cannot hold." Across Africa, it turns out that the center never was. And only when the dust from the half-century of inauthentic fail states clears will a dynamic, assured, post-national public shine through.

We are beginning to see a host of hybrid institutions that work in Africa to improve lives. The lean techniques and talents of the periphery are creeping closer to the center. Large institutions playing in Africa are beginning to use more *kanju* tools to reach the periphery. The most innovative development initiatives are harder to characterize as public or private.

Sometimes the new maps are literal. When Google passed over Kibera, the citizens struck back with the perfect balance of engagement and independence. Kepha Ngito, one of Kibera's estimated 170,000 residents, reminded me that his neighborhood "hasn't been recognized by the government or anybody else. They still think of it as a forest" —the English word for Kibera. Indeed, the official Survey of Kenya has neither the capacity nor the energy to trace the slum's constantly changing infrastructure and economy. Even a special urban planning team from the University of Nairobi threw up their hands, classifying Kibera's jangle of kiosks and tin homes as broadly "residential."

Against this logic, committed residents like Ngito, armed with simple GPS devices and Open Street Map—a sort of geographic Wikipedia—created not only a detailed online map of Kibera, but a business and services directory for the residents. In addition to mapping Kibera's built environment, digital atlases layer information on health, education, security, and land use. If you want to know which clinic offers free immunizations, how many trained teachers are at a given school, or which streetlights are operational, Map Kibera will tell you. It's Yelp for development.

The map epitomizes the new narrative of twenty-first-century Africa. It defines a universe smaller than the state—as well as a larger,

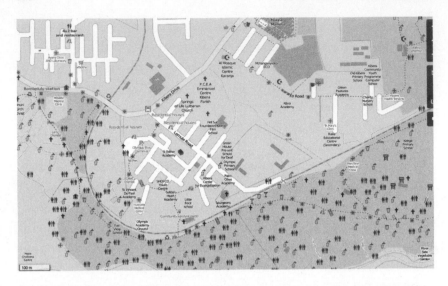

Map Kibera offers a detailed cartography of Nairobi's largest informal settlement,
layering information about amenities and living conditions
atop an open-source, community-edited map.

potentially global community, invited into the map on the residents'
terms. As such, it's a useful model for anyone who cares about making
it in Africa: students, religious NGOs, smallholder farmers, fledgling
businesses, booming corporations, and small-scale social entrepreneurs trying to make a difference.

But in modern Africa, scale is everything. Even as ordinary people
rewrite stale cartography, we need allies. Good ideas that languish in
local clinics or tech hubs will never reach their generative potential.
These ideas are borne along diverse and complementary vectors: family, technology, commerce, nature, and youth. Like the motorcycle
taxis bringing word of change across Lagos, our maps help bridge the
two publics. They can accelerate traditional efforts to build wealth,
strengthen formal institutions, and aid the least fortunate. These maps
change the equation for what is possible. And in most cases, their only
subsidy is their utility to ordinary people. Compared with "stuff we
don't want," they are elementary ingredients of Africa's bright future.

ACKNOWLEDGMENTS

THANKS FIRST AND forever to my family, especially my parents, Sola and Funmi — who every day define what it means to be both good and great. I honor your wisdom and cherish your trust. This book could not be without you. To my siblings, Feyi and Tobi: you are my first friends, best teachers, and vice versa. I am so lucky to have you, and four generations of Olopades and Falusis, at my back. I am grateful for your exuberance and your example.

Thank you to the brilliant teachers and mentors who prepared me for this task, especially Jada Hebra, Mark Oppenheimer, Ann Biersteker, Fred Strebeigh, Jill Abramson, Caryl Phillips, Elizabeth Alexander, Mike Vazquez, and Skip Gates.

Thank you to the people and publications who took a flyer on me as a young writer in Washington. I'm grateful to Frank Foer at *The New Republic;* Lynette Clemetson, Donna Byrd, and Jacob Weisberg at *The Root;* Tina Brown at *The Daily Beast;* and Steve Coll and Andres Martinez at the New America Foundation, for the long leash. I likewise thank my many talented editors, and the generation of inspiring fellow journalists who trained alongside me in the DC gymnasium.

From the day I landed in Kenya it felt like home. Thank you to my Nairobi family for your commitment to adventure, your patient instruction, and countless Tuskers. Special thanks to Nneka Eze and Walter Lamberson, who saw it all. I appreciate you in advance.

Reporting this book was a village effort. Thank you to my tipsters, sherpas, real-talkers, and fellow travelers: Tope, Tayo, Ibukun, and Tade Abidoye, Rebecca Abou-Chedid, Dupe and Konyin Ajayi, Semhar Araia, Elizabeth Ashamu, Bibi Bakare-Yusuf and Jeremy Weate, Rick

Bennet, Elana Berkowitz, Richard Brooks, Jon Castro, Teresa Clark, Jessica Colaco, Will Connors, Robbie Corey-Boulet, Laurent Corthay, Eme Essien, Eve Fairbanks, Howard French, Ann Friedman, Rachel Gichinga, Dana Goldstein, Serigne Gueye, Fitsum Hagos, Christopher Hayes, Erik Hersman, Angelo Izama, Paul Matiru Kago, Mary Catherine Lader, Jonathan Ledgard, Stefan Magdalinski, Mike McKay, Katherine Michonski, Jacqueline Muna Musiitwa, Marlene Ngoyi, Isis Nyong'o, Emeka Okafor, Ory Okolloh, Sasha Polakow-Suransky, Dupe Pupoola, Alec Ross, Teddy Ruge, Reihan Salam, Nicholas Schmidle, Anne-Marie Slaughter, Faith Smith, Aminatou Sow, Farah Stockman, Suraj Sudhakhar, Angela Wachuka, Binyavanga Wainaina, Tim Wu, Andrew Youn, Bill Zimmerman, Jamie Zimmerman, and Ethan Zuckerman. I owe you great ideas.

Thank you to the team that believed me when I said I had a book to write: my stylish and superlative agents, Howard Yoon and Gail Ross, and Deanne Urmy for her early encouragement. Special thanks to my gifted editor, Courtney Young, and research assistant, Sarah Yager. You massaged every phrase and chased down the trickiest facts with grace.

Thank you to the institutions who made this ambition possible: the New America Foundation, the Rockefeller Foundation, the German Marshall Fund, the Yale Journalism Initiative, and the Yale Law School.

Thanks most to everyone who agreed to share their stories with me. And to Chinua Achebe, who insisted, "If you don't like someone's story, write your own."

NOTES

FRONTMATTER

viii *A man who uses an imaginary map:* E. F. Schumacher, *Small Is Beautiful: Economics as If People Mattered* (Harper Perennial, 1973).

1. ORIENTATION

1 *"I am astonished":* Herodotus, *The History of Herodotus,* 440 BCE, trans. George Rawlinson.

2 *At the time of Speke's trip:* Alan Moorhead, *The White Nile* (Penguin, 1965), 124.

12 *Abundance is the average:* All gross national income figures in this section are from the World Bank.

13 *The Umande Trust:* "Bio-centres Change the Lives of Locals," *The Standard* (Kenya), March 9, 2009.

15 *Don't get bogged down with precise descriptions:* Binyavanga Wainaina, "How to Write About Africa," *Granta* 92 (Winter 2005).

2. KANJU

17 *From 1995 to 1998:* "$242m 419 Scam Trial Collapses," *The Register* (UK), July 20, 2004; and Benjamin Weiser, "Nigerian Accused in Scheme to Swindle Citibank," *The New York Times,* February 20, 2009.
Secretary of state Colin Powell: "Colin Powell Digs African Hip Hop," BBC News, October 15, 2008.

19 *"I come from a poor family in Lagos, Nigeria":* "Interview with a Scammer Part One," ScamDetectives.co.uk, January 22, 2010.
"I know from my own education": Daniel Morrow, "Excerpts From an Oral History Interview with Steve Jobs," Smithsonian Institution, April 20, 2005.
Academic writer Louis Chude-Sokei: Louis Chude-Sokei, "Invisible Missive Magnetic Juju: On African Cybercrime," The Fanzine, October 24, 2010.

22 *Political scientist Joel Migdal:* Joel Migdal, *Strong Societies and Weak States: State-Society Relations and State Capabilities in the Third World* (Princeton University Press, 1988).

22 *Dutch architect and planner Rem Koolhaas:* Bregtje van der Haak with Rem Koolhaas, interview, "Lagos Wide and Close," July 5, 2002.

23 *The local film industry . . . universally low budget:* Norimitsu Onishi, "Step Aside, L.A. and Bombay, for Nollywood," *The New York Times,* September 16, 2002. See also Mridul Chowdhury et al., "Nollywood: The Nigerian Film Industry," Harvard Business School and Harvard Kennedy School, May 2, 2008.

26 *deep, neurobiological roots:* Laurie Leitch and Loree Sutton, "The Missing Link: The Biology of Human Resilience," Threshold Global Networks, April 2012.

27 *Author Paul Tough:* Paul Tough, "What If the Secret to Success Is Failure?" *The New York Times Magazine,* September 18, 2011.

29 *the informal economy experience:* David Lingelbach et al., "What's Distinctive About Growth-Oriented Entrepreneurship in Developing Countries?" UTSA College of Business Center for Global Entrepreneurship Working Paper No. 1, March 2005.
    Globally, the gray economy: TheInformalEconomy.com.
    a study by the Institute for Liberty and Democracy: "Country Diagnosis: Lagos, Nigeria," Institute for Liberty and Democracy, 2009. www.ild.org.pe.

30 *Steve Daniels in his book* Making Do: Steve Daniels, *Making Do: Innovation in Kenya's Informal Economy* (Analogue Digital, 2010), 19.

31 *A story on bad flour:* Nicholas Schmidle, "Smuggler, Forger, Writer, Spy," *The Atlantic,* October 4, 2010.

3. FAIL STATES

36 *Sixty percent of the government's budget:* "Draft Somaliland National Development Plan (NDP) 2012–2016," Somaliland Ministry of National Planning and Development, October 2011.

37 *living without foreign aid and intervention:* Nicholas Eubank, "Taxation, Political Accountability, and Foreign Aid: Lessons from Somaliland," Stanford Graduate School of Business, March 26, 2011. See also Mary Harper, *Getting Somalia Wrong? Faith, War and Hope in a Shattered State* (Zed Books, 2012).

38 *Ghanaian George Ayittey:* George Ayittey, *Africa in Chaos: A Comparative History* (Palgrave Macmillan, 1997).

39 *In Swaziland:* "Strikers Demand Democracy and Pay Raises in Swaziland," *The New York Times,* August 1, 2012.

40 *even the judicial institutions:* Joseph M. Isanga, "Rethinking the Rule of Law as Antidote to African Development Challenges," in *Legitimacy, Legal Development and Change: Law and Modernization Reconsidered,* ed. David K. Linnen, 59–80 (Ashgate Publishing, 2012).
    In Malawi, for example: WikiLeaks cable 05ROME3782 (2005-11-16), USUN ROME TRIP REPORT SOUTHERN AFRICA OCTOBER 13–20, 2005.

41 *In his cheekily titled* Lawlessness and Economics: Avinash K. Dixit, *Lawlessness and Economics: Alternative Modes of Governance* (Princeton University Press, 2004).

44 *Eighty years later, the Organization of African Unity:* Organization of African Unity Secretariat, "Resolutions Adopted by the First Ordinary Session of the Assembly of Heads of State and Government Held in Cairo, UAR, From 17 to 21 July 1964."

Seventy-three percent of households in Africa: Pierre Englebert, *State Legitimacy and Development in Africa* (Lynne Rienner Publishers, 2000), 47.

"part-time" refugees: Mary Schenkel, "Congo-Kinshasa: Part-Time Refugees Commute Between Congo and Uganda," Radio Netherlands Worldwide, June 18, 2012.

45 *Across Africa, Englebert notes:* Englebert, *State Legitimacy and Development in Africa,* 77.

46 *"extractive" institutions:* Daron Acemoğlu and James Robinson, *Why Nations Fail: The Origins of Power, Prosperity, and Poverty* (Crown Business, 2012).

In far smaller Sierra Leone: Robert Bates, *When Things Fell Apart: State Failure in Late-Century Africa* (Cambridge University Press, 2008), 102.

47 *in every year that a single African political party:* Ann E. Harrison, Justin Yifu Lin, and L. Colin Xu, "Explaining Africa's (Dis)advantage," NBER Working Paper No. 18683, January 2013.

The African National Congress: Eve Fairbanks, "You Have All the Reasons to Be Angry," *The New Republic,* March 4, 2013.

Since the 1990s, aid interventions: Stephen Knack, "Does Foreign Aid Promote Democracy?" Munich Personal RePEc Archive, July 1, 2003.

48 *Morgan Tsvangirai:* Brian Hungwe, "Has Zimbabwe's Morgan Tsvangirai Been Tarnished by Power?" BBC News, July 28, 2013.

Take GDP: Abhijit Banerjee and Esther Duflo, "Growth Theory Through the Lens of Development Economics," Massachusetts Institute of Technology, 2004. See also Alwyn Young, "The African Growth Miracle," draft paper, London School of Economics, August 2012; Laura Gray, "How to Boost GDP by 60%," BBC News, December 8, 2012; and Morten Jerven, "Lies, Damn Lies, and GDP," *The Guardian* (UK), November 20, 2012.

49 *Incumbents in Kenya:* Edwin Mutai, "Treasury Releases Sh10bn Balance for CDF Projects," *Business Daily* (Kenya), January 2, 2013.

50 *"Everywhere," writes Achille Mbembe:* Bates, *When Things Fell Apart,* 53.

51 *In "Bangladesh":* Will Ruddick, "Bangla-Pesa Turmoil," Koru Kenya, June 3, 2013; and Ritchie King, "Kenyan Authorities Are Mistaking a New Local Currency for a Separatist Movement," Quartz, June 11, 2013.

4. STUFF WE DON'T WANT

52 *Jason Sadler:* Nick Wadhams, "Bad Charity? (All I Got Was This Lousy T-Shirt!)," *Time,* May 12, 2010.

Investor and philanthropist Jacqueline Novogratz: Jacqueline Novogratz, *The Blue Sweater: Bridging the Gap Between Rich and Poor in an Interconnected World* (Rodale, 2009), 3.

53 *secondhand clothes are bad for business:* Garth Frazer, "Used-Clothing Dona-
tions and Apparel Production in Africa," *The Economic Journal,* October 2008.
See also Sally Baden and Catherine Barber, "The Impact of the Second-hand
Clothing Trade on Developing Countries," Oxfam, September 2005; and Laura
Seay, "Why World Vision's Free T-Shirts Will Hurt the Poor," EthicsDaily.com,
February 24, 2011.

colorful names for the secondhand swag: Meri Nana-Ama Danquah, "Dead
White People's Clothes," The Root, March 5, 2009.

Kenyan economist James Shikwati: "For God's Sake, Please Stop the Aid!" interview with *Der Spiegel International,* July 4, 2005.

SWEDOW: "#SWEDOW," Tales From the Hood, April 20, 2010.

TOMS Shoes: Richard Stupart, "The 7 Worst International Aid Ideas," Matador
Network, February 20, 2012. See also "FHI 360 announces that Kenya will be
the second country to participate in TOMS Shoe-Giving initiative," Press Release, August 16, 2013.

55 *In an open letter to Sadler:* Mariéme Jamme, "Another Bad Aid Idea for Africa,"
MariemeJamme.com, April 30, 2010.

Zambian economist Dambisa Moyo: Dambisa Moyo, *Dead Aid: Why Aid Is Not
Working and How There Is a Better Way for Africa* (Macmillan, 2009), 27.

56 *Most international NGOs:* Nancy Birdsall and Homi Kharas, "Quality of Official
Development Assistance Assessment (2010)," Center for Global Development,
October 2010.

57 *per capita income decreased:* Moyo, *Dead Aid.*

aid flows are inversely related to government function: Deborah Bräutigam, "Aid
Dependence and Governance," Expert Group on Development Issues, 2000.
See also C. Lu, M. T. Schneider, P. Gubbins, K. Leach-Kemon, D. Jamison, and
C.J.L. Murray, "Public Financing of Health in Developing Countries: A Cross-
National Systematic Analysis," *The Lancet,* April 17, 2010.

In exchange for World Bank aid: Paul Collier, *The Bottom Billion: Why the Poorest Countries Are Failing and What Can Be Done About It* (Oxford University
Press, 2007), 109.

58 *"D.I.Y. Foreign-Aid Revolution":* Nicholas Kristof, "D.I.Y. Foreign-Aid Revolution," *The New York Times Magazine,* October 20, 2010.

59 *The simplistic narrative:* Michael Wilkerson, "Joseph Kony Is Not in Uganda
(and Other Complicated Things)," *Foreign Policy* 7 (March 2012).

60 *"armchair cynics":* Nicholas Kristof, "Viral Video, Vicious Warlord," *The New
York Times,* March 14, 2012.

"White Savior Industrial Complex": Teju Cole, "The White Savior Industrial
Complex," *The Atlantic,* March 21, 2012.

Millennium Development Declaration: United Nations Resolution A/RES/55/2,
"United Nations Millennium Declaration," September 18, 2000. See also UNDP
Human Development Report 2003, *Millennium Development Goals: A Com-
pact Among Nations to End Poverty* (Oxford University Press, 2003).

61 *African countries have been sprinting toward this goal: Africa Renewal/Afrique Renouveau* 24, nos. 2–3 (August 2010): 4.
more-in-sorrow-than-in-anger analysis: Jeff Waage et al., "The Millennium Development Goals: A Cross-Sectoral Analysis and Principles for Goal Setting After 2015," *The Lancet* 376, no. 9745: 991–1023.

62 *the interconnected nature of progress:* See generally Amartya Sen, *Development as Freedom* (Oxford University Press, 1999).
2009 debate: Munk Debates, "Foreign Aid Does More Harm Than Good," June 1, 2009. www.MunkDebates.com.

63 *Millennium Villages Project:* "A Solution to Extreme Poverty: Millennium Villages," UNDP, Earth Institute at Columbia University.

64 *But the program is expensive:* Michael Clemens, "New Documents Reveal the Cost of 'Ending Poverty' in a Millennium Village," Center for Global Development, March 30, 2012; and Michael Clemens, "Why Careful Evaluation of the Millennium Villages Is Not Optional," Center for Global Development, March 3, 2010. For a counterargument from the MVP, see Paul Pronyk, "The Costs and Benefits of the Millennium Village Project: Correcting the Center for Global Development," April 3, 2012.
In a 2004 speech to African heads of state: Jeffrey Sachs, "Statement to the African Leaders at the Closed Session of NEPAD," African Union Summit, Addis Ababa, Ethiopia, July 7, 2004.

65 *the keynote address:* www.VillagesinAction.com.
In his book Getting Better: Charles Kenny, *Getting Better: Why Global Development Is Succeeding—and How We Can Improve the World Even More* (Basic Books, 2011), 79–80.

66 *The multidimensional poverty index:* "Policy—a Multidimensional Approach," Oxford Poverty and Development Initiative. www.ophi.org.uk.

5. THE FAMILY MAP

69 *Bowling Alone:* Robert D. Putnam, *Bowling Alone: The Collapse and Revival of American Community* (Simon and Schuster, 2000).
one in four Americans had no close friends or confidants: Miller McPherson et al., "Social Isolation in America: Changes in Core Discussion Networks Over Two Decades," *American Sociological Review* 71, no. 3 (June 2006).
In Join the Club: Tina Rosenberg, *Join the Club: How Peer Pressure Can Transform the World* (W. W. Norton, 2011).

71 *a Canadian working on water projects in Malawi:* Owen Scott, "The Things We Rely On," Barefoot Economics, December 8, 2010.
When the Gates Foundation earmarked: Donald G. McNeil Jr., "Ghana: A Grant Meant to Curb Infant Mortality Focuses on Getting Mothers to the Hospital," *The New York Times,* October 29, 2012.

73 *families either owe or are owed:* Christopher Udry, "Risk and Insurance in a Ru-

ral Credit Market: An Empirical Investigation in Northern Nigeria," *Review of Economic Studies* 61, no. 3 (1994).

"My inner circle now includes an entire village": "Keep Out! The Disadvantages to Living in a Rural Community," LizzyTravelz, September 15, 2011.

73 *In Ghana, researchers found:* Timothy Conley and Christopher Udry, "Learning About a New Technology: Pineapple in Ghana," *American Economic Review* 100, no. 1 (2010): 35–69.

76 *a public declaration:* Sarah Kopper, "Female Genital Cutting in the Gambia: A Case Study of Tostan," PhD dissertation, Oregon State University, June 2010, pp. 22–25. See also Celia Dugger, "Senegal Curbs a Bloody Rite for Girls and Women," *The New York Times,* October 15, 2011.

77 *"prosperity gospel":* Philip Jenkins, *The New Faces of Christianity: Believing the Bible in the Global South* (Oxford University Press, 2006), 91–92.

Islamist movements: The recent diffusion of Boko Haram in Nigeria, Al-Qaeda in the Islamic Maghreb, and strict Islamist aggressors like Ansar Dine in Mali have each provoked religiously motivated insecurity among the general population. See Jean-Pierre Filiu, "Could Al Qaeda Turn African in the Sahel?" Carnegie Endowment for Peace, June 2010; Adam Nossiter, "Islamists' Harsh Justice on Rise in Mali," *The New York Times,* December 28, 2012; and "Analysis: Understanding Nigeria's Boko Haram Radicals," IRIN News, July 18, 2011.

"People do throw back lifelines": Rosenberg, *Join the Club,* 45–46.

78 *Directly observed treatment, short course:* R. Bayer and D. Wilkinson, "Directly Observed Therapy for Tuberculosis: History of an Idea," *The Lancet* 345, no. 8964 (June 17, 1995): 1545–48. See also Katherine Floyd et al., "Comparison of Cost Effectiveness of Directly Observed Treatment (DOT) and Conventionally Delivered Treatment for Tuberculosis: Experience From Rural South Africa," *BMJ,* 1997.

AIDS patients in Mozambique: Celia Dugger, "Sharing Burdens of Living With AIDS," *The New York Times,* September 26, 2011.

79 *the lack of remote clinical services:* "Task Shifting to Tackle Health Worker Shortages — Global Recommendations and Guidelines," World Health Organization, January 2008. See also "Task Shifting in Uganda: Case Study," USAID, Washington, DC: Futures Group, Health Policy Initiative, Task Order 1 report, 10; and "Tanzanian Surgeon With a 500,000-Child Waiting List," Africa Review, May 14, 2012.

80 *non-physician clinical workers:* Kathryn Chu et al., "Surgical Task Shifting in Sub-Saharan Africa," *PLOS Medicine* 6, no. 5 (2005). See also Centro Evangelico de Medicina do Lubango, www.ceml.net.

traditional healers: "Guidelines for Registration of Traditional Medicines in the African Region," World Health Organization Regional Office for Africa, 2010. See also "WHO Traditional Medicine Strategy 2002–2005," World Health Organization, 2002.

81 *Treatment Action Campaign:* Mark Heywood, "South Africa's Treatment Ac-

tion Campaign: Combining Law and Social Mobilization to Realize the Right to Health," *Journal of Human Rights Practice* 1, no. 1 (2009): 14–36.

a study aiming to prevent new HIV infections among teens: O. Shisana et al., *South African National HIV Prevalence, Incidence, Behaviour and Communication Survey 2008: A Turning Tide Among Teenagers?* Human Sciences Research Council, 2009; and Pascaline Dupas, "Do Teenagers Respond to HIV Risk Information? Evidence From a Field Experiment in Kenya," *American Economic Journal: Applied Economics* 3 (January 2011): 1–34.

McKinsey asked over 1,300 growing businesses: David Fine et al., "Africa at Work: Job Creation and Inclusive Growth," McKinsey Global Institute, August 2012.

82 *President Ian Khama's family:* Yvonne Ditlhase, "All the President's Family, Friends and Close Colleagues," Mail and Guardian Centre for Investigative Journalism, November 2, 2012.

voters in dozens of African countries: Daniel N. Posner, "Regime Change and Ethnic Cleavages in Africa," *Comparative Political Studies* (2007): 40. See also Michael Bratton et al., "Voting Intentions in Africa: Ethnic, Economic or Partisan?" *Commonwealth & Comparative Politics* 50, no.1 (2012): 27–52.

clashes . . . of economic and environmental interests. See generally Eliza Griswold, *The Tenth Parallel: Dispatches From the Fault Line Between Christianity and Islam* (Farrar, Straus and Giroux, 2010).

83 *in rural northwest Tanzania:* Mahmood Mamdani, *Citizen and Subject: Contemporary Africa and the Legacy of Late Colonialism* (Princeton University Press, 2006), 206.

"parliament of Soweto": Michelle Obama, "Remarks by the First Lady During Keynote Address at Young African Women Leaders Forum," June 22, 2011. www.whitehouse.gov.

"Brain drain": Bernard Mumpasi Lututala, "The Brain Drain in Africa: State of the Issue and Possible Solutions," The Council for the Development of Social Research in Africa and the Woodrow Wilson Center, 2012. See also Richard M. Scheffler, "Estimates of Health Care Professional Shortages in Sub Saharan Africa by 2015," *Health Affairs* 28, no. 5 (September/October 2009).

84 *conference on diaspora engagement:* Hillary Clinton and Maria Otero, US State Department Global Diaspora Forum, May 17–18, 2011.

Guinean immigrants to the United States: Abdulai Bah, "Free Conference Call 'Radio' for African Immigrants," Feet in 2 Worlds, August 10, 2011.

86 *Diaspora remittances:* "World Migration Report 2011: African Regional Overview," International Organization for Migration, 2011.

87 *Diaspora African Women's Network:* www.dawners.org.

88 *The Eritrean civil war:* Mike Pflanz, "Eritrea Accused of Planning Terrorist Attacks on Its Neighbours," *The Telegraph* (UK), July 28, 2011.

many streamed back to start afresh: Kate Eshelby, "'It's Hard Here but This Is My Country': Thousands Return to South Sudan After Independence," *Metro* (UK), December 12, 2012.

6. THE TECHNOLOGY MAP

91 *an American plane touched down in Côte d'Ivoire:* Lawrence Summers, "Remarks of Lawrence H. Summers at the Presidential Summit on Entrepreneurship," April 27, 2010. www.whitehouse.gov.

92 *sharp increase in new users over the past decade:* Jenny Aker and Isaac Mbiti, "Mobile Phones and Economic Development in Africa," *Journal of Economic Perspectives* 24, no. 3 (Summer 2010).
Safaricom projected: Ibid.

93 *"the AK-47 of communication":* J. M. Ledgard, "Digital Africa," *The Economist: Intelligent Life Magazine,* Spring 2011.
In northern Mali: "Mali Music Culture Defined by the Cell Phone," WBUR, February 25, 2013.
SEACOM: Michael Wilkerson, "Tuesday Map: Broadband Hits Africa," *Foreign Policy,* June 23, 2009.
Africa's Internet capacity: Ledgard, "Digital Africa." See also Alex Perry, "Silicon Savannah: Mobile Phones Transform Africa," *Time,* June 30, 2011; Opera, State of the Mobile Web, June 2011.

95 *"Wires warp cyberspace":* Neal Stephenson, "Mother Earth Mother Board," *Wired,* December 1996.
"centralized means 'remote'": Sokari Ekine, ed., *SMS Uprising: Mobile Activism in Africa* (Fahamu/Pambazuka, 2010), 37.

98 *Phones change market behavior:* Aker and Mbiti, "Mobile Phones and Economic Development in Africa."
10 percent of their daily wage: Nathan Eagle, Guardian Activate Summit, 2011.
Jim Balsillie: Simon Dingle, "SA Top BlackBerry Growth Market," Fin24, March 15, 2010.

99 *The undersea cable business:* Okuttah Mark, "State Plans Shared Cable to Cut Internet Costs," *Business Daily* (Kenya), July 11, 2011.
Huawei introduced the IDEOS: Wayan Vota, "Celebrate the IDEOS vs. Samsung $100 Smartphone Price War in Kenya," ICTWorks.org, July 20, 2012.
impact on economic development: L. Waverman, M. Meschi, and M. Fuss, "The Impact of Telecoms on Economic Growth in Developing Countries," in *Africa: The Impact of Mobile Phones,* Vodaphone Policy Paper Series 2 (March 2005).

100 *In 2005, Safaricom rolled out:* Idd Salim, "A Brief Life History of the Mpesa Phenomena," July 21, 2012.

101 *credit and banking services barely exist:* "Half the World Is Unbanked," McKinsey on Society, March 2009.
M-Pesa offers security, convenience, and empowerment: William Jack and Tavneet Suri, "The Economics of M-Pesa," August 2010. See also Gatonye Gathara, "Women Rival Men in Cash Transfer," *The Daily Nation* (Kenya), July 8, 2012.
too risky: Paul Makin, "Regulatory Issues Around Mobile Banking," Consult Hyperion, 2009.

102 *A 2012 survey of global financial habits:* "Press 1 for Modernity," *The Economist,*
April 28, 2012.
Kopa Chapaa and M-Shwari: "Safaricom Launches New Micro-Credit Prod-
uct," NTV Kenya, November 27, 2012.

103 *A 2010 study of M-Pesa:* Jack and Suri, "The Economics of M-Pesa."
BRCK: Anthony Wing Kosner, "BRCK Keeps the Power On When the Internet
Goes Off, Even in Africa," *Forbes,* May 5, 2013.
"an intricate web of relationships and transactions": Daniels, *Making Do,* 22.

104 *Similar spaces:* www.mobilehackaf.com.

105 *strong ties among micro-enterprises:* Lingelbach et al., "What's Distinctive
About Growth-Oriented Entrepreneurship in Developing Countries?"; and
Daniels, *Making Do.*

107 *"Groupon clone after Groupon clone":* Hermione Way, "The Problem With Silicon Valley Is Itself," The Next Web, July 13, 2011.

108 *a quartet of Nigerian teenaged girls:* Emil Protalinsky, "Forget Apps and Other
Useless Startups," The Next Web, November 7, 2012.

109 *"It has to kill something":* Mark Graham, "Will Broadband Internet Establish a
New Development Trajectory for East Africa?" *The Guardian* (UK), October 7,
2010.

110 *Distributed data management:* Ruth Simmons, Peter Fajans, and Laura Ghiron,
"Scaling Up Health Service Delivery," World Health Organization, 2007.

111 *biggest virtual social network you've never heard of:* "Bringing the Medical
Cloud to Africa With Hello Doctor & MXIT," Entegral, July 20, 2012.

112 *The project was born of dire straits:* Gerald P. Douglas et al., "Using Touchscreen
Electronic Medical Record Systems to Support and Monitor National Scale-Up
of Antiretroviral Therapy in Malawi," *PLOS Medicine,* August 10, 2010. See also
Peggy MacKenzie, "Malawi's $1 million eHealth Miracle," *Toronto Star,* April 10,
2010.

115 *I got malaria:* All information about malaria in this section is from *World Malaria Report 2011,* World Health Organization, 2011; and David Bell et al., "En-
suring Quality and Access for Malaria Diagnosis: How Can It Be Achieved?"
Nature Reviews Microbiology 4, S7–S20 (September 1, 2006).

116 *Even designer drugs are suspect:* "84 Percent of Anti-Malaria Drugs in Lagos Are
Fake," *The Guardian* (Nigeria), March 30, 2012.

119 *Moving a container inland:* Fine et al., "Africa at Work," 43.

7. THE COMMERCIAL MAP

121 *South African Stanbic Bank:* "CfC Stanbic Breaks Even in South Sudan in 9
Months," *The Star* (Kenya), March 8, 2013.
Even Melinda Gates: Melinda Gates, "What Nonprofits Can Learn From Coca-
Cola," TEDxChange, October 12, 2010.

122 *Good African coffee:* "A Good African Tale," *The Economist,* May 11, 2010.

122 *"political risk" is overstated:* "Economic Tools Mapping Multilateral Investment Guarantee Agency (MIGA)," The Aspen Institute Market Building Initiative, 2012.

prosperity porn: "Lions on the Move: The Progress and Potential of African Economies," McKinsey Global Institute, 2011.

the "Bottom of the Pyramid": C. K. Prahalad and Stuart L. Hart, "The Fortune at the Bottom of the Pyramid," *strategy+business* 26 (First Quarter 2002).

123 middle *of the pyramid:* "The Middle of the Pyramid: Dynamics of the Middle Class in Africa," African Development Bank, April 20, 2011.

"A low GDP per capita": Zain Latif interview with Isoko Institute.

124 *Home Depot and Best Buy embraced the "haggle economy":* Matt Richtel, "Even at Megastores, Hagglers Find No Price Is Set in Stone," *The New York Times,* March 23, 2008.

125 *In the book* Portfolios of the Poor . . . Poor Economics: Daryl Collins, Jonathan Morduch, Stuart Rutherford, and Orlanda Ruthven, *Portfolios of the Poor: How the World's Poor Live on $2 a Day* (Princeton University Press, 2009); and Abhijit Banerjee and Esther Duflo, *Poor Economics* (Public Affairs, 2012), 135.

126 *Africa's emerging consumer class:* Janice Kew, "Wal-Mart Brand Favored in Massmart's Africa Growth Drive," Bloomberg News, April 16, 2013; and Ingrid Lunden, "Summit Partners Sinks 26m Into Samwer Brothers African Amazon Clone Jumia," TechCrunch, March 6, 2013.

128 *"entrepreneurial leaders are now as important":* Katrina Manson, "Kenya's 'Silicon Savannah' to Challenge India on IT," *Financial Times,* June 6, 2011.

A long-running debate among development hands: For the debate on bed nets, see Jessica Cohen and Pascaline Dupas, "Free Distribution or Cost-Sharing: Evidence From a Malaria Prevention Experiment in Kenya," Brookings Institution Working Paper, December 2007; "Scaling Up Insecticide-Treated Netting Programs in Africa," Roll Back Malaria, August 2005; and April Harding, "The Economist Succumbs to the Siren Song of Universal Bednet Giveaways," Center for Global Development, February 1, 2008. For a general discussion of incentives and public/private/charity alternatives, see Kara Hanson et al., "Is Private Health Care the Answer to the Health Problems of the World's Poor?" *PLOS Medicine,* November 25, 2008.

130 *cost of "free" schooling:* Frances Vavrus and Goodiel Moshi, "The Cost of a 'Free' Primary Education in Tanzania," *International Critical Childhood Policy Studies* 2, no. 1 (2009).

non-public schools: Kenny, *Getting Better,* 83. See also James Tooley and Pauline Dixon, "Private Education Is Good for the Poor: A Study of Private Schools Serving the Poor in Low-Income Countries," Cato Institute, 2005.

independent missionary and community schools: Donna Bryson, "Private Schools for the Poor Fill Gap in S. Africa," Associated Press, January 2, 2011.

131 *For years in Uganda:* Banerjee and Duflo, *Poor Economics,* 235.

132 *privately schooled young Africans:* Tooley and Dixon, "Private Education Is Good for the Poor."

136 *African health care expenditure:* World Bank Development Indicators. See also Pablo Gottret and George Schieber, "Health Financing Revisited: A Practitioner's Guide," World Bank Group, 2006.

137 *When fees were abolished in Burundi:* Adam Nossiter, "In Sierra Leone, New Hope for Children and Pregnant Women," *The New York Times,* July 17, 2011. *According to a report from the International Finance Corporation:* "The Business of Health in Africa: Partnering With the Private Sector to Improve People's Lives," International Finance Corporation, 2008.

139 *private outpatient clinics:* For many examples, including Unjani and Livewell Clinics, see the Center for Health Market Innovations website.
Open Capital Advisors: "The Next 33 Million," Open Capital Advisors, October 2012.
lack of health insurance: Marius Gamser, "Heath Insurance Coverage Debated in Africa," *International Insurance News* 17 (November 2011). The Africa Reinsurance Company maintains updated statistics about insurance in Africa.

140 *a study of insurance providers:* J. L. Carapinha et al., "Health Insurance Systems in Five Sub-Saharan African Countries: Medicine Benefits and Data for Decision Making," *Health Policy,* 2010.
uninsured in Namibia: Emily Gustafsson-Wright et al., "Low Cost Health Insurance in Africa Provides the Poor With Antiretroviral Drugs," Brookings Institution, November 29, 2007.

141 *The ARV debates:* "AIDS, Drug Prices and Generic Drugs," Avert.org. See also Donald McNeil Jr., "Study Finds Generic AIDS Drug Effective," *The New York Times,* July 2, 2004; and Elizabeth Whitman, "Rich Nations Wage Assault on Generic AIDS Drugs," Inter Press Service, June 7, 2011.

142 *Quality Chemical Industries Ltd.:* "Kenya May Buy Ugandan ARVs," Kenya Medical Research Institute, January 28, 2010.

143 *"Social entrepreneurship":* www.Ashoka.org, www.Enablis.org, www.aspeninstitute.org, and www.EchoingGreen.org.

144 *a steady job:* Claire Melamed, "Does Development Give Poor People What They Want?" Overseas Development Institute, February 2011.

145 *Husk Power Systems:* Andrew Revkin, "Husk Power for India," *The New York Times,* December 24, 2008.

146 *Microfinance has been instrumental:* All information about microfinancing in this section comes from MIX Market, which keeps updated general statistics on microfinance institutions in Africa. "Microlending and the Profit Motive," a debate between Alex Counts and Vikram Akula at the Asia Society on October 25, 2010, provides an overview of the controversy about for-profit microfinance.

147 *small and medium-size enterprises:* "Small and Medium Sized Enterprises," Corporation for Enterprise Development, 2013.
big banking: "Scrambled in Africa," *The Economist,* September 16, 2010.

148 *Brazilian megabank BTG Pactual:* Andrew England, "International Banks Ramp Up Presence in Africa," *Financial Times,* January 2, 2012.
an aluminum can factory in the city of Agbara: Bukola Idowu, "Nigeria: Fidelity

Bank Financed Africa's Largest Aluminium Can Factory," *Leadership* (Nigeria), March 3, 2013.

149 *formal continent-wide unemployment rate:* Fine et al., "Africa at Work."

150 *"not always a priority":* "SME Trade Finance: Review of Facilities Available in Kenya," Financial Sector Deepening, 2008.

informal finance: Lingelbach et al., "What's Distinctive About Growth-Oriented Entrepreneurship in Developing Countries?"

Impact investing: "Impact Investments: An Emerging Asset Class," J. P. Morgan Global Research and Rockefeller Foundation, November 29, 2010, offers a summary of impact investment and projects its potential scale globally.

151 *superfluous meta-bureaucracies:* Among the new secondary monitoring organizations: the Global Impact Investing Network (GIIN), ImpactBase, the Impact Reporting and Investment Standards (IRIS), the Global Impact Investing Rating System (GIIRS), and Mission Measurement.

152 *"we've seen several strong for-profit enterprises":* Paula Goldman ("The Distortion Risk of Impact Investing," Stanford Social Innovation Review Blog, May 7, 2012) offers a view on the risk that donors can crowd out market-based solutions and how the Omidyar Network seeks to manage that risk.

loan guarantee facility: Alex Duval Smith ("Is Trade, Not Aid, the Answer for Africa?" *The Guardian* [UK], May 25, 2009) describes a discussion of what became the African Guarantee Fund at the World Economic Forum meeting in Cape Town in 2009.

153 *The nimbler African banks: African Business,* August/September 2011, p. 31.

"Just give money to the poor": David Hulme, Joseph Hanlon, and Armando Barrientos, *Just Give Money to the Poor: The Development Revolution From the Global South* (Kumnarian Press, 2012).

154 *Diaspora bonds:* Ngozi Okonjo-Iweala and Dilip Ratha, "A Bond for the Homeland," *Foreign Policy,* May 24, 2011.

diaspora investment office in Liberia: James Butty, "Liberia Diaspora Debates Reconstruction, Dual Citizenship," Voice of America, July 26, 2012.

155 *Ethiopia's recent diaspora bond:* "Milking Migrants," *The Economist,* August 20, 2011.

Dambisa Moyo's big plan: Paul Collier, "Review: Dead Aid, by Dambisa Moyo," *The Independent* (UK), January 30, 2009.

8. THE NATURE MAP

157 *The African continent has a power problem:* Anton Eberhard et al., "Underpowered: The State of the Power Sector in Sub-Saharan Africa," World Bank Africa Infrastructure Country Diagnostic, June 2008. See also "Key World Energy Statistics," International Energy Agency, 2012.

158 *Peter DiCampo's "Life Without Lights" project:* www.lifewithoutlights.com.

159 *energy poverty in Africa:* "Energy Poverty: How to Make Modern Energy Access Universal," International Energy Agency and United Nations Development

Programme, September 2010. See also Charles Kenny, "A Thousand Points of Light," *Foreign Policy*, July 11, 2011.

lowest carbon footprint in the world: Eberhard et al., "Underpowered."

400 liters of water per day: Fareed Zakaria, *The Post-American World* (W. W. Norton and Company, 2008), 30.

"K-strategists": William Rees, "What's Blocking Sustainability? Human Nature, Cognition and Denial," *Sustainability: Science Practice and Policy* 6, no. 2 (Fall 2010): 4.

160 *the world's biggest power plant:* John Vidal, "DR Congo Waits on Funding for World's Largest Hydropower Project," *The Guardian* (UK), May 21, 2013; and John Irish, "Bidding Nears for $9–14 bln Congo Hydropower Plant," Reuters News, May 18, 2013.

In Guinea-Bissau: "Energy Poverty in Africa," OPEC Fund for International Development, June 2008.

In Tanzania: Jacques Morisset, "Tanzania Can Benefit From Natural Gas by Empowering People," World Bank, March 16, 2012; and Isis Gaddis, "Only 14% of Tanzanians Have Electricity: What Can Be Done?" World Bank, October 31, 2012.

the Cahora Bassa Dam in Mozambique: See generally Allen F. and Barbara S. Isaacman, *Dams, Displacement and the Delusion of Development: Cahora Bassa and Its Legacies in Mozambique, 1965–2007* (Ohio University Press, 2013). See also "Mozambique Power Supply Constrained Until 2020," *News-Day* (Zimbabwe), April 26, 2012; and Rowan Moore Geraty, "New Coal Giant Mozambique Facing Rising Public Anger," *Christian Science Monitor,* April 27, 2012.

163 *dirty energy:* Bryan Walsh, "The Worst Kind of Poverty: Energy Poverty," *Time,* October 11, 2011. See also "Coal Mining in Africa — Overview," Mbendi Information Services.

164 *new renewable energy investments:* "Global Trends in Renewable Energy Investment 2011," United Nations Environmental Program, July 7, 2011. See also "Lighting Africa" annual reports.

maintaining power to the wireless towers: Adeola Yusuf, "Nigeria: The Country's Expensive Darkness," *The Daily Independent* (Nigeria), June 27, 2011.

165 *solar-powered "cell site":* "IHS Opens Africa's Largest Solar Cell Site," *BusinessTech* (South Africa), April 30, 2012.

fuel subsidy: "Nigeria Fuel Subsidy Report 'Reveals $6bn Fraud,'" BBC, April 24, 2012.

166 *William Kamkwamba:* "William Kamkwamba: How I Built a Windmill," TED Global, July 2007.

167 *All told, agriculture makes up:* Calestous Juma, *The New Harvest: Agricultural Innovation in Africa* (Oxford University Press, 2011), 11.

Africa's farm production: Keith Fuglie and Alejandro Nin-Pratt, "A Changing Global Harvest," International Food Policy Research Institute, 2012. See also "Africa's Pulse," The World Bank, October 2012.

only 4 percent of it is irrigated: The World Bank keeps up-to-date reports on agricultural water management.

168 *World Bank–led structural adjustment programs:* Lee R. Lynd and Jeremy Woods, "Perspective: A New Hope for Africa," *Nature* 474, S20–S21 (June 23, 2011). See also James S. Guseh, "The Public Sector, Privatization, and Development in Sub-Saharan Africa," *African Studies Quarterly* 5, no. 1 (2001).
Marketing and commodity boards: Anna Laven, "Marketing Reforms in Ghana's Cocoa Sector," Overseas Development Institute, December 2007.
80 percent of African countries spent: Juma, *The New Harvest,* 13.

169 *tractors per thousand farmers:* Ibid.
food insecure: Heather Murdock, "Nigeria Tries to Curb Appetite for Imported Food," Global Post, April 27, 2012.

170 *balance global consumption:* Lynd and Woods, "Perspective."
large-scale industrial farming: See Juma, *The New Harvest.*
"one acre" plots: "Smallholders, Food Security and the Environment," International Fund for Agricultural Development, 2013; and Shenggen Fan, "G20 Ministers of Agriculture Must Focus on Smallholder Farmers to Achieve Food Security and Prevent Food Price Volatility," Institute for Food Policy Research, June 15, 2011.

172 *famine killed hundreds of thousands of Ethiopians:* See generally Peter Gill, *Famine and Foreigners: Ethiopia Since Live Aid* (Oxford University Press, 2010).

173 *droughts in the Horn:* "Horn of Africa: Fast Facts About the Drought," IRIN News, August 5, 2011.
The pan-African food market: Juma, *The New Harvest.*

174 *large-scale, private industrial farms:* Peter Gibbon, "Experiences of Plantation and Large-Scale Farming in 20th Century Africa," Danish Institute for International Studies, 2011.
Congo-Brazzaville: Arsène Séverin, "Congo-Brazzaville: South African Farmers Set Up in Congo," Inter Press Service, March 26, 2011.

176 *Africa-based mobile ventures:* For an overview, see Jaco Maritz, "How Mobile Phones Are Transforming African Agriculture," How We Made It in Africa, March 28, 2011. See also "New Mobile Applications Help Ugandan Communities," ITU News, September 2009.

179 *Crop insurance . . . index insurance:* Ruth Vargas Hill, "Agricultural Insurance in Sub-Saharan Africa: Can It Work?" International Food Policy Research Institute, September 2010. See also Tina Rosenberg, "Doing More Than Praying for Rain," *The New York Times,* May 9, 2011; Shawn Cole, "Index Insurance — a Free Lunch for African Farmers," This Is Africa, November 19, 2012; and "Index-Based Weather Insurance: Project Briefing Note," Rockefeller Foundation.

182 *Rural populations are streaming into African mega-cities:* "Africa's Cities to Triple in Size," BBC, November 24, 2010.

184 *the number of slum dwellers:* Ibid.
Ougadougou: John Vidal, "Africa Warned of 'Slum Cities' Danger as Its Population Passes 1bn," *The Guardian* (UK), November 24, 2010.

"charter cities" movement: Sebastian Mallaby, "The Politically Incorrect Guide to Ending Poverty," *The Atlantic,* June 8, 2010. See also www.chartercities .org.

185 *ground has broken at Konza:* Katrina Manson, "Konza City to Challenge India's Tech Giants," *The Standard* (Kenya), January 26, 2013. See also www.konzacity .co.ke.

Oyala, the capital built by Teodoro Obiang Nguema Mbasogo: Stephen Sackur, "Equatorial Guinea: Obiang's Future Capital, Oyala," BBC News Magazine, December 17, 2012.

186 *one formal brick home for every forty-three black residents:* "Africa Action Stands in Solidarity with South Africa's Poor," Africa Action, October 5, 2009.

government housing: "South Africa Since Apartheid," Reuters, June 24, 2012.

187 *hysterically corrupt former governor:* "Fayose: Profile of Corruption," *Tell Magazine* (Nigeria).

Samsung laptops: "A Story Untold: Something Is Happening in Ekiti — for Real!" Information Nigeria, December 24, 2012.

British Petroleum is considering Ekiti: Okwy Iroegbu-Chikezie, "Ekiti, BP to Partner on Biofuel," *The Nation* (Nigeria), July 5, 2012.

188 *Ethanol produced from local sugar:* All information about ethanol production in Ethiopia in this section comes from "Ethiopia Saves 24 mln USD From Ethanol Blended Fuel," Walta Info; "Ethiopia to Increase Ethanol Capacity, Raises Mandate From 5 to 10 Percent," *Biofuels Digest,* January 19, 2011; and "Ethiopia Has 207,180 Hectares Designated for Biofuels Projects," *Biofuels Digest,* December 29, 2010.

Trade-offs with food production: Duncan Graham-Rowe, "Beyond Food Versus Fuel," *Nature* 474, S8 (2011)

189 *Growing power becomes profitable:* Horand Knaup, "Green Gold Rush: Africa Becoming a Biofuel Battleground," *Der Spiegel* (Germany), September 5, 2008.

the Guardian counted one hundred projects: Damian Carrington, "Biofuels Boom in Africa as British Firms Lead Rush on Land for Plantations," *The Guardian* (UK), May 31, 2011.

Ethiopia spends: Dennis Gathanju, "Ethiopia Sets Its Sights on Biodiesel," *Renewable Energy World,* December 3, 2010.

avenues for small-scale farmers to benefit: "Biofuels in Africa: Growing Small-Scale Opportunities," International Institutes for Environment and Development, November 2009.

9. THE YOUTH MAP

191 *the 2012 Olympic Games:* All information about the Olympic Games in this section comes from Beatrice Debut, "Youngest Olympic Competitor Keeps It Simple," *The Daily Star* (Lebanon), August 6, 2012; and Sam Jones, "London 2012's Oldest Competitor, Hiroshi Hoketsu, Takes the Reins," *The Guardian* (UK), August 2, 2012.

demographic dividend: "Regional Overview: Youth in Africa," United Nations Economic Commission on Africa; and Fred Swaniker, "Lifting Africa Up by Empowering Its Youth," McKinsey on Society, Voices on Society, vol. 1.

192 *median age of the public and the age of its leaders:* Todd Moss, "The Generation Chasm: Do Young Populations Have Elderly Leaders?" Center for Global Development, February 3, 2012.

193 *"hippo generation":* George Ayittey, "George Ayittey on Cheetahs Versus Hippos," TEDGlobal, 2007.
  global youth unemployment rate: "The Youth Employment Crisis: Time for Action," International Labor Organization, 2012. Many of the analyses and statistics from this report inform the rest of the chapter.

195 *"waithood":* All information about "waithood" in this section comes from Alcinda Honwana, "'Waithood': Youth Transitions and Social Change," International Institute for Social Studies, University of Rotterdam, 2012.

197 *"It breaks down waste":* Kyle Brown, "Why Africa's Young Thinkers Are Headed to Prestigious US Colleges," *Christian Science Monitor,* October 25, 2010.

199 *"deliberate practice":* K. Anders Ericsson et al., "The Role of Deliberate Practice in the Acquisition of Expert Performance," *Psychological Review* 100, no. 3 (1993).

200 *"The Talented Tenth":* W.E.B. Du Bois, "The Talented Tenth," in *The Negro Problem: A Series of Articles by Representative Negroes of To-day* (New York, 1903).

202 *Africa-based outsourcing ventures:* Imara Africa Securities Team, "Why Outsourcing Could Be Africa's Next Big Opportunity," How We Made It in Africa, May 11, 2011.

203 Up From Slavery: Booker T. Washington, *Up From Slavery: An Autobiography* (Doubleday, Page, 1901).
  Informal "attachment" employment: "The Youth Employment Crisis," ILO report.

205 *Free schooling schemes:* Jocelyn Sambira, "African Schools Keep an Eye on the Prize," Africa Renewal (UN), August 1, 2012. See also Kenny, *Getting Better,* 104.

206 *Overcrowding:* All information on overcrowding in this section comes from "Cost, Financing and School Effectiveness of Education in Malawi," Development Research Group, The World Bank, 2004; and "When Will Our Children Learn?" Twaweza Policy Note, August 2010.

209 *dropout rates:* "Primary Completion Rate, Total," World Bank World Development Indicators, 2008–2012; and "Access to Education in Ghana: The Evidence and the Issues," University of Sussex Consortium for Research on Educational Access, Transitions and Equity, June 2007. See also Lucy Holborn, "Education in South Africa: Where Did It Go Wrong?" Africa in Fact, September 1, 2013.

211 *the longer a mother attends school:* Twaweza Policy Note.

212 *the youngest elected official in Africa:* David Smith, "Twenty Year Old Ugandan Becomes One of Youngest MPs in African History," *The Guardian* (UK), September 26, 2012.

proportion of female representatives: "Women in National Parliaments," Inter-Parliamentary Union, 2013.

"Parliament is not a daycare centre": Edward Ssekika, "Work Cut Out for New 19-Year-Old Usuk MP," *The Observer* (Uganda), September 14, 2012.

213 y'en a marre: Ethan Zuckerman, "Y'en A Marre: Music and Mobilization in Senegal," EthanZuckerman.com, April 15, 2013.

215 *"manipulated by the elites into fighting ethnic and religious conflicts":* Alcinda Honwana, *The Time of Youth: Work, Social Change, and Politics in Africa* (Kumarian Press, 2012).

10. TWO PUBLICS

217 *The late economist Albert Hirschman:* See generally Albert O. Hirschman, *Exit, Voice, and Loyalty: Responses to Decline in Firms, Organizations, and States* (Harvard University Press, 1970).

218 *"I Paid a Bribe":* www.ipaidabribe.com.

Freedom House: All Freedom House statistics in this section come from www .freedomhouse.org/. Freedom House maintains useful and up-to-date statistics on press freedoms, civil rights, and other civil society issues, not limited to sub-Saharan Africa.

enabling repressive media environments: Rodney Sieh, "Jailed for Journalism," *The New York Times,* August 30, 2013.

219 *a 60 percent salary hike:* "Kenyan MPs Settle for Lower Pay Rise," Al Jazeera, June 12, 2013.

"shrinking space" for non-state voices: Elissa Jobson, "Civil Society Exclusions Dampen Mood at African Union Summit," *The Guardian* (UK), May 28, 2013.

220 *legal pluralism:* For a general introduction to the concept of legal pluralism as well as specific applications to the field of development, see Brian Z. Tamahana et al., eds., *Legal Pluralism and Development: Scholars and Practitioners in Dialogue* (Cambridge University Press, 2012).

221 *ease of doing business:* "Doing Business," The World Bank. Rwanda was ranked third in Africa in 2013.

224 *Paul Kagame:* For this and many other details of Paul Kagame's biography and Rwanda, pre- and post-genocide, see Stephen Kinzer, *A Thousand Hills: Rwanda's Rebirth and the Man Who Dreamed It* (John Wiley and Sons, 2009).

225 gacaca: "The Gacaca Tribunals in Rwanda," in *Reconciliation After Violent Conflict,* International Institute for Democracy and Electoral Assistance, 2003.

226 *domestic development fund:* www.agaciro.org.

$400 million bond to international investors: Carolyn Cohn, "Bond Yields Too Low? There's Always Rwanda," Reuters, May 3, 2013.

227 agaciro: "Opening Speech by H. E. President Paul Kagame at the 9th Leadership Retreat," March 4, 2010; and "Speech by H. E. Paul Kagame, President of the Republic of Rwanda, at the Young Achiever Awards," December 11, 2011.

mixed results: "Rwanda Human Development Report," United Nations Development Programme.

"the Singapore of Africa": "Africa's Singapore?" *The Economist,* February 25, 2012.

228 *military adventurism:* In addition to the 1997 march to the DRC that deposed Mobutu, Rwandan special forces are said to be launching continual attacks, targeted killings, and human rights violations in the DRC today. A series of UN Security Council reports have more details.

"organizations of civil society in Rwanda": Kinzer, *A Thousand Hills,* 222.

229 *"The real custodian of democratic order":* Mahmood Mamdani, "The State, the Private Sector, and Market Failures: A Response to Prof Joseph Stiglitz," *Pambazuka News* 595 (July 25, 2012).

a market test: Bilal Siddiqui and Justin Sandefeur, "Delivering Health Justice to the Poor: Evidence From a Field Experiment in Liberia," working paper, Stanford University Program for International Policy Studies and Center for Global Development, 2013.

"expensive, corrupted, discriminatory": Olivier Sterck and Olivia d'Aoust, "Who Benefits From Customary Justice: Rent-Seeking Bribery and Criminality in Sub-Saharan Africa," Université catholique de Louvain, Institut de Recherches Économiques et Sociales (IRES), 2012.

230 *formal legal systems are designed for punishment:* Siddiqui and Sandefeur, "Delivering Health Justice to the Poor," 9.

231 *economist Avinash Dixit:* Dixit, *Lawlessness and Economics.*

"the nation appears increasingly like a straitjacket": Jean-Marie Guéhenno, *The End of the Nation-State* (University of Minnesota Press, 1995), 4, 13.

232 *"entanglement" . . . "to account for time* as lived": Achille Mbembe, *On the Postcolony* (University of California Press, 2001).

Global Pulse: All information on Global Pulse in this section comes from "Big Data for Development: Opportunities & Challenges," UN Global Pulse, May 2012.

233 *full government data sets online:* "Open Data for Africa," OAfrica, September 20, 2012.

national education survey: www.uwezo.net/assessments.

234 *"Development 3.0":* Shanta Devarajan, "Development 3.0," Africa Can . . . , November 5, 2010.

"creative thinking is needed to find alternatives": "Africa's Growth Tragedy: An Institutional Perspective," World Bank Country Note G, 2000.

235 *special urban planning team:* Andrew Thiaine Imwati, "Investigating the Potential of Modern Geo-Info Technologies in Planning Urban Community Settlements: The Case of Nairobi-peri Urban Settlements," University of Nairobi College of Humanities and Social Sciences, 2010.

Accra, Ghana: growth of, 183
ActivSpaces, 103–104
advertising: commerce and trade and,
    127
Africa: arbitrary boundaries in, 44–46,
    64, 185
  Brazil invests in, 148
  carbon footprint in, 159
  Chinese commercial ventures in,
    117
  development assistance in, 5, 7, 10,
    64–66
  digital technology innovations in,
    101–103, 106–108
  electrical power supply in, 157–58,
    160
  ethnic and language boundaries in,
    43–45, 65
  food production in, 169
  health care in, 60–62, 65, 84, 116
  Herodotus and, 1–2
  internal migration in, 44–45, 181–82
  mapping of, 1–2, 3, 15
  natural resources in, 11, 160–61
  precolonial boundaries in, 42, 45
  public education in, 11, 60–61, 63, 65
  self-development and assistance in,
    5, 7–8, 11
  self-identity in, 70–71
  separatist movements in, 34–36,
    45–46
  stock markets in, 155
  urbanization in, 181–84

  Western perception of, 1–3, 4–5, 10,
    11–12, 14–15
Africa Commission, 152
African Development Bank, 122–23,
    147
African diaspora: as brain-drain, 83–84,
    90
  communications within, 84–85
  finances liberation struggles, 88
  Guinea in, 84–85
  and investments at home, 154
  kanju in, 85
  remittances in, 85–87, 150, 181
  social solidarity in, 87–88
  and ties with home, 84, 85–88, 90, 172
  U.S. State Department and, 88
  women in, 87–88
African Leadership Academy (ALA),
    196, 201, 205, 214
  teaches African Studies, 214–15
  teaches deliberate practice, 199–200
  teaches leadership, 197–98, 215
  teaches risk management, 198–99
  teaches time management, 199, 202
African National Congress, 47
African Studies: ALA teaches, 214–15
African Union, 34, 234
African Venture Capital Association,
    149
Africa Unchained (Ayittey), 38
age: cultural assumptions about, 193,
    194–95
  and heads of state, 192–93

agriculture, 65
  and biofuels, 187–89
  cell phones in, 176
  climate change's effects on, 134, 176,
      181, 188–89
  cooperation in, 180
  corrupt and dysfunctional
      government and, 168–69
  crisis in, 167–70, 173–74
  and crop insurance, 180
  "fat" vs. "lean" economies and,
      173–74, 190
  foreign aid and, 169–70, 178–79
  growth in, 167
  irrigation and, 134
  kanju in, 177, 179
  in Kenya, 176–79
  and market access, 180
  mega-farming model in, 170–71,
      173–74
  in Nigeria, 135, 167–68, 174–75
  in Rwanda, 135
  scalability of, 170
  smallholder model in, 174–79,
      189–90
  technology revolution and, 176
  training in, 176–78
  in Uganda, 180–81
  urban farming in, 6–7
  water management and, 134–35,
      168
Ahiabenu, Kwame, 49
AIDS: education programs and, 81
  in Malawi, 112
  philanthropy and, 58
  and prescription drugs, 141–42
  in South Africa, 80–81
  and Treatment Action Campaign,
      81
Akamanzi, Clare, 224, 225, 226
Aladesuru, Olamide, 213–14, 215
Alao, Abiodun, 205
Alemu, Bethlehem Tilahun, 54–55
Alliy, Mbwana, 106–107
Al-Shabaab terrorists, 34–35, 77, 214

Anas, Anas Aremeyaw, 175, 217
  investigative journalism by, 31–33, 50
Angola: government corruption and
      dysfunction in, 39–40, 57
  health care in, 80
Annan, Kofi, 170
Araia, Semhar, 87
Ayittey, George, 193
  Africa Unchained, 38
Aylward, David, 109

Balsillie, Jim, 98
Banda, Hastings, 50
"Bangla-Pesa," 51, 121, 143
banking and financial services. See also
      microfinance institutions
  cell phones and, 100–102, 108, 109,
      153
  in commerce and trade, 147
  in entrepreneurship, 144–45, 149–50,
      156
  "fat" vs. "lean" economies and, 145
  shortcomings of, 149–50
  in Zimbabwe, 145
Banks, Ken, 95, 110
Baobab Health (nonprofit), 111–14, 151
Barclays, 86
Barry, Mamadou, 84–85
beds: manufacture and distribution of,
      124–26
Berlin Conference (1884), 3, 41, 42
biofuel industry, 187–89
  impact on food production, 187–89
  and petroleum imports, 189
Biya, Paul, 48, 192
Blue Sweater, The (Novogratz), 52
Boko Haram terrorists, 77, 214
Bono, 58
Botswana, 82
"Bottom of the Pyramid" consumers,
      123, 129, 146
Bowling Alone (Putnam), 69
Bragiel, Paul, 107
Bräutigam, Deborah, 57
Brazil: African investments by, 148

Bridge International Academies, 200
    funding of, 131–32
    instructional model of, 132–33, 206
    philosophy of, 131–32
broadband connectivity: in technology
    revolution, 93–95
BTG Pactual, 148
Buffett, Warren: and development
    assistance, 64
Burnet, Rob, 207–209, 210
business. *See* commerce and trade
Businge, Milly, 65
Busoga Rural Open Source and
    Development Initiative, 176

Cahora Bassa Dam (Mozambique),
    160–61
Cameroon: foreign aid in, 59
    government corruption and
        dysfunction in, 48
    social lending and credit circles in,
        126
capital: foreign aid and, 151, 233
    from grants, 151
    and investment, 144–45
carbon footprint: in Africa, 159
caregiving. in health care, 79–80
cell phones: in agriculture, 176
    and banking and financial services,
        100–102, 108, 109, 153
    in commerce and trade, 97–98,
        100–103
    cultural impact of, 93, 98, 100–101,
        109–10
    and economic development, 99–100
    in health care, 110
    in Nigeria, 123
    and public health, 116–18
    recharging of, 69, 97, 98, 160, 162,
        163
    in retail distribution and supply
        chains, 119–20
    social solidarity and, 8–9, 10, 93
    and technology revolution, 85, 92–93,
        97–98, 129

Centre for Democracy and
    Development, 77
Centre for Development and
    Enterprise, 130
"charter cities" movement: controversy
    over, 184–85
Cheeseman, R. E.: on the Nile, 2
Chikakula, Blessings, 49–50, 131
China: commercial ventures in Africa,
    117
Chiura, Munya, 145, 156
Chude-Sokei, Louis, 19–20
Cipla, 141–42
cities: attitude toward addresses and
    directions in, 3–4
Cleary, Siobhan: on stock markets, 155
climate change, 61
    effects on agriculture, 134, 176, 181,
        189
clinical services: health care and lack of,
        79–80
Clinton, Bill, 91
Clinton, Hillary, 84
Clinton Global Initiative, 63, 118, 224
Clueless (film), 54
cluster economies: and technology
    hubs, 103–105
cocoa farming, 167–68
Colaco, Jessica, 104
Cold War: foreign aid as strategy in,
        57, 58
Cole, Teju, 60
Collins, Darryl: *Portfolio of the Poor*, 125
Colong, Valery, 105
colonialism and imperialism, 10, 14,
        34–35, 37, 41–44, 45–46, 47, 67,
        130, 185, 193
    foreign aid as continuation of, 56–57,
        59–60, 62
    and natural resources, 160–61
commerce and trade. *See also* informal
    economy
    and advertising, 127
    banking and financial services in, 147
    cell phones in, 97–98, 100–103

commerce and trade *(cont.)*
  and community financing, 126
  corruption and dysfunction in, 97,
      165–66
  and economic development, 123, 128,
      156
  electrical power supply in, 164–65
  and free markets, 128–29
  haggling and flexibility in, 123–24,
      126
  health care in, 137, 142–43
  innovation in, 127, 129–30
  and investment opportunities,
      122–23, 126–27, 136, 148
  kanju in, 127, 149
  nature of, 123–25
  nepotism and cronyism in, 81–82
  product placement in, 129–30
  responds to dysfunctional
      government, 121, 127–28
  in Rwanda, 223
  scalability in, 129
  universality of, 127–28
  Western misunderstandings of,
      121–22, 123
  women in, 74–75, 101
community financing: commerce and
      trade and, 126
  of education, 71–72, 73, 126
  and investment, 149–50
community norms: social solidarity
      and, 75–77, 229–31
Congo, Democratic Republic of, 44, 57,
      228
  government corruption and
      dysfunction in, 46, 57, 223
Conrad, Josef, 3
construction industry: innovation in,
      185–86
  urbanization and, 183–84, 185
consumerism, 10–11, 128–29
  and demand for education, 134, 136,
      139, 230
  poverty and, 122–23, 129–30
  and private health care, 137, 139, 230

Conté, Lansana, 5
cooperation: in agriculture, 180–81
  and social solidarity, 67–69
corruption and dysfunction: in
      commerce and trade, 97, 165–66
  in elections, 8–10, 38–39, 47–48, 49,
      207
  in government. *See* government,
      corrupt and dysfunctional
  in health care, 116–17
  and informal economy, 31–33
  journalism and, 31–33, 218
  in public education, 130, 131, 205–206
  in retail distribution and supply
      chains, 119
  Tiger Eye and, 32–33
Côte d'Ivoire: water management in,
      91–92
credit. *See also* social lending and credit
      circles
  and entrepreneurship, 144–45, 152,
      153
crime: and entrepreneurship, 19, 24–25
  in public health, 117
crop insurance, 180
crowdfunding: as investment, 156

Dahabshiil: money transfers by, 85–88,
      127
Dangote, Aliko, 19, 183
Daniels, Nick, 178–79
Daniels, Steve: *Making Do*, 30, 103
Deacon, Bridget, 207
Dead Aid (Moyo), 55–56
deliberate practice: ALA teaches,
      199–200
demographics: in "fat" *vs.* "lean"
      economies, 11, 191–93
Denny, Lynette, 23, 139
Devarajan, Shanta, 48–49, 234
development assistance: in Africa, 5, 7,
      10, 64–66
Diaspora African Women's Network
      (DAWN), 87
Diawara, Demba, 76–77

DiCampo, Peter: "Life Without Lights" project, 158–59
Diligent Tanzania Ltd, 189
Directly Observed Treatment, Short Course (DOTS): in health care, 78
Dixit, Avinash, 231
  Lawlessness and Economics, 41
Dlamini-Zuma, Nkosazana, 219, 234
d.light Design, 163
donations in kind. *See also* non-governmental organizations; philanthropy
  impact on manufacturing sector, 53–55
  by TOMS Shoes, 53–54
Dondo, Aleke, 38, 153
donor economy. *See* foreign aid
Douglas, Gerry, 111
drugs, fake: health care and, 116–18
drugs, prescription: AIDS and, 141–42
  costs of, 141
  in health care, 140–41
Duale, Abdirashid, 85–86, 127, 154
Du Bois, W. E. B.: "The Talented Tenth," 200–201, 203
Duflo, Esther & Abhijit Banerjee: *Poor Economics,* 125–26
Dugger, Celia, 78

East African Community, 221, 234
Economic Community of West African States, 234
economic development: cell phones and, 99–100
  commerce and trade and, 123, 128, 156
  grass-roots model of, 120, 232–34
  technology revolution and, 109, 120
education, informal: digital technology and, 211
  kanju and, 211
  Obami and, 210
  Shujaaz and, 206–207, 208–10
  telenovelas and, 207

education, private: competes with public schools, 129–31, 204–205
  consumer demand for, 134, 136, 139, 230
  poverty and, 132
  and social elite, 200
  spread of, 129–31
  technology revolution in, 133
education, public: in Africa, 11, 60–61, 63, 65
  community financing of, 71–72, 73, 126
  corruption and dysfunction in, 130, 131, 205–206
  dropout rates in, 209–10
  and inadequate teacher-training, 131
  instructional models in, 131, 193, 195
  Jitegemee and, 201–202, 204–205
  in Malawi, 205–206
  MDGs and, 130–31, 205
  private schools compete with, 129–31, 204–205
  UN mandate for, 201, 205
education, vocational: and apprenticeships, 204–205
  as empowerment, 202–203
  Jitegemee and, 201–202, 204–205
  relevance of, 203
EGG-energy, 162–63
Ekwage, Fritz, 96, 108–109, 113
elections. *See also* government
  corruption in, 8–10, 38–39, 47–48, 49, 207
electrical power supply: in Africa, 157–58, 160
  alternatives to, 158–59, 161–62, 166–67
  in commerce and trade, 164–65
  and dysfunctional government, 160–61, 162, 164–66
  entrepreneurship and, 69, 97–98, 160, 162–63, 165
  generators and, 158–59, 165
  in Ghana, 158–59
  and hydroelectric dams, 160–61

electrical power supply (*cont.*)
  and informal economy, 162–63
  kanju and, 162, 166
  in Mozambique, 160–61
  in Nigeria, 164–65
  and poverty, 159, 162
  solar energy and, 163–64, 165
  in Tanzania, 161–63
  technology revolution and, 164–65
  in Uganda, 163
  in U.S., 157
Elumelu, Tony, 64
e-mail fraud: Nigeria and, 16–20, 24,
    26, 33
Emmy Award: *Shujaaz* wins, 209
employment: investment and, 148–49,
    150, 153
  poverty and, 143–44
  youth and, 193–95, 201
End of Poverty, The (Sachs), 95
End of the Nation-State, The
    (Guéhenno), 231–32
Enemies of the State (film), 33
energy sources, alternative, 158–59,
    161–62, 166–67
Englebert, Pierre, 45–46, 49
Enonchong, Rebecca, 126, 150, 193
  on foreign aid, 59
  on microfinance institutions, 147
entrepreneurship: banking and financial
    services in, 144, 149–50, 156
  credit and, 144–45, 152, 153
  crime and, 19, 24–25
  in digital technology, 107–108
  and electrical power supply, 69,
    97–98, 160, 162–63, 165
  in health care, 139
  Ibrahim on, 21
  in informal economy, 29–30, 98
  and investment opportunities,
    126–27
  kanju and, 20–22, 104, 108, 143,
    197
  matatu buses and, 27–29
  microfinancing and, 145–46

  in movie industry, 25–26
  in Nigeria, 104–106, 108
  technology hubs and, 104–105
  women and, 74–75, 113, 147
  youth and, 197–98, 215
entrepreneurship, social: and foreign
    aid, 142–43
  impact of, 150
Ericsson, Anders, 199
Eritrea, 87, 88
Esteves, André, 148
ethanol industry, 188
Ethiopia: civil war in, 172–73
  food production in, 170–72, 234
  footwear industry in, 54–55
  government corruption and
    dysfunction in, 41, 57, 154–55,
    172–73
ethnic conflicts: economic roots of,
    82–83
Eubank, Nicholas, 37
Eze, Elizabeth, 73
Ezekwesili, Obiageli, 38, 193, 194, 231

Fabolade, Dejo, 105
FACE Africa, 89–90, 151
family: and social solidarity, 10, 70–71,
    73
"fat" *vs.* "lean" economies, 11–14, 49
  and agriculture, 173–74, 190
  and banking and financial services,
    145
  demographics in, 11, 191–93
  and development assistance, 5, 7, 10,
    64–66
  and formality bias, 231
  and health care, 115–16
  and innovation, 107–108, 119–20
  and philanthropy, 53–55, 56, 57–60,
    97
  and recycling, 22, 111–12, 114
  and social solidarity, 69–70
Fayemi, Kayode, 187
Fenix International, 163
Feruzi, Emanuel, 198, 215–16

fiber-optic cables: in technology
        revolution, 93, 95–96, 99,
        148
financing, community
    commerce and trade and, 126
    of education, 71–72, 73, 126
food production: in Africa, 169
    biofuel's impact on, 187–89
    and dysfunctional government,
        172–73
    in Ethiopia, 170–72, 234
    and inadequate distribution, 172–73
    in South Sudan, 176
    and world demand, 170, 171–72,
        173
footwear industry: in Ethiopia, 54–55
foreign aid: and agriculture, 169–70,
        178–79
    in Cameroon, 59
    and capital, 151, 233
    as Cold War strategy, 57, 58
    as continuation of colonialism, 56–57,
        59–60, 62
    design flaws in, 55–56, 57, 58, 61–62,
        66, 173, 179, 233
    economically tied to donor nations,
        56, 141
    Enonchong on, 59
    grass-roots model of, 57–58, 89–90
    and health care, 79, 136–37
    Ismail on, 58–59
    in Kenya, 57
    Kristof and, 58, 60
    in Mozambique, 57
    paternalism in, 129
    in Rwanda, 226
    and social entrepreneurship, 142–43
    in Somaliland, 58–59, 113
formality bias, 8, 14, 37, 44, 49, 54,
        60–62, 66, 80, 155, 185, 205,
        219
"fat" vs. "lean" economies and, 231
Freedom House, 218
free markets: commerce and trade and,
        128–29

Frei, Phil, 131
FrontlineSMS, 110

Gadabu, Oliver, 112
Gadio, Cheikh Tidiane, 45
Garrick, Nosarieme, 195
Gates, Melinda, 64, 121
Gates (Bill and Melinda) Foundation,
        58, 65, 71, 151
    and development assistance, 64
"Generative Internet, The" (Zittrain),
        102
generators: and electrical power supply,
        158–59, 165
genital mutilation: women and, 75–76,
        77
Getting Better (Kenny), 65
Ghana, 73–74, 117
    electrical power supply in, 158–59
    government corruption and
        dysfunction in, 31–33, 41, 49
    health care in, 140
GiveDirectly, 153
Global Fund to Fight AIDS,
        Tuberculosis and Malaria, 65,
        115, 141
globalization, 10, 52–53, 57–58, 232
Global Pulse project, 232–33
Godfrey, Godwin, 79
Gogo, Ashifi, 118–19, 149, 150
Goldman, Paula, 152
Google, 3, 235
government. See also elections
    ages of heads of state in, 192–93
    disinterest in, 213
    distrust of, 38–41, 47, 49–50, 65,
        219–20, 223
    and legal pluralism, 220–21
    loyalty model of, 219–20, 223, 227,
        228, 232
    movement for openness in, 233
    nepotism and cronyism in, 82
    organizational models, 220–21
    women in, 61, 212, 222
    youth and, 192–93, 212–14

government, corrupt and dysfunctional,
        34–49, 57, 68–69, 82, 98, 101,
        109, 116, 120, 121, 130–31, 154–55,
        172, 186, 213, 218–19, 224–25
    and agriculture, 168–69
    commerce and trade respond to, 121,
        127–28
    and electrical power supply, 160–61,
        162, 164–66
    and food production, 172–73
    kanju as response to, 30–31, 37,
        50–51, 104–105, 221, 232
    and oil industry, 163–64
    social solidarity as response to,
        68–71, 83
Grameen Bank, 146
"green revolution," 134
Green Revolution in Africa (AGRA),
    170
gross domestic product (GDP): as
        measurement standard, 48–49,
        149, 183, 194
Grow Biointensive Agriculture Center
    (Kenya), 176–77
Guéhenno, Jean-Marie: *The End of the
    Nation-State*, 231–32
Guinea: in African diaspora, 84–85

haggling and flexibility: in commerce
        and trade, 123–24, 126
Hagos Fitsum, 170–72, 173
health care: in Africa, 60–62, 65, 84, 116
    in Angola, 80
    caregiving in, 79–80
    cell phones in, 110
    in commerce and trade, 137, 142–43
    consumerism and private providers
        of, 137, 139, 230
    corruption and dysfunction in, 57,
        116–17
    DOTS in, 78
    entrepreneurship in, 139
    and fake drugs, 116–18
    "fat" *vs.* "lean" economies and, 115–16
    foreign aid and, 79, 136–37

investment opportunities in, 139,
        142–43
    kanju in, 110
    and lack of clinical services, 79–80
    in Mauretania, 79
    Mxit and, 111
    pay-as-you-go model in, 137
    poverty and, 137, 139–40
    prescription drugs in, 141
    private providers of, 137
    in Rwanda, 225
    shortcomings of, 116
    social solidarity and, 77–78, 110–11
    in South Africa, 139
    in South Sudan, 138
    in Tanzania, 80
    technology revolution and, 111–14
    in Uganda, 141–42
    varying quality of, 137–39
health insurance, 139–40
Henshaw Capital Partners, 152
Herodotus: and Africa, 1–2
Hersman, Erik, 103, 104, 107
Hirschman, Albert, 217
HIV. *See* AIDS
Honwana, Alcinda, 195, 215
Horne, Spencer, 197
Hospice Africa Uganda, 141
"How to Write About Africa"
        (Wainaina), 14–15
Hulme, David, 153
"hustling." *See kanju*
hydroelectric dams: electrical power
        supply and, 160–61

Iba One, 92
Ibrahim, Jibrin, 77
Ibrahim, Mohammed, 30, 64, 98
    on entrepreneurship, 21
identity politics: Posner on, 82
iHub, 104
Ije (film), 25
Ikegwuonu, Nnaemeka, 174–75
Imperial British East India Company,
    124

informal economy, 8, 14, 21, 127, 140,
        232. *See also* commerce and
        trade
    apprenticeships in, 204–205
    corruption and, 31–33
    electrical power supply and, 162–63
    entrepreneurship in, 29–30, 98
    investment in, 153
    kanju and, 28–29, 143
    in Kenya, 103
    nature of, 28–30
    in Nigeria, 29
    in Rwanda, 222
    transportation in, 27–30, 236
    youth and, 203–204
informal justice: in Rwanda, 225–26
informal settlements, 13, 89, 235–36
Information and Communication
        Technologies for Development
        (ICT4D), 109–10, 119
information networks: social solidarity
        and, 73–75, 78–79
innovation: in African digital
        technology, 101–103, 106–108
    in commerce and trade, 127, 129–30
    in construction industry, 185–86
    "fat" vs. "lean" economics and,
        107–108, 119–20
    in investment, 150–51
Institute for Liberty and Democracy, 29
interdependence. *See* social solidarity
International Labor Organization
        (ILO), 193, 195, 204
International Monetary Fund (IMF), 57,
        62–63
Internet: economic impact of, 95–96,
        103
    in technology revolution, 93, 95–96,
        148
Internet cafés: spread of, 18
investment: capital and, 144–45
    community financing and, 149–50
    crowdfunding as, 156
    and employment, 148–49, 150, 152
    in informal economy, 152–53

    innovations in, 150–51
    James on, 149, 152, 156
    kanju in, 154
    in Nigeria, 148, 152
    opportunities for, 122–23, 126–27,
        136, 139, 142–43, 148–49, 187, 189
    private equity firms and, 148, 152
    program-related investment (PRI),
        151
    public-private partnership (PPP), 152
    SMEs and, 148, 150, 152
    social impact investing, 150–51
Invisible Children, 59
Inyumba, Aloysia, 222, 224–25
iROKOtv, 25–26
irrigation: and agriculture, 134
Isanga, Joseph, 40
Islam, 75, 77
Ismail, Edna Adan, 36, 60, 138
    on foreign aid, 58–59
Iwere, Ngozi, 9, 65, 70, 81, 220–21

Jacob, Teresia, 133, 134
Jacques Roger Show, The (TV program),
        85
Jah, Jenneh, 198, 215
James, Barbara: on investment, 149,
        152, 156
Jamme, Marième, 55
Jitegemee: and public education,
        201–202, 205
    and vocational education, 201–202,
        204–205
JMI initiative, 189
Jobs, Steve, 19
Johannesburg, South Africa
    growth of, 183
Join the Club (Rosenberg), 69
Jones, Saran Kaba, 40, 88–89
journalism: and corruption, 31–33, 50,
        218
    kanju in, 33
    repression of, 218–19, 227–28
Juba Medical Complex (South Sudan),
        138

Juhudi Kilimo, 153
Jumia *(website)*, 127

Kagame, Paul, 88, 224–28
Kamau, Linda, 9
Kamau, Regina, 136, 151
Kamkwamba, William, 166, 174, 196
kanju: in African diaspora, 85
    in agriculture, 177, 179
    in commerce and trade, 127, 149
    and electrical power supply, 162, 166
    and entrepreneurship, 20–22, 104,
        108, 143, 198
    and flexibility, 107
    in health care, 110
    and informal economy, 28–29, 143
    and informal education, 211
    in investment, 154
    in journalism, 33
    in Kenya, 50–51
    nature of, 20–21, 33
    and recycling, 22–23, 177
    and resilience, 27, 190
    as response to dysfunctional
        government, 30–31, 37, 50–51,
        104–105, 221, 232, 235
    and social solidarity, 70
    in Somaliland, 37–38
    in technology revolution, 95, 100–
        101, 102–103
Karambi, Davis, 71–72, 73, 90, 126
Karambisi, Pasquale, 223
Karanja, Muchiri, 64
Kayihura, Manzi, 223, 225–26
Kennedy, John F., 91
Kenny, Charles: *Getting Better,* 65
Kenya: agriculture in, 176–78
    election corruption and violence in,
        8–9, 38–39, 49, 207
    foreign aid in, 57
    government corruption and
        dysfunction in, 41, 57, 213, 218
    informal economy in, 103
    kanju in, 50–51
    nationalism in, 51

prostitution in, 68
technology revolution in, 100–101,
    109
Kerawa *(website)*, 96–97
Khama, Ian, 82
Khan Academy, 211
Kibera, Kenya, 93, 235–36
Kibet, Trevor, 196
Kibki, Mwai, 93
KickStart, 135–36, 151, 174
Kim, Jim Yong, 234
Kimbo, Liza, 139, 145–46
Kimmelman, Jay, 131–32, 134
King-Akerele, Olubanke, 154
Kludjeson, Prince, 203
Kony, Joseph, 59
Kony 2012 (film), 59, 110
Konza, Kenya, 185
Koolhaas, Rem, 22
Kristof, Nick: and foreign aid, 58, 60

Ladd, Holly, 59
land rights and reforms, 169
Latif, Zain, 123, 142
Lawlessness and Economics (Dixit), 41
leadership: ALA teaches, 197–98, 215
legal pluralism: government and,
    220–21
    in Liberia, 229–31, 232–33
    social nature of, 230
Lewis, Stephen, 62–63
liberation struggles: African diaspora
    finances, 88
Liberia: civil war in, 88–89, 229
    government corruption and
        dysfunction in, 40, 41
    legal pluralism in, 229–31, 232–33
    water management in, 89–90
"Life Without Lights" project, 158–59
Lighthouse Trust, 112
Live Aid, 172–73
Living in Bondage (film), 23–24, 25
Lord's Resistance Army, 59
loyalty model: of government, 219–20,
    223, 227, 228, 232

Luna Farm Export and Slaughterhouse
    PLC, 170–71, 173

Main One, 95–96
Maintain, Olu, 18
Maker Faire Africa, 108
Making Do (Daniels), 30, 103
malaria: effects of, 115–16
Malawi, 166–67
    AIDS in, 112
    government corruption and
        dysfunction in, 40, 49–50
    public education in, 205–206
    technology revolution in, 111–12, 114
Mali, 48
Mallinson, Barbara, 210–11
Mamdani, Mahmood, 229
Mandela, Nelson, 47
manufacturing sector: impact of
    donations in kind on, 53–55
Massmart, 126–27
matatu buses: and entrepreneurship,
    27–29
Mauretania: health care in, 79
May, Shannon, 131, 133
Mbembe, Achille, 50, 232
McKinsey Global Institute, 81
Medic Mobile, 110
Mexico: mobile money in, 153–54
Mhlaba, Nolizwe, 214
microfinance institutions (MFIs). *See
    also* banking and financial
    services
    Enonchong on, 147
    and entrepreneurship, 146
    shortcomings of, 147
middle class: growth of, 122–23
Migdal, Joel, 22
migration, internal: in Africa, 44–45,
    181–82
Millennium Development Goals
    (MDGs), 4, 15, 66, 111, 223,
    227
    design flaws in, 61–65, 130–31
    and public education, 130–31, 205

Ruge on, 63
    in Rwanda, 62
Millennium Villages Project (MVP)
    Sachs and, 63–64
mobile money, 108, 127, 132
    economic impact of, 101–103, 153
    in Mexico, 153–54
mobile technology. *See* cell phones
Mobisol, 163
Mobutu, Joseph, 46, 57, 228
Moladi, 185–86
moneylending: and poverty, 145–46
    social solidarity and, 72–73
Moon, Nick, 134, 135, 136, 174
Motsepe, Patrice, 64
movie industry: entrepreneurship in,
    25–26
    in Nigeria, 23–26
    piracy in, 24–25
Moyo, Dambisa, 62, 155
    Dead Aid, 55
Mozambique, 67–68, 80
    electrical power supply in, 160–61
    foreign aid in, 57
mPedigree, 116–19, 218
M-Pesa: money transfers by, 100,
    101–103, 107, 109, 127, 153
Mugabe, Robert, 48, 192
Muganza, Janine, 197, 205
Mulangala, Vanessa, 71
Mumba, Soyapi, 111, 114
Murenz, Denis, 225
Musembi, Wilson, 201–202, 204–205
Museveni, Yoweri, 192, 212, 228
Mutesi, Betty, 62, 223
Mutiso, Alex, 201
Mwangi, James, 127–28, 153
Mwanjisi, Jamillah, 219
Mwaura, Moses, 145, 150
Mwenda, Andrew, 130
Mwende, Gladys, 6–7, 8, 21, 50, 169, 217
Mxit: and health care, 111

Nairobi: navigation in, 4
Namara, Evelyn, 75

Namibia, 48
natural resources: in Africa, 11, 160–61
   colonialism and, 160–61
   consumption of, 159–60
Ndemo, Btange, 109
Nderitu, Samuel, 176–79
Nelson, Akan, 198
nepotism and cronyism: in business,
      81–82
   in government, 82
Ngito, Kepha, 235
Nigeria: agriculture in, 135, 167–68,
      174–75
   cell phones in, 123
   Economic and Financial Crimes
      Commission, 18
   election corruption and violence in,
      9–10
   electrical power supply in, 164–65
   and e-mail fraud, 16–20, 24, 26, 33
   entrepreneurship in, 104–106, 108
   government corruption and
      dysfunction in, 39, 41, 154–55,
      187
   informal economy in, 29
   investments in, 148, 152
   military dictatorship in, 84
   movie industry in, 23–26
   textile industry in, 53
Nile River: Cheeseman on, 2
   exploration of, 1–3, 15
Njoku, Jason, 25
Nnebue, Kenneth, 23–24
Nobel Peace Prize: Yunus wins, 146
Nollywood, 23–26, 175, 208
non-governmental organizations
      (NGOs), 62, 89, 129. See also
      donations in kind; philanthropy
   compete with private equity firms,
      151–52
   and donor fatigue, 151
   funding models in, 55–56, 57–58,
      64
   program-related investment (PRI),
      151

Novogratz, Jacqueline: The Blue
      Sweater, 52
Nuru Energy, 163

Obama, Barack, 32
Obama, Michelle, 7, 83
Obami (social network): and informal
      education, 210
Odufuye, Dele, 105–106
oil industry: boom in, 160
   and dysfunctional governemt, 162–63
Okonjo-Iweala, Ngozi, 154
Olagunju, Segun, 214–15
Omidyar, Pierre, 132
Omidyar Network, 104, 132, 152
One Acre Fund, 178–79
"One Laptop Per Child" program, 114,
      211, 224
"1 Million Shirts" project
   Sadler and, 52, 55, 61
Opeke, Funke, 95–96, 99
Open Capital Advisors, 139
Organization for Economic
      Co-operation and Development
      (OECD), 12, 161
Organization of African Unity (OAU),
      34, 44
Oromait, Proscovia Alengot, 212
Orun Energy, 165
Osege, Angeline, 212
Otero, Maria, 88
Oviosu, Tayo, 108

Partners in Health, 234
paternalism: in foreign aid, 129
Peace Corps, 58
philanthropy. See also donations
      in kind; non-governmental
      organizations
   and AIDS, 58
   and direct payments to the poor, 153
   "fat" vs. "lean" economies and, 53–54,
      56, 57–58, 97
   micro-funding model in, 58, 78
   Sadler on, 55

piracy: in movie industry, 24–25
Poor Economics (Duflo & Banerjee),
      125–26
Portfolio of the Poor (Collins), 125
Posner, Daniel: on identity politics, 82
poverty: and consumerism, 122–23,
      129–30
   and direct philanthropy, 153
   electrical power supply and, 159, 162
   and employment, 143–44
   and health care, 137, 139–40
   moneylending and, 145–46
   and private education, 132
   urbanization and, 183–84
Powell, Colin, 17–18
Prahalad, C. K. & Stuart L. Hart:
      and "Bottom of the Pyramid"
      consumers, 123, 129, 146
President's Emergency Plan for AIDS
      Relief (PEPFAR), 141
privacy: social solidarity and lack of, 73
private equity firms: and investment,
      148, 151
   NGOs compete with, 152
   World Bank competes with, 152
(PRODUCT) RED, 58
program related investment (PRI), 151
prostitution: in Kenya, 68
public health, 12, 13, 114–15, 138
   cell phones and, 116–18
   crime in, 117
public-private partnership (PPP), 152
Putnam, Robert: *Bowling Alone*, 69

Quality Chemical Industries Ltd., 142,
      144

radio: as educational medium, 175,
      207–209
Ratha, Dilip, 154
Reclaim Naija, 9
recycling: "fat" *vs.* "lean" economies
      and, 22, 111–12, 114
   kanju and, 22–23, 177
   in technology revolution, 114

Rees, William, 159
religion: effects of, 76–77
remittances: in African diaspora, 85–87,
      150, 181
resilience, 26
   kanju and, 27
   youth and, 27
retail distribution and supply chains,
      124–26
   cell phones in, 119–20
   corruption and dysfunction in, 119
   costs of, 119
risk management: ALA teaches, 198–99
Romer, Paul, 184–85
Rosenberg, Tina: *Join the Club*, 69
   The Social Cure, 77–78
Rotich, Juliana, 120
Rugasira, Andrew, 122
Ruge, Teddy: on MDGs, 63
Rwanda, 88, 218
   agriculture in, 135
   commerce and trade in, 223
   foreign aid in, 226
   genocide in, 88, 221–23, 224, 225–26
   government innovations and reforms
      in, 221–24, 232
   health care in, 140, 225
   inclusiveness and unification in,
      226–27
   informal economy in, 222
   informal justice in, 225–26
   MDGs in, 62
   technology revolution in, 225

Sachs, Jeffrey: *The End of Poverty*, 95
   and Millennium Villages Project
      (MVP), 63–64
Sadler, Jason, 58
   and "1 Million Shirts" project, 52,
      55, 61
   on philanthropy, 55
Safaricom, 92, 99, 100, 101
Sambaza, 100–101
Sandy *(hurricane, 2012)*, 157, 190
sanitation, 13–14

Savannah Fund, 107
SEACOM, 93, 148
"Second Coming, The" (Yeats), 235
Seeds for Needs project, 233–34
self-identity: in Africa, 70–71
Senegal, 76–77
    government corruption and
        dysfunction in, 213
separatist movements: in Africa, 34–36,
    45–46
Shikwati, James, 53
Shire, Saad, 36
Shujaaz (graphic novel): and informal
    education, 206–207, 208–10
    radio program based on, 209
    wins Emmy Award, 209
Sierra Leone: government corruption
    and dysfunction in, 46–47
Silicon Valley: technology hubs'
    connections with, 106–107
Simmons, Russel, 107
Simons, Bright, 117–18
Sirleaf, Ellen Johnson, 90, 192, 218
Skosana, Elizabeth, 196, 197, 199, 214
slavery, 10
small and medium-size enterprises
    (SMEs): and investment, 147–48,
    150, 152
Smith, Kwabena, 164–65
Snoad, Nigel, 109
Social Cure, The (Rosenberg), 77–78
social lending and credit circles,
    146–47. *See also* credit
    in Cameroon, 126
social solidarity: in African diaspora,
    87–88
    and cell phones, 8–9, 10, 93
    and community norms, 75–77,
        229–31
    cooperation and, 67–69
    family and, 10, 70–71, 73
    "fat" *vs.* "lean" economies and,
        69–70
    feedback loops in, 73–74, 78
    and health care, 77–78, 110–11

and information networks, 73–75,
    78–79
    kanju and, 70
    and lack of privacy, 73
    and moneylending, 72–73
    as response to dysfunctional
        government, 68–71, 83
    social and psychological effects of,
        69–70
    solar energy and, 74–75
solar energy: and electrical power
    supply, 163–64, 165
    and social solidarity, 74–75
Solar Sister, 74–75, 78, 151, 163
Somalia, 49, 85–86
    invaded by Ethiopia and Kenya
        (2011), 35, 37
    political collapse in, 41
    Transitional Federal Government, 37
Somaliland, 217, 221, 223–24, 228
    foreign aid in, 58, 113
    freedom from foreign interference, 37
    kanju in, 37–38
    legal pluralism in, 229
    nationalism in, 36
    as secessionist state, 34–36, 49, 51
Sound Princess, 13–14, 108
South Africa: AIDS in, 80–81
    apartheid in, 47, 83, 196, 214
    government corruption and
        dysfunction in, 41, 47, 186, 224
    health care in, 139
    legal pluralism in, 229
Southern African Development
    Community, 234
South Sudan: food production in, 176
    government corruption and
        dysfunction in, 40, 224
    health care in, 138
    war for independence in, 88, 121
Speke, John Hanning, 2
Sproxil, 118, 149
Stanbic Bank, 121
Stanley, Henry Morton, 1
Starr, Jonathan, 206, 208

State of the Union, 219
Stevens, Siaka, 46–47
Stockman, Farah, 201
stock markets: in Africa, 155
    Cleary on, 155
Stupart, Richard, 54, 56
sub-Saharan Africa. *See* Africa
Summers, Larry, 91–92, 95, 120
Swaniker, Fred, 196–98
Swaziland: government corruption and
    dysfunction in, 39

"Talented Tenth, The" (Du Bois),
    200–201, 203
TANESCO, 162
Tanzania: electrical power supply in,
    161–63
    government corruption and
        dysfunction in, 39
    health care in, 80, 140
teachers: inadequate training of, 131
Tech4Africa conference, 107
technology, digital, 10, 13–14
    African innovations in, 101–103,
        106–108
    entrepreneurship in, 107–108
    foreign investments in, 106–107
    and ignorance of policymakers,
        193
    and informal education, 211
technology hubs: cluster economies
    and, 103–105
    connections with Silicon Valley,
        106–107
    and entrepreneurship, 104–105
    venture capital and, 107
technology revolution: and agriculture,
    176
    broadband connectivity in, 93–95
    cell phones and, 85, 92–93, 97–98,
        129
    and economic development, 109,
        120
    economics of, 98–99, 100
    in education, 133

and electrical power supply, 164–65
    fiber-optic cables in, 93, 95–96, 99,
        148
    and health care, 111–14
    Internet in, 93, 95–96, 148
    kanju in, 95, 100–101, 102–103
    in Kenya, 100–101, 109
    in Malawi, 111–12, 114
    recycling in, 114
    in Rwanda, 225
TEDGlobal conference, 103, 104
telenovelas: and informal education,
    207
textile industry: in Nigeria, 53
Tiger Eye: and corruption, 32–33
time management: ALA teaches, 199,
    202
Tinkasiimire, Barnabas, 212
TOMS Shoes: donations in kind by,
    53–54
Tostan *(advocacy group)*, 75–76
Tough, Paul, 27
Touré, Ali Farka, 92
transportation: in informal economy,
    27–30, 236
Tsvangirai, Morgan, 38, 192

Uganda, 59
    agriculture in, 180–81
    electrical power supply in, 163
    health care in, 141–42
    legal pluralism in, 229
Ulimwengu, Jenerali, 203
Umande Trust, 13
UNACOFF, 180–81
United Kingdom Department for
    International Development
    (DFID), 179
United Nations, 4–5, 7, 60
    Africa Human Development Report,
        66
    Global Pulse project, 232–33
    mandates free education, 201, 205
United States: electrical power supply
    in, 157

United States Centers for Disease
    Control and Prevention, 114
United States State Department
    and African diaspora, 88
UN Women, 59
Up from Slavery (Washington), 203
urbanization: in Africa, 181–84
    and construction industry, 183–84,
        185–86
    and poverty, 183–84
USAID, 91, 114, 152, 179, 233
Ushahidi *(nonprofit)*, 107, 108, 120
    and cell-phone applications, 8–9

venture capital: and technology hubs,
    107
Villages in Action, 63, 65, 217–18
Virtual City, 119

Waibochi, John, 119–20
Wainaina, Binyavanga: "How to Write
    About Africa," 14–15
Warsame, K'Naan, 37
Washington, Booker T.: *Up from
    Slavery,* 203
water management, 159
    and agriculture, 134–35, 168
    in Côte d'Ivoire, 91–92
    foot-powered pumps in, 135–36, 144
    in Liberia, 89–90
Way, Hermione, 107
"We Are the World," 172
"White Man's Burden," 60
Williams, Abiodun, 182, 184, 186, 190
wind power, 166–67
Winter, Shawn, 90
Wittgenstein, Ludwig, 5
women: in African diaspora, 87–88
    in commerce and trade, 74–75, 101
    and entrepreneurship, 74–75, 113, 147
    and genital mutilation, 75–76, 77

in government, 62, 212, 222
    health of, 23, 81
World Bank, 47–49, 57, 62, 65, 66, 147,
    154, 159, 179, 226, 233–34
    competes with private equity firms,
        152
    International Finance Corporation,
        137, 142, 147
    Multilateral Investment Guarantee
        Agency, 122
    structural adjustments by, 168
World Economic Forum, 118, 224
World Health Organization (WHO), 57,
    78, 80, 142
World Vision, 56
Woro, Ronald, 138

"Yahoo Boys," 17–20, 22, 104, 166
Yang, Jamie, 162
Yeats, William Butler: "The Second
    Coming," 235
youth, 11, 191–92
    and apathy, 214
    and employment, 193–95, 201
    and entrepreneurship, 197–98, 215
    and government, 192–93, 212–14
    and informal economy, 203–204
    rejects old cultural assumptions, 193
    and resilience, 27
Yunus, Muhammad: wins Nobel Peace
    Prize, 146

Zaire. *See* Congo, Democratic
    Republic of
Zimbabwe: banking and financial
    services in, 145
    government corruption and
        dysfunction in, 41, 48
Zimmerman, Bill, 103
Zittrain, Jonathan: "The Generative
    Internet," 102